WALK IN
THEIR SHOES

Can One Person Change
the World?

JIM ZIOLKOWSKI, founder of buildOn
with JAMES S. HIRSCH

Simon & Schuster
New York London Toronto Sydney New Delhi

WALK IN THEIR SHOES

Can One Person Change
the World?

JIM ZIOLKOWSKI, founder of buildOn

with JAMES S. HIRSCH

SIMON & SCHUSTER

New York   London   Toronto   Sydney   New Delhi

Simon & Schuster
1230 Avenue of the Americas
New York, NY 10020

Library of Congress Cataloging-in-Publication Data
Ziolkowski, Jim, author.
Walk in their shoes : can one person change the world? / Jim Ziolkowski,
with James S. Hirsch.
pages cm
1. Fundamental education—Developing countries. 2. School buildings—Developing
countries—Design and construction. 3. Humanitarian assistance, American—Developing
countries. 4. After-school programs—United States. 5. BuildOn (Organization)
6. Ziolkowski, Jim—Travel. I. Hirsch, James S., author. II. Title.
LC5163.D44Z56 2013
370.11'1091724—dc23   2013007991

ISBN 978-1-4516-8355-4
ISBN 978-1-4516-8357-8 (ebook)

To Sunshine, Jack, and Quinn

Contents

Prologue

When I was twenty-four, I entered GE's Financial Management Program, a fast-track position that all but guaranteed a lucrative career in corporate finance. GE liked to hire ambitious young graduates, work them hard, then reward them with the perks and prestige that befit a corporate behemoth. My parents were proud.

But fifteen months later I quit. I'm not the first person to have walked out on the GE program; its rigorous demands have caused others to reconsider their career goals. But I doubt many have quit to pursue a mission as improbable as the one I envisioned. I had traveled abroad to developing countries after college, and what I saw had lit a fire within me that I couldn't put out. In visiting India, Thailand, and Nepal, I had seen cities and villages mired in extreme poverty. When I was in New Delhi, I saw the beggars and the street children, destitute and hungry, without any hope for a better life. When I was in a village in Nepal, I saw families living in mud huts without running water or electricity. The more I traveled in regions of poverty, the more clearly I saw that those conditions were directly related to rampant illiteracy and the general lack of education. But I also saw that these communities desperately wanted their own children to read and write. If I could help in that regard, I was certain their commitment to this cause would surpass my own.

My experiences in developing countries made me more sensitive to the poverty in my own country, particularly affecting urban youth. The problems of our inner cities are intimidating, and many adults had given up, but I had a different idea: that the kids themselves wanted to build a better community, shape their own destiny, and disprove the cynics. They wanted to be part of the solution. I didn't have direct proof initially but was convinced that all kids, regardless of class or circumstance, have the same dreams. The troubled kids, most of them anyway, just need a little guidance from people who believe in them.

I knew there was no silver bullet to cure our social ills, but I was also starting to consider more earnestly what it meant to live my faith as a Roman Catholic. Christ had served the poor and the hungry, and I saw that as our responsibility as well. Over time, I would integrate ideas from other traditions, but the Christian tenets of service to others and social justice motivated me from the start.

I left GE to start a nonprofit organization that offered afterschool programs for high school students in America's most impoverished inner cities. Enrichment programs, which typically involve academic clubs or the arts, abound in affluent schools but are rare in poor ones. I wanted to offer a different kind of program to engage students in community service so they would be distributors of goodwill instead of only recipients. I wanted them to visit senior centers, help the disabled, clean up parks and abandoned lots, and work at the very food pantries on which some of their own families depended. And perhaps most audaciously, I wanted these same students to help us build schools in the world's poorest countries so children there would receive long-overdue educational opportunities. This seemed like a natural fit. What better way to give hope to American kids than by having them renew the lives of people in their own neighborhoods while also uplifting children in other parts of the world?

It was quite a plan, but when I left GE Capital, the CFO thought that I'd be back in six months. After all, I had no background in education, no background in youth development programs, and no background in construction. I had never worked as a fundraiser, nor had I ever managed anyone or anything. I had a business degree, a passport, and a few thousand dollars in the bank. My younger brother Dave, who had even less experience than I, would be my partner. Was our dream a long shot? Of course. But I believed in the cause, in the power of service to redeem and transform, and that was all I needed. That's all anyone needs.

Twenty-one years later, I have journeyed though deprivation and despair. Hostile soldiers in South Africa have aimed their rifles at me while I documented the injustices of apartheid. I've been arrested at gun point in Harlem for stealing my own car. I've been stung by a scorpion in Brazil and was nearly poisoned by deadly snakes in Africa and South America. I've had dysentery on four continents. Malaria almost killed me in Malawi.

But this story is also about hope and redemption. I've drawn great strength from the most disadvantaged and courageous among us. I have roamed with street children through the shantytown *favelas* of Brazil, danced with *campesinos* in Nicaragua, and listened to all-night drumming vigils for the dead in Malawi. I've worked in African communities where more than a third of the population was HIV-positive, tried to comfort American students whose families were on the losing side of the drug war, and watched my own son battle for his life against a rare and unpredictable disease. I've been inspired by teachers in the Bronx and humbled by former slaves in Nepal. I interviewed Mother Teresa just before she passed away and the Dalai Lama in his home in Dharamsala. This story is not only mine; it's the story of the thousands of people who have let me into their communities and into their lives. It's the story of buildOn, an organization that has confounded expectations and continues to grow, and it's the story of my son's bravery to defy all odds. I hope it causes you to laugh, cry, cringe, and think—not about whether one person or even a few can save the world but about how each of us can step forward, step up, and change it.

CHAPTER 1

The Sleeping Sickness
of the Soul

My teammates surrounded the mat, waving their arms and screaming. My coach was yelling too, but I couldn't make out what they were saying. All I felt was my body wearing down, until the sounds faded, my vision blurred, and my shoulders hit the mat.

I was on the wrestling team in seventh grade, all 117 pounds of me, and this had been one of the most furious matches of the season. My opponent and I kept working for take-downs and reversals, until the third and final period, when he began pressing me to the mat. My teammates were urging me on, and I tried to resist, but my energy was gone.

He pinned me. At first I was just relieved the struggle was over. Breathing heavily, I then looked up and discovered why my teammates had been so loud and animated. I had been winning the match and was pinned with just three seconds to go. *Three seconds!* I lost because I had quit.

I was devastated, and while it may seem ridiculous, the lesson of that day has stayed with me all these years. What I learned had less to do with the shame of giving up (though that was terrible) than the unpredictability of events. Even when all seems lost, you keep going because you don't know what's coming next. You might be three seconds away from victory.

I grew up in Jackson, Michigan, a small, working-class community about seventy-five miles west of Detroit. We were a traditional Catholic family: my parents had five kids in seven years and sent us all to Catholic schools. Each day we had breakfast (usually plain oatmeal) and dinner together, and all seven of us had to be at the table for each meal. One of us would say a short prayer before we could eat, and sometimes my dad would extend his prayer to a ten-minute discussion of the gifts we receive from God. We traveled on occasion; my dad would pile us into the station wagon and drive to Florida to visit our grandparents, and when I was older, we'd drive to Colorado to ski. But my world didn't stray far beyond Jackson. My father built a lake house with his brother, Bob, who had eight kids, and all the cousins descended there in the summer. We tooled around on motorcycles, developed a love for sailing, and swam until night fell.

When I was about six or seven, my mother started taking me regularly to the Vista Grand Villa, a nursing home. My mom explained that these elders didn't have family or friends to visit them, so our coming made a difference in their lives. I can't say that going to Vista Grand Villa was my favorite activity of the week, but I didn't object to it either. We went almost every week and spent time with a woman in a wheelchair who couldn't talk and had lost control of her limbs. Her name was Mrs. Marshall, and whenever we showed up, she broke into a smile and gave me a hug. Her words were incoherent, but it didn't matter. I sat next to her and fed her applesauce, and she patted me on my head.

Those were probably the first times I realized that I enjoyed being around people for whom I could make a difference, and I believe it helped me to respect and feel comfortable around senior citizens.

My mother, Pat, had a degree from the University of Pittsburgh, but she was a traditional stay-at-home mom. Both she and my dad, John, loved all of us unconditionally and showed it. But Dad was sometimes too intense, impatient, or confrontational, and he wasn't always close to us—four boys and a girl. But he did connect with me. At six feet two and 220 pounds, he was larger than life, a man who expressed his emotions freely and unapologetically. He would cup my face in his hands, look me straight in the eye, and say, "I love you, my son." And I would look straight back and say, "I love you too."

I hated to disappoint him. When I was sixteen, I begged him to loan me his car, and I drove to Detroit with some buddies to see my first concert, the Who and the Clash at the Silverdome. I had just gotten my driver's license and didn't pay attention to the time. All the way home I was hoping he would be asleep or else I was certain the shit would hit the fan. Sure enough, when I tried to quietly sneak through the kitchen at 3:30 a.m., my father was waiting there. But he was more disappointed than upset. "You could have called," he said. Then he went to bed. I couldn't believe he wasn't angry, but I realized, and appreciated, how much he trusted me.

My mom is sensitive and compassionate and instilled those values in me, but my father was my mentor. He came to all of my baseball and football games, played catch with me, taught me how to sail and ski, and advised me on everything from the value of hard work to girls. "Don't let the blood rush out of your head in the heat of the moment," he would joke. But our most powerful connection revolved around faith, and his came easily. He didn't have to puzzle over the meaning of God or work to feel His presence. It was always there, like an eternal gift, and it came from a very deep place within. As a kid, I used to walk with my dad to church, but he was moving so fast, with his long, intense strides, that I could barely keep up. Afterward he would leave the church relaxed, at peace. He had found union with God and the Eucharist, and I could return home with him at a much slower pace. "You have to nurture and exercise your faith," he often told me, "in order for it to grow and sustain you."

My father and uncle were extremely close, raised by parents with a strong work ethic and a deep religious and moral code. Their father, a carpenter, didn't use the word *darn* because it was too close

3

to *damn*. Growing up in Grand Rapids, they had a younger brother, Tommy. Early one morning when Tommy was nine, he left for his paper route. As he was bundling his papers on the sidewalk, a taxi jumped the curb, hit him, killing him, and left the scene. Later that day, my uncle and my dad rode their bikes to the site of the accident and saw the blood on the sidewalk.

Some people would have been so angry with God they would have abandoned their beliefs. Not so with my father, who never questioned his faith and lived his life as if he knew every day was "a gift from God," as he liked to say.

A philosophy major at Aquinas College, he was also deeply influenced by *The Seven Storey Mountain*, the autobiography of Thomas Merton, which describes how Merton's search for God led him to convert to Roman Catholicism. My father, in turn, exposed me to Merton's ideas when I was young. In his early writings, Merton devoted himself to his search for spiritual meaning in a world that had been badly shaken by so much death and destruction, and as his views evolved, he became more outspoken about nonviolence, social justice, and civil rights, and my father conveyed those ideas to me.

I knew from a young age that I wanted to develop a faith as strong as my father's. He gave me my spiritual foundation. Then, my years in high school and college broadened and shook my world in ways that shaped the rest of my life.

I was a typically insecure teenager. I was decent at sports and loved music and all the revolutionary bands of the 1960s and '70s that celebrated the raucous youth movement of sex, drugs, and social protest. But some of the music also left me attuned, literally, to spirituality. My sister had a cassette of a live concert by Crosby, Stills, Nash & Young, and Stephen Stills's exuberant wail "Jesus Christ was the first nonviolent revolutionary!" opened my eyes to an entirely different perspective on Christ. Until then, I had seen Christ as a gentle source of unconditional love, of strength. The notion of Christ as a nonviolent revolutionary was new and exhilarating, and gave me a completely different prism through which to view the world: Christ as an agent of change, a role model for peaceful transformation.

Stephen Stills ignited one type of vision, but J. R. R. Tolkien sketched another one of much greater depth and possibility, a world of sacrifice and salvation as an epic adventure. In high school I read the *Lord of the Rings* trilogy, mesmerized by Tolkien's ability to weave his selfless characters into a spellbinding warrior tale of good versus evil. The books struck a deep chord. At the time, I lived in fear of being different and just wanted to fit in. Tolkien's characters (hobbits, dwarves, wizards, and men) were all outcasts, but they also had the traits that I wanted for myself: courage, humility, and the willingness to sacrifice for others. They overcame their fears, took enormous risks, and were rewarded with redemption. That sounded pretty good to me.

I attended Michigan State University and loved the intellectual stimulation, the clash of ideas, and the search for truth that define college. I also loved the parties, the beer, and the freedom. I envisioned taking over my father's company someday—he and his brother ran a restaurant supply firm—so I entered business school and chose finance as my major. Reading about religion and philosophy fulfilled a spiritual need, but finance appealed to my desire for precision and logic, and I reveled in the unassailability of numbers.

My college years also opened my eyes to new possibilities beyond my planned career in business. I met kids with diverse backgrounds and experiences, and I took time off to travel the country.

The summer of my sophomore year, I wanted to take a month-long road trip with a friend and my brother Dave, who is fifteen months younger than I. We hadn't always been close, as we're both intensely competitive and clashed while we were growing up. But in high school, we moved past that and became much tighter, with many of the same friends and a shared desire for adventure. Dave also enrolled at Michigan State, where we both majored in business, partied together, and were roommates in the same house. At six foot three and with superior upper body strength, Dave was a gifted athlete. His freshman year at Michigan State, he made the varsity track team as a walk-on, but he quit after one year. He didn't like structure or hierarchy or early morning practices, especially after late nights drinking. He was a free spirit who attracted women in droves and took school far less seriously than I, but we would do anything for each other, even coming to the other's defense in a couple of beer-induced scraps at keg parties.

For our summer road trip I asked our dad if we could use his van. He agreed on one condition: that he come with us. So we packed our tents, our hiking boots, and our music cassettes and headed west. We made our way through the Black Hills and the Tetons, whose peaks stretched across the sky like God's sculptures and where we hiked from Lake Jenny to the exquisitely named Lake Solitude. It was so peaceful you could hear every breath you took.

My dad brought his 35 mm SLR camera, a good one in its day, and I began experimenting with it. He let me use the camera during the trip (he made me read the manual first), and at the end, he said, "It's yours." I was grateful, of course, though I had no idea how critical that camera would become to my work.

The highlight of the trip, at least for my dad, was our excursion to see the massive mountain sculpture of Crazy Horse in South Dakota. Dad didn't have any particular affinity for the iconic Lakota leader, but he wanted to see this giant memorial, still under construction, because it was sculpted by a New Englander named Ziolkowski.

Dave and I went on another trip the following summer, without our dad. (This time he forgot to invite himself.) We windsurfed in the Columbia River Gorge and then headed down the California coast all the way to Tijuana. I began meeting young travelers from abroad, who shared their backpacking or rock-climbing stories from Australia, Brazil, England, France, Germany, or New Zealand. They didn't just visit these places. They *lived* them, and I wanted to as well. College now struck me as overly structured and tedious. So I spent the next three winters in Vail, Colorado, where I worked nights waiting tables so I was free to ski during the day. I mostly skied the back bowls, pounded moguls, and occasionally dropped into steep narrow passages known as backcountry chutes. When I was a student, my dad urged me, "Test your outer limits," which I did, but I was now following the same advice in Colorado—launching off forty-foot cliffs, hurtling off the cornices, or competing on the pro mogul tour, where I wiped out and exploded on unforgiving bumps. "No falls, no balls" was my philosophy.

I was still going to school, studying finance and spreadsheets, but because I spent my winters in Colorado I took five years to graduate. I received some good job offers, but my wanderlust got the better of me. I had no real desire to make money or to save the world. I wanted adventure, and I knew that now was the time to find it.

After graduating in 1989, I flew to Europe with Dave. We went paragliding in France, walked the Berlin Wall in Germany, and hiked the Alps in Switzerland. Poland was still behind the Iron Curtain, but we got visas and visited Krakow, where we entered a post office and asked if there were any Ziolkowskis in the city. We envisioned tracking down some long-lost relatives. The postmistress just laughed, pulled out a thick book, and showed us page after page of entries of our last name.

We had a serious purpose in going to Poland: to see the Auschwitz and Birkenau concentration camps. The buildings had been left standing like vacant tombs. We saw where the rail cars pulled up with the prisoners and where an SS officer would decide who would go to the barracks and who would go to the "showers." We saw the sign that read "Work Makes You Free" and the bins stuffed with eyeglasses, hair, shoes, pants, and other clothes. We saw the ovens where the bodies had burned and the grounds where the prisoners had been blindfolded in front of a firing squad.

There was something otherworldly and demonic about these camps, which made my visit to Maximilian Kolbe's starvation cell all the more meaningful. Kolbe was a Catholic priest who provided shelter to Jewish refugees in Poland, until his arrest in 1941. He was sent to Auschwitz and was there when three prisoners escaped. In response, the deputy camp commander picked ten men to be starved to death in an underground cell. When one of the men yelled, "My wife! My children!" Kolbe volunteered to take his place and was granted his wish. In the cell, he led Mass each day and sang hymns with the other prisoners. They say he was the last of the ten prisoners to die.

That cell is open to visitors, and when I walked inside, I saw that Kolbe had carved a cross into the stone wall. I thought: That is the truest form of Christianity, sacrificing your life for others. I was nearly overwhelmed by emotion. To visit Auschwitz is to come face to face with evil. What Kolbe represented was a potent sliver of hope amid the darkness.

Dave returned home, and I continued on to hitchhike across Australia, where I went scuba diving off the Great Barrier Reef, and then on to New Zealand, where I bungee-jumped 290 feet off a deserted canyon bridge. I returned to Colorado and over several months scraped together enough money for another trip. This time I was traveling solo and planned to see Thailand, India, Nepal, and China, then take the Siberian Express through the USSR and into Berlin and beyond. I intended to meet up with a friend in Sweden at the end. I was going to land in Bangkok, strap on my backpack, and just improvise. But a few days before I left, I started feeling nervous. These were beautiful countries but far less developed than what I was used to. I was about to land in a country with crushing poverty, thick jungles, and a population in which few spoke English. My father detected my unease. "You don't need to do this," he told me. "I'll reimburse you for your ticket."

That snapped me out of it. His kind suggestion was a challenge, and I wasn't going to back out now. "Of course I'm going," I told him. And I did.

I was trying to escape a life, and maybe even a future, that felt constricted and predictable. But it wasn't just about the adventure.

I wanted to immerse myself in different cultures. So in Thailand I took a bamboo raft down a jungle river, using a long stick to push off sand bars, because that was how the Thais transported their food and other goods. I rode working elephants through the jungle and trekked up hills to visit the tribes. I smoked a lot of marijuana and even once smoked opium with a shaman once in a tribal den. It was part of the culture, and though I didn't know it fully at the time, these experiences were the beginning of my wanting to understand the world around me from the inside out. Only then, I felt, could I do anything useful in another country or even my own.

Nothing prepared me for New Delhi, India's teeming, multiethnic capital. It was early August, and the temperature had to be over 100 degrees, a suffocating heat that seemed to rise from the asphalt. As soon as I left the airport, I knew I was in another world. I rode a tuk-tuk, a three-wheeled minicab, into town, where the streets were mayhem: careening rickshaws pulled by runners, rambling trucks blaring their horns, and lumbering cows on their afternoon stroll down the middle of a congested avenue. Hindus view the cows as sacred, so we were all dodging and swerving, trying not to hit each other or an animal.

Stepping onto the sidewalk, I was immersed in a sweaty mass of humanity. There was no personal space, no degree of separation, and I got a glimpse of abject poverty that exceeded anything I had ever imagined. Beggars without legs dragged themselves along the ground. Men with leprosy bared their ghastly abrasions beneath the hot sun. If someone wanted to sell you something, he was in your face. Only the pickpockets acted discreetly. I walked through the shantytowns and saw families living in shacks and children scavenging in mountains of waste. I had seen the homeless and the hungry in America, but they were nothing like this. America's big cities have shelters and food kitchens and hospitals. However limited, those cities have resources. In New Delhi, starvation, disease, and neglect were all killers. The city's most destitute appeared to have no one to advocate for their needs and nowhere to go but the street.

I had never seen anything like it and suddenly felt a jarring, helpless sensation. I had always read or heard that you can't do anything to assist the shockingly poor, or that giving anything to beggars would only encourage them. But I wondered if that was an excuse for complacency. How better to relieve yourself of any responsibility for a problem than to say the problem is insolvable? The question festered. I was just a backpacker, but I was beginning to see that many people, in this city and elsewhere, were numbing themselves to their environment so they wouldn't have to confront the suffering around them. The more I thought about our detached view of poverty, the more insane I thought it really was.

There was great beauty and religious depth in New Delhi as well. The majestic Hindu temples were oases of spiritual calm and focus amid the tumult. I had walked into plenty of churches in the States and in Europe, in which you might see a few older folks in the back praying intently. In these Hindu temples, which offered a sumptuous riot of colorful murals, fresco paintings, and cascading waterfalls, numerous faithful of all ages prayed and bowed in front of their deity with complete devotion. They lit incense and performed *pujas*. Prayer seemed to be the fabric that held everyone and everything together. What peace there was, as I saw it, could be traced to the stepwells of those temples.

I had now been exposed to far more of the world than I had ever seen on television or read about. I knew I was on a search for meaning in my own life but had no idea what trail would get me there.

The link between suffering and spirituality came to a head when I packed myself into a crowded third-class car on a train to Varanasi. The spiritual vortex of India, Varanasi is a place of sacred pilgrimage. Many Hindus travel there to die so they might break the cycle of death and rebirth, in hopes that they will no longer have to endure the suffering of earthly existence. They don't just wait for death; they celebrate it, blessed to be liberated spiritually and to have made it to their eternal resting place, the Ganges River. I watched as these pilgrims bathed in the sacred water. Family members carried the dead bodies of loved ones, wrapped in white cotton, to the ghats and reverently placed them atop piles of wood. The closest male relative of the deceased, dressed in white, his head shaved except for a short ponytail, sprinkled holy river water on the body as he walked around it three times. Then the fires were lit. With smoke whipping in the stiff breeze, the cremation lasted several hours. When the fires died, the mourners scooped the ash in their hands and scattered it in the swift currents of the river.

Salvation awaits the dead. But what about the living?

I was still processing what I had seen when, days later, I was riding on top of a truck from Varanasi all the way to Kathmandu in Nepal, where I planned to climb up into the Himalayas. Many hikers would fly in rickety double-engine planes to the Solo Khumbu (Everest) Region and start their trek from the dirt runway in Lukla. But I had little money for airfare and believed that hiking through the rain forest would get me in shape for the high altitude. So I trudged through the jungle during a monsoon, drenched by the rains for eighteen hours a day. The muddy, miserable trip took me eleven days, but it was worth it; had I not walked, I would never have stumbled across a village called Kari Kola.

Inside a large communal hut, I dried out, peeled the leeches off my body, and drank some hot tea. Outside in the rain, the villagers were singing boisterously, drinking rice wine, and reveling in a celebration. Members of a British expedition were also in the hut, some of whom had been partying as well. I asked what was going on, and they explained that they were here a year ago, when they had given the village the equivalent of $5,000 toward building a school. Now back on another trip, the Brits were being feted for their contribution.

As I spoke to others in the hut, I learned that the villagers did not have running water or electricity. The children suffered from preventable diseases. Most of the villagers were illiterate, they didn't have enough to eat, and their huts, made of stone, mud, and thatch, could be wiped out by mudslides. Yet they were celebrating the construction of a tiny school and dormitory for children who would otherwise need to walk hours to get to class. I saw the pride, determination, and hope of a community that had been neglected. I had never seen anything like that in the "developed" world. It was a revelation.

About a week later and farther up the trail, I met two other trekkers, Scott from Colorado, a quiet mountaineer with dark hair and a thick beard, and Claude from France, a strong, gregarious climber with a giant red beard. After hiking together over some high-altitude passes and viewing the sunrise on Mount Everest, we decided to climb the 20,000-foot summit of Imja Tse, better known as Island Peak because it appears as an island of ice when viewed from a distance. It's breathtaking but daunting, with steep slopes and narrow ridges, a mountain sometimes used by climbers preparing for Everest. We were required by Nepalese law to have permits and a guide, as well as Sherpas, to carry our supplies. We had none. We rented mountaineering equipment, including crampons, ice axes, and ropes, and then spent two days hauling it to our makeshift base camp at 18,000 feet. At that level the air is quite thin—the highest peak in the continental United States is a little over 14,000 feet—and as the three of us rested in our two-man tent, it felt as though we were stealing oxygen from each other.

The plan was to begin climbing at midnight so we could reach the summit by dawn, which would allow us to return before the sun's heat increased the risk of an avalanche. But almost as soon as we began, Scott said he couldn't continue. Then, about a hundred steps later, Claude said he had to stop because his rented boots were killing his feet. He handed me the rope and said, "You try it."

It was dark, and also snowing, but I thought I could do it alone. I could follow the pinpoints of light from a Swiss expedition about an hour and a half ahead of me. But I soon lost them in the valleys and folds of the great peak, and I didn't know which route to follow. After a few hours of climbing, confused and disoriented, I sat down in the frozen darkness, closed my eyes, and fought off panic. I did what came naturally to me: I prayed, and it gave me a great sense of tranquility and purpose, a way to fend off my fear. I placed my faith in God and vowed to look up and take whichever route I saw. It was perhaps the first time I completely surrendered myself and put all my trust in Him.

When I opened my eyes, what I saw was a steep 60-degree chute. Though forbidding, it had some promising footholds leading up its side. I made the long climb until I finally reached the top, where I edged around a rock face and found myself in a snowfield. The soft, purple light of predawn crept over the peak, and I could suddenly see the footprints from the previous expedition. But with so little oxygen and no tank, I was growing light-headed. I had been climbing for more than seven hours and had to push myself just to go twenty steps before needing a rest.

Eventually I came to a crevasse, about six feet wide, whose bottom I couldn't see. I knew an abyss here could easily be a thousand feet deep; to jump across it in the exhausted state I was in would be a true leap of faith. I saw, though, that the Swiss had left behind a rope tied to a mountaineering stake that they had planted on the far side of the divide. The other end of the rope was on my side. I wrapped it around my waist, tied myself off, and launched myself across the crevasse to relative safety.

I looked up and had my first clear view of the summit. The early morning sun was hitting the snow peaks, framed by a purple-blue sky. An exhilarating sight, but now I saw that to climb that final face up to the peak, I would need to navigate a vast, and blinding, snow-field while avoiding any crevasses that may have been hidden by the freshly fallen snow. This would be the most dangerous part of my ascent.

To avert the risk of falling into crevasses, mountaineers climb with partners and attach themselves to each other with a strong length of rope. If one of the climbers falls into a crevasse, his partner on the other end can "hit the deck," dig in with her ice ax, and save her partner from falling to his death. But I was climbing alone.

I slowly made my way across the snowfield to the base of the peak.

I took off my backpack, pulled out my crampons, and strapped them to my boots. Exhausted, I decided to leave my pack at the base, taking only my camera and a pair of ice axes to begin the final climb up the nearly 70-degree face. I had never used an ice ax or worn a pair of crampons, but both seemed pretty straightforward: climb the face of the mountain just as you would a ladder; dig in with the teeth of each crampon, one after the other, and dig in with the blade of each ice ax, one after the other. Methodically, if not gracefully, I reached the top.

There I found the team of Swiss climbers I had been trailing. They had had no idea I was climbing below them and gave me baffled looks. After they headed down, I sat and enjoyed the view for a long time, probably longer than I should have. I didn't want to lose that feeling of exhilaration.

While I was in Nepal, I read Peter Matthiessen's acclaimed travel book, *The Snow Leopard*. I found it drudgery, but Matthiessen, a practicing Buddhist, quoted a proverb: "A snowflake never falls in the wrong place." There is a reason, perhaps divinely inspired, why each of us is on this Earth. I didn't give the line much thought at the time, but I soon would. I spent over eighteen hours on the mountain that day, and the trip was a turning point for me. I wanted to defy convention, to chart a unique path for myself, and climbing Imja Tse proved that I could do just that.

The sun was rising and heating up the snow and ice, increasing the risk of avalanche. I made my way back to our base camp by late afternoon, where Claude cooked me some eggs before I reloaded my backpack so we could continue down.

I next flew from Kathmandu, over Mount Everest, to Hong Kong, where I stayed long enough to buy some film for my camera. I took a boat to the port city of Guangzhou on mainland China, found a train station, and got on a train to Beijing so I could visit Tiananmen Square only months after the demonstrations there had led to the bloody government crackdown. I wanted to find some evidence of the atrocities, but the Square had been cleaned up, even sanitized, and all I could do was make small talk with some soldiers who were on patrol.

I'm usually bored by museums and tourist sights. I visited the Forbidden City in Beijing and the Great Wall but couldn't relate to either of them. For me, the real thrill of traveling is connecting with people from around the world, exchanging ideas and stories and traditions. I preferred talking with the locals whenever I could or meeting other travelers from different parts of the world. I liked the monasteries, the gompas, the churches, and the temples.

From Beijing I took the Siberian Express to Berlin, sharing a tiny sleeping car with four Chinese traveling to Europe to study. When we rolled into Moscow, I got off to stretch my legs. I met a couple of Russians on the platform, and they invited me to hang out with them, so I ended up staying in Moscow for a week. This was before the fall of the Berlin Wall, during the reign of the Soviet Union, which I had grown up being taught was an "evil empire." I was now there without a visa, illegally, but I made fast friends with several Russians who shared everything they had, including their vodka.

I then spent a week in Leningrad, and one evening when I was walking alone, I came upon tens of thousands of Soviet troops marching in the darkness and practicing for an enormous military parade. The soldiers, accompanied by tanks and missiles, looked intimidating from afar, but as I approached I saw how young they were, maybe seventeen or eighteen. As they marched by in formation, most would smile or even wink, and I thought how ridiculous the Reagan administration's scare talk was about the Soviet Union's ruthless military. The soldiers were just kids dressed in adult uniforms.

Though I didn't fully realize it, the vision that I had for my life, the one that I had developed in college, was gradually being obliterated with every mile I traveled.

After eleven months of traveling the world, I landed back in the United States broke, exhausted, and filled to the brim with experiences that I did not yet know what to do with. I could not integrate

15

everything I had seen, smelled, and felt into my real life. For lack of a better idea, I decided to take the job offer from GE that I had turned down when I graduated college. The woman I spoke to in Human Resources couldn't have been nicer.

"I'm ready to settle down," I told her.

"What if you decide to go travel around the world again?" she asked.

"That's out of my system. I swear it is." And I thought it was. I was finally embarking upon the career, the life, that had always been intended for me and for which I had worked so hard in college.

GE offered me a nice salary, and I moved to Stamford, Connecticut, to begin my job in December 1990. I joined the company right in the middle of Jack Welch's storied tenure as chief executive officer. "Neutron Jack" grew the company's profits unlike any executive before or since, and GE became the model for how to slim down a bloated corporate giant and run it like a gazelle. The parent company nurtured a kind of survivor mentality—underperforming managers didn't last long—but those in the Financial Management Program weren't there to just survive. They were highly ambitious, intensely competitive, and aiming for the top jobs.

The Financial Management Program is part of GE Capital, and in 1994 *Fortune* wrote, "GE Capital pours wealth into the corporate coffers by doing just about everything you can do with money except print it."

I had landed in the right spot at the right time. I knew about the generous salaries and lavish perks for GE managers. But I never saw myself as a GE lifer. I still planned on returning home and taking over my father's business or starting my own. I knew the farther down I went on this corporate track, the harder it would be for me to get off. But toward what end? GE had an exceptional training program, but I didn't have the same passion for it that the other FMPs had. I was holding my own and, because of my own competitive streak, slowly getting drawn into it. At the same time, though I would work fifty-five or sixty hours a week, my peers would work seventy-five or eighty. They would never consider leaving work early on a Friday, while I would cut out early to go to Lake George for the weekend, where I would mountain bike and windsurf with a friend. I took an unpaid vacation and headed back out to Colorado to ski; I also went to Pamplona, Spain, to run with the bulls with my brother Dave and my friend Erik Dorf. A native of Vail, Erik was a competitive skier, and we had bonded on the mountain and drank a lot of beer in dive bars from Colorado to Sweden.

I couldn't reconcile the intense work in the comfortable offices in Connecticut with the harsh suffering I had seen in those overwhelmed cities in India. Here we were, modeling complex economic forecasts when so many people in the world couldn't even read or write their own name. Even for a numbers guy, that seemed unacceptable. In my travels abroad, I loved waking up in the morning and not knowing where I'd sleep that night. Now I knew what time I'd wake up, what time I'd eat, what time I'd go to bed. I found myself sitting at my desk wondering: Why am I here? If "a snowflake never lands in the wrong place," there must be a reason. I just didn't know what it was.

Around this time, I was reading Albert Schweitzer's classic *Reverence for Life*, in which he described a "sleeping sickness" in Central Africa that led to death. "There also exists," Schweitzer wrote, "a sleeping sickness of the soul." He warned against living "superficially" and called on his readers to "persevere in action."

> *You cannot imagine how important action is to the inner life. . . . The interior joy we feel when we have done a good deed, when we feel we have been needed somewhere and have lent a helping hand, is the nourishment the soul requires. Without those times when man feels himself to be part of the spiritual world through his actions, his soul decays.*

For me, those words were a call to action. I would not let my soul fall victim to sleeping sickness.

I shared some of these feelings with Dave, who was working on a fishing boat in Alaska. He had his business degree, but the Alaska venture appealed to his outdoor sensibilities. Disdainful of corporate America, he wasn't surprised when I told him that I found company life a bit too structured.

Dave was fascinated by my recent visits to Thailand, India, and Nepal, and he wanted to make that trip as well. I too wanted to return, and in a series of telephone calls, we discussed how we could convert those travel experiences into something that was more than just a journey, into something altruistic – and if we had adventures along the way, all the better. We had certain themes in mind: poverty, illiteracy, education, hope. I remembered the British mountaineers who had financed the school in Nepal. I sent one of them a fax, saying I was inspired by their work and wondered if he had any advice for us. He sent a fax back and explained the logistics of making a financial contribution for a school. But Dave and I wanted to go further. Instead of making a donation, we wanted to build the actual school.

Dave moved to Stamford and got a job waiting tables, and over several months, we sketched out how we could actually make this work. We envisioned traveling by motorcycle and talked in general terms about building schools on three different continents. We also talked to our friends, many of whom—to our surprise—wanted to be part of it. We realized together that we could also address needs in our own communities. One friend, a high school teacher, wanted to get her students involved, either in building schools abroad or in doing public service in their own community. We started talking to high school students and realized how excited they were about this whole notion of service. That they could help build schools in developing countries and make a lasting impact in their own cities was powerful motivation. Slowly our plans to create a nonprofit took shape.

Dave and I founded Building with Books (BwB) in August 1991, when I was still at GE. Erik Dorf was completing his class work at

Middlebury College in Vermont, but he signed on too. We drafted a mission statement and a business plan, which called for building three schools on three different continents while engaging students from three American high schools in intensive service and youth development programs. It struck me as the right combination of compassion, idealism, and social change. We also named a three-person board of directors—Dave, myself, and our friend Don Epperson, who, as a banker and ardent Republican, was the most mature person in our group.

I thought I could work on BwB in my off-hours while I completed the Financial Management Program. But six months after BwB was incorporated, I was set to begin a new rotation at GE that would have demanded eighty hours a week, and I could no longer divide my loyalties between the two jobs. I had to make the biggest decision of my young life: Should I quit GE and devote myself entirely to the nonprofit?

I consulted with a friend, Marc Friedman, who was my cousin's college roommate and in many ways a perfect sounding board. Lean, with dark hair and blue eyes, he was one of our first volunteers, dedicating a huge amount of time to fundraising. He was also six years older than I, cautious by nature, and already part of the business establishment. He had moved to Connecticut to work in his uncle's electrical wire and cable business. The job paid well, even better after he became the company's chief operating officer. I knew Marc, if he were in my shoes, would never quit GE to work at a nonprofit that paid no salary. He was too reasonable. But that's why I wanted his opinion. We talked for hours, often at his house over beers, until finally one night I asked him, "What do you think I should do?"

He thought for a moment, then shrugged. "I think you should go for it."

That was quite meaningful, but I had never made an important decision without talking to my father. This matter, however, was different. I knew how proud he was that I was with GE, and I didn't want to disappoint him. He had reminded me more than once that, even if I didn't stay at GE forever, the training program would be enormously valuable for the rest of my career. At Christmas that year I finally spoke to him in person about what I was thinking. We were at our house in Michigan on a cold winter night. The lake was frozen, and all the cousins were running around. Christmas was a big deal in our family, but I finally got my dad's attention and told him I wanted to have a serious conversation, so we stepped into a private room.

I explained that I wanted to quit GE and work full time at Building with Books. My dad listened patiently and began asking questions.

How would we fund the new enterprise?

Who would build the schools?

Would I be able to return to GE once I left?

How would this affect my career?

Risk management had been my dad's strength in business. He wasn't going to tell me what to do, but he wanted me to see my career, and my life, like a chess game: every move I made would trigger other, opposing moves. My job was to assess the entire board, to avoid the traps, and to understand the interconnections of all my decisions. "Just remember," he told me, "what you do now will have a direct impact on where you will be ten years from now."

I think he was also trying to scare me a little. He was right, of course. Years later he told me that he thought the organization was certain to fail. But for now, he just wanted to make sure that I understood the opportunity, the career, and the money that I was giving up. Though I had no apparent means of supporting myself, I told him I was determined to help the poor.

"Oh?" he said.

"That's right. Christ was an ascetic who fought for social justice and lifted up the poor, and now that's our responsibility. That is what you taught me. This is our faith."

It was a pivotal moment for me. Until then, I really hadn't thought about this endeavor as a matter of faith, but when my dad challenged me, it became clear: *this* is what Christ is all about, and this is a God that I can live for.

"You're right," my dad said. "It's your decision, and you will have my love and support no matter what."

In February 1992 I walked into the GE offices and told the HR manager that my brother and I had started a nonprofit organization and that I couldn't stay at the company if we were going to get it off the ground.

"How much money do you have in the bank?" she asked.

"Three or four thousand dollars."

She said she wanted me to return to GE after I was done with the project, so she would call this detour a "sabbatical." She would give me half of my salary for six months and medical benefits for a full year. "I can't have you out there shooting squirrels for dinner," she said.

I thanked her for her generosity, but then I said, "Just so you know, I have no intention of coming back."

CHAPTER 2

Fear Is Useless

Many ideas die before they have a chance to succeed; others perish before they're even born. That was our challenge. Could our nonprofit bring educational opportunities to villages abroad and create public service curriculums at high schools in this country? Maybe a better question was this: Could our nonprofit even survive long enough to have its own address? One thing was certain: *I* was going to need a new address. I had to leave the house that I was sharing with several friends (which cost me $400 a month) and move into Marc Friedman's house. He charged me a discounted rent of $200.

Initially we were a ragtag operation. Dave and I worked out of the kitchen in the house where he lived, and Erik joined us when he could make it down from Vermont. The three of us made a commitment that we would give three years to the organization, and then we would "return to life"—though, in my case, I wasn't sure what that life would be. I thought our good intentions would be enough to win people over. In the first few months after I quit GE I approached a half dozen high schools about allowing us to run community-service programs, such as working in senior centers or homeless shelters, but the administrators all said no. Our complete lack of experience was an obvious strike against us. Back then, we didn't have the data we have now, which show that kids who are involved in after school programs are twice as likely to graduate from high school and that involvement in community service for low-income students shrinks the achievement gap and increases academic engagement.

Meanwhile, we had attracted dozens of volunteers in Connecticut and New York, many of whom were associated with GE. Before I left, I was asked to talk to the incoming class of FMPs, as GE thought that my departure to start a nonprofit reflected well on the company. After I spoke, some of the FMPs asked if they could help out on weekends or at night with fundraising, communications, and, of course, generating our financial statements.

After only four or five weeks, Building with Books had close to forty young professionals volunteering—writers, artists, corporate trainees, even a lawyer, Missy Taub, whom we convinced, over beers, to draw up our bylaws pro bono and to register us as a nonprofit. She later joined our board of directors. We held our meetings in the evenings at Dave's house, and as our team grew, we moved into a large conference room at GE Capital. We didn't really have permission, but no one at Security said anything, so we kept coming in every week. The volunteers worked hard and were there for all the right reasons, but we also had a good time together. After the meetings, we'd always go for a few drinks, and several couples who met there later got married. As we made plans for the first high school program to be launched or the first school to be built, a growing sense of common purpose brought us all together.

Back in Michigan, my cousin Joe was a student at my alma mater, Lumen Christi Catholic High School. When he heard what we were trying to do, he spoke to the principal of his school, who agreed to let me make my case to the students. These middle-class kids were by no means the population Building with Books was ultimately trying to reach, but it was a place to start. I camped out in the library with Joe and his best friend, Brendan Kelly, and I spoke to about a hundred students at a time until I had reached the entire student body. Using slides from India and Nepal, I told them that these were two of the poorest countries on the planet. I showed them photos of

Mount Everest but talked mostly about the Nepalese and the impact of extreme poverty on the children, and I recounted how the villagers had celebrated their new school. At the end of the presentations, I talked about the need for education and the importance of stepping up and doing something. I then asked any interested students to meet with me at the end of the day.

We expected a dozen or so kids, but more than 120 showed up. Frankly, a good many came because Joe and Brendan recruited them. I was astonished, and I wasn't entirely sure how to work with that many students—especially when I lived in a different state. But we learned. We recruited a volunteer teacher advisor who ran weekly meetings while the students nominated officers and formed leadership committees. They held fundraisers to help our school-building efforts abroad—Battle of the Bands contests, dances, car washes—and reached out to the community to volunteer on service projects. The students themselves decided what projects were most important to them.

Getting one high school on board made us legitimate, and I was able to sign up two others in that first year as well. One was in Mahopac, New York, where we were friends with a teacher; the other was in Stamford, where a student heard about us, recruited two teaching advisors, and helped convince the principal to implement our after-school service program. I initially visited the New York and Stamford schools about once a week, the Michigan school less often, and was constantly communicating with all three by telephone. I was encouraged by what I saw. The students had energy and passion for the work—helping out at soup kitchens, visiting nursing homes, planting community gardens, removing graffiti—but what struck me most was their confidence, their belief that they could really make a difference in their community and change the world. We were seeing our young organization's mission come to life.

Amid all the good energy, and with a foothold in three high schools in the United States, we pursued our goal of building three schools overseas. We targeted countries based on their poverty index and illiteracy rates, and we initially identified Brazil, Malawi, and Nepal—three different countries on three different continents. Dave and I began to develop partnerships with two international organizations, Habitat for Humanity International and Save the Children, which helped us find villages but would leave the rest up to us. We were looking for communities that not only needed a school but were willing to help build it. That was essential, in part because we needed the manpower but also because we knew the school would only succeed if the community truly wanted it and was willing to work for it.

Though we had committed to building the three schools, we asked our partners not to make any announcements until we had the funding. The director of Habitat for Humanity in Malawi didn't get the message. One morning he sent us a fax that said he had notified the village of Misomali that we'd be constructing a school there. "The kids immediately broke out in song and dance," the director wrote. "The celebration went on for hours. Needless to say, if you fail to make it here to build the school, they'll be equally disappointed."

We had already been feeling the pressure of our mission, but this news made it all the more acute. It had been six months since I left GE, and we hadn't even raised enough to cover the cost of our phone bill. We were failing indeed. We had contacted foundations, philanthropists, and corporations. We had applied for grants, sent letters, made phone calls, cajoled, and begged. We had developed a slide show for meetings with potential funders (which were rarely held). The response we kept getting was this: Our inner cities are wastelands, suffering from intractable social problems, impervious to government initiatives, effectively ignored by most Americans. Developing countries, meanwhile, are on no one's radar. Who are you to solve all these problems? No one else seemed to see that the issues at home and abroad could be intertwined. But we believed that they were.

I tried to rally friends, family, and acquaintances, but there was only so much they could do. We were stuck. I felt terrible for our volunteers, who had given so much. We were about to betray a group of impoverished children in Malawi, and we were also going to fail hundreds of students in the United States who believed in our mission and who were trying to raise money so these villages could build a school.

Some weeks after the fax arrived from Malawi, a GE executive allowed Dave and me to use one of the company's basement offices. We called it the "cube farm." Only one other person ever went down there, a recently laid-off manager who muttered obscenities about GE as he fruitlessly searched for a job on a computer. It was in the cube farm that my downward spiral began. I knew I was foundering, but I couldn't say so because our volunteers had invested so much time and hope in us. As the rejections to our pleas for money piled up, I started asking myself, Why did I have to create something new? Why didn't I just join the Peace Corps? Or why didn't I stay at GE?

I was having trouble sleeping. When the phone rang, I wouldn't answer it because I didn't want to confront the simple question "How's it going?" I avoided certain friends because I knew they would ask about BwB. I couldn't even confide in Dave, who still believed we could do this. The only person I could talk to was Marc; we would have late night strategy discussions and sometimes I would wake him up in the early hours of the morning to bounce ideas off of him. He tried to reassure me but had no idea how to find the money we needed.

At some point, I was driving with a friend on a 100-degree day, when we got stuck in traffic in a construction zone. As I sat in the air-conditioned car, I watched one worker pouring blacktop, drenched in sweat, and thought out loud, "I'd do anything to trade positions with him right now." I was so lost, I might have traded places with anyone.

On another day, I woke up at 3:30 a.m. and began running potential scenarios through my head. We had solicited money from so many organizations, but even if most of them came through, we still wouldn't have enough to build the schools. I envisioned a $100,000 budget, but we were applying for $2,500 here and $5,000 there. I needed a Niagara but could only ask for droplets. And even if we got the money, we didn't know the first thing about building schools, mobilizing communities, or even how to get to the villages where we'd do the work. Yet I had convinced everyone involved that I knew what I was doing.

I just lay there in the dark, alone with reality. Minutes seemed like hours, until finally, just before the sun came up, I flipped on a light, reached over to my night stand, and picked up a Bible that my father had given me. I opened it up to a random page and began to read from the Gospel of Mark (5:36–41), where one of the rulers begs Christ to come to his house and heal his dying daughter.

> *He had not finished speaking when people from the official's house arrived saying, "Your daughter is dead. Why bother the Teacher further?"*
>
> *Jesus disregarded the report that had been brought and said to the official: "Fear is useless, what is needed is trust."*

When Christ reached the house, he saw the girl and declared that she was not dead but asleep. They ridiculed him, but Christ, taking the child's hand, told her:

> *"Little girl, get up."*
>
> *The girl, a child of 12, stood up immediately and began to walk around.*

"Fear is useless, what is needed is trust." I read that line over and over again and realized that I was being crippled by *fear*.

My problem wasn't so much that I lacked money or expertise or experience. My problem was that I was afraid I was going to let down the children in Misomali and all the American students and volunteers who believed in me, including my own brother. And that fear was debilitating. What I needed was trust—in Christ, in the Holy Spirit, and in God. I came back to that verse in the days and weeks ahead, and I started going to Mass more often, even on weekdays. I now understood that only through faith could I overcome my fear, and as my father told me, I would have to nurture and exercise that faith every day.

I had felt alone, exposed, and humbled; I was empty. But that is when God finds you.

My faith wasn't my only defense in restoring the chances of our non-profit. Before I had left GE, Jamie Hauge, the Human Resources manager, had asked if I would give the company a copy of our business plan. I sent it in and thought nothing more of it. Nearly six months later, just after I had hit rock bottom, Jamie called me out of the blue and said that Jim Parke, the chief financial officer of GE Capital, had read the plan, and I should try to meet with him. It was a long shot, but I had nothing to lose. I set up an appointment, though my friends at GE warned me not to be surprised if Parke ended up canceling.

He didn't.

His was the biggest office I had ever been in. I couldn't believe how far his desk was from the door. But he couldn't have been more professional and gracious. The product of a small town in Montana, he had attended college in Minnesota and then competed against the Ivy Leaguers when he joined GE. He liked underdogs. He listened intently and didn't waste words.

I told him what our goals were: we wanted to build three schools on three continents, and we wanted to run afterschool programs dedicated to community service in America's poorest cities. I told him we had 501(c)(3) status, that we had begun work in three high schools, and that we had identified villages abroad in which to build the schools. We even had a lawyer.

I then told him about a kid in a leather jacket who had joined our program. He was an older student, big shoulders and tough, who was in the special education program at the high school; he may have had a learning disability but he definitely had a behavior problem. He had been suspended numerous times, and his teachers didn't know where to turn. But after we arrived, he began to get involved in community service. He was now coming to school regularly, doing the work, and avoiding trouble. "I talk with these students personally and see it for myself," I told Parke. "This kid can turn his life around."

Parke smiled. "This is good," he said. "What can we do to help?"

I couldn't believe my ears. Sure, Habitat for Humanity had agreed to help find a place to build a school, but Parke was the first person with any authority, or at least access to money, to say anything positive about our idea. He actually believed in us. Until now, our support had come from idealistic young people, but Parke was a high-ranking executive. "We need funding," I said. "Can you help us get funding?"

He picked up the phone and called Dennis Dammerman, the chief financial officer of the parent company and the head of the GE Foundation, which donates money to charities. Parke told him, "I've got this crazy kid here who'd like to get some funds from you. Can we come up and talk?"

I was stunned by how quickly we were to meet with Dammerman: in one week. A meeting was set, and I left Parke's office determined not to let the newest member of our team down.

Meeting with Parke had made me nervous, but Dammerman petrified me. He had a reputation for brilliance as well as toughness, a man who enforced the ultimate meritocracy that was GE: he rewarded the high achievers and fired the underperformers. I had assumed that Parke would explain what I wanted. But right before we entered Dammerman's office, Parke told me, "You're doing the talking. I'm just listening." I gulped and we went in.

We sat down at his conference table, and I tried to explain what our organization did and what the goals were, but I didn't get anywhere. I was jittery, and Dammerman was so intense and direct.

Sensing my discomfort, Parke told me to describe the kid in the leather jacket, which I did.

Dammerman nodded.

I looked out the window and saw Jack Welch's helicopter descending to land on a copter pad. Moments later, he popped into our meeting and asked what we were doing. Dammerman motioned to me to tell him about the organization, which I did. Welch appeared interested but not exactly inspired. "God bless you for stepping up to this," he said. Then he was gone.

I wrapped up my presentation and waited to hear Dammerman's verdict. "Why do you think you can do this?" he asked. "You have no track record. You have no other model you can replicate or even point to. Why are you so convinced you can do this? And why should I be convinced?"

It was a familiar litany of questions and doubt. I had no answer and didn't try to fake one. I just looked him in the eye and heard myself say, "I will never give up. I will never give up. I will never give up."

The words hung in the air for a few long moments.

Then Dammerman smiled. "What do you need?"

"Our budget is $100,000."

He shook his head. "That's not going to happen, but here's what you can do." He told me to submit a grant application to the GE Foundation.

I was crushed. I thought I'd walk out of there with a fat check, and instead I got invited to request another grant we probably wouldn't receive. A meeting with the CEO of McGraw-Hill, Joe Dionne, led to the same outcome: submit a grant application, but no money. Only six months after we started, Building with Books was dying a slow death, and I wanted to quit.

But before we shut the whole thing down, Dave suggested we make one last-ditch effort to raise some money. We had held some small fundraisers at bars, but now we were going to put all of our savings, roughly $3,500, into the Global Gala 1992. It would be a black-tie event, never mind that we couldn't afford the black ties for ourselves. A tuxedo shop gave us two free tuxes in exchange for advertising their store on our invitation. We rented the Stamford Center for the Arts for $500, hired a band, ordered a dozen kegs of beer, and convinced A Little Slice of Heaven Pizza, among other small restaurants, to provide some food.

Of course, we also needed people to come—we were charging $45 a person—so we mailed hundreds of invitations. We canvassed the area, hung up posters, handed out invitations at festivals, put up fliers in restaurants and bars, talked up the event at parties, called friends and strangers alike. One volunteer, Jennifer Nix, wrote press releases and sent stories about us to local newspapers. With a true fervor and growing excitement, we were running all over Stamford and New York trying to save our nonprofit.

We had just one problem: virtually no one was responding. Each day, Dave or I would go to the post office and open our box, expecting it to be stuffed with RSVPs. We must have had the loneliest P.O. box in the system. Day after day, that damn box was empty. We couldn't figure out why no one was interested. We called everyone we could think of and asked if they were coming. They told us they were, but no one was sending in their checks. We needed 120 people to break even, but the night before the event we had only forty responses. What an embarrassment. Even worse, Jim Parke would be there, and I was convinced he would witness our defeat. Our big fundraiser was going to be a funeral instead. Maybe Parke would deliver our eulogy.

Dave and I reached the Stamford Center about an hour before the event was to start, and we saw people milling around out in front. They were wearing tuxes and gowns, and it turned out that they were there for us. Inexplicably, more people arrived, and then more, and by the time we were ready to open, a line ran out the door and around the block. And they just kept coming. More than four hundred people showed up.

I watched people drinking beer and eating pizza and pasta, and I realized that I was witnessing something very special. Almost everyone there had a similar profile: they were young, well-educated professionals (accountants, lawyers, bankers, journalists, teachers), mostly white, who had the means to spend this particular Saturday night a hundred different ways. They could have traveled, gone clubbing in the City, attended a concert or a Broadway show. But instead they were here. They were with us because they wanted to be part of something bigger. They wanted to find a way to make a difference. They were moved to help out because the act of giving, of service, is too powerful to ignore, too gratifying to deny.

At one point I was standing off to the side with Jim Parke, and I admitted that I had had no inkling that this many people were going to attend. He said he was surprised as well. We both had a good laugh, and then he told me it was his birthday. I was amazed that someone of his stature would spend his birthday with us.

I hadn't thought to prepare any remarks, so I found a quiet place and scribbled down some ideas. I spoke for four minutes, expressing my gratitude and sharing my passion, but I was unable to truly express what was in my heart: I had witnessed a miracle.

That night, our fortunes turned. We netted $17,000 for the gala. A few days later, GE sent us a check for $25,000 and McGraw-Hill wired us $10,000: from zero to $52,000 in one week!

During that first year after I left GE, I came very close to giving up, despite my faith and all the people who believed in me. I thought we were down for the count—but we had been three seconds away from our first victory. We could now begin building schools.

CHAPTER 3

The Village of Liberty

We had barely survived our first year as an organization—but none of those challenges would compare with building our first schools overseas. We had incorporated as a 501(c)(3) not-for-profit, elected a board of directors, recruited a core of volunteers, established partnerships with Habitat for Humanity and Save the Children, and established programs in three high schools. But now, we had to make some decisions that would define our organization: Were we a group of ambitious do-gooders who were seeking travel and adventure as part of some vague humanitarian mission, or were we serious organizers and advocates who were committed to education and service? The motorcycles were an early test.

I had met a representative for Honda at a motorcycle rally in upstate New York, and suggested that Honda donate three giant 750cc dirt bikes that were designed specifically for the overland race from Paris to Dakar, Senegal. These machines could handle anything, and I thought they'd be perfect to help us get around. I followed up with the rep, quite a few times in fact, and he finally sent a letter confirming that Honda would provide us with bikes. What a sight we would be! Dave, Erik, and I loved the idea of tearing through the African plains or the Nepalese countryside on our way to the next work site.

But a couple weeks after hearing from Honda, I began to have my doubts. This wasn't supposed to be *Easy Rider* joins the Peace Corps.

The bikes would be a distraction, or worse; if they broke down or if we were pulled over by the authorities, the delay could jeopardize our ability to build the schools. We were having a hard enough time raising money, and the image of us on those bikes wouldn't make it any easier. Suddenly they seemed an indulgence. Even though we had had our hearts set on it, Dave, Erik, and I decided to turn down Honda's offer.

That decision was a kind of turning point: it said—to the outside world, but also to ourselves—that we were dedicated to our cause more than to our own desire for fun.

Though we had many volunteers, only the three of us were willing to travel to three different continents and spend eighteen months living in remote villages and building schools. In addition to the village in Malawi, Habitat for Humanity International identified one in Brazil, while Save the Children directed us to a village in Nepal. Neither Dave nor Erik nor I had been to any of these countries, and none of us knew how to speak the native languages.

In February 1993 we flew to Brazil. During the previous six months, we had been in contact, mostly by fax, with Izary Lizias, the country director for Habitat for Humanity International, and a Methodist missionary named Gordon Greathouse. A serious man with straight blond hair and dark eyes, Gordon had moved to Brazil from Oregon in the 1970s as part of his missionary work. He then met a woman, married, and stayed, and he and his wife, Teca, ran a community center near a shantytown to help residents become more economically independent.

Gordon picked us up at the airport at Belo Horizonte in the eastern part of Brazil, the country's third largest metropolitan area. Unlike in America, where the inner cities are often home to the poor and the suburbs attract the wealthy, in Brazil the opposite was true: the rich lived in the urban centers, and the slums were on the outskirts. We were heading for the outskirts.

Beneath a warm sun and blue sky, we drove through beautiful mountains and rolling hills, reminiscent of Vermont in summer. We arrived at a village that was part of a new settlement still under construction. The families were poor—the adults eked out a living as day laborers in Belo Horizonte—but it wasn't a slum. About fifty houses had been built, simple concrete structures, about 800 to 1,000 square feet, with ceramic tile roofs, two bedrooms, plumbing, and basic electricity. The village already had a primary school, but it needed a *crèche*, or preschool, for the children ages three to six. Building it would be our job, and the kids who would attend rushed to meet us when we arrived, along with older children and a group of women. They welcomed us with warmth and gratitude. The more bashful children smiled and shook hands or waved, but the bolder kids gave us hugs. Until now, our desire to build a school had been well intentioned but abstract; those young children made everything real, leaving me both excited and fearful.

The initial adjustment to the village was jarring—I had never eaten chicken stew with the animal's claw still in the bowl—but on our first day, a group of us gathered in a circle on an empty lot, and with the help of Teca Greathouse we talked about the project, and then we held hands and said a prayer. We still had no idea what we were doing, but we knew there was something special about this community.

Favela is a lyrical Portuguese word for a place that is quite inhumane: the shantytowns, or slums, of Brazil. Most modern *favelas* emerged in the 1970s, when many Brazilians left the countryside and moved to the cities; unable to find housing, they ended up building their own makeshift quarters on the edge of town. These were grim whirlpools of crime, open sewage, and disease. They were also on private property and therefore illegal. At the time, the country was ruled by a military dictatorship, and at best the government ignored the settlements; at worst, it bulldozed them, placating the landowners while forcing the occupants, often well over five thousand of them, onto some other patch of land with less than twenty-four hours' notice.

By the time we arrived in 1993, Brazil was no longer under military rule, so the government's most egregious assaults on the *favelas* had ended. What's more, the authorities were making land available for those who lived in slums like São Gabrielle. Located on the edge of Belo Horizonte, it was little more than a collection of tired shacks made of plastic bags and sticks, erected on dirt paths that in a rainstorm turned to mud and streams of raw sewage. São Gabrielle was also the site of Gordon and Teca Greathouse's community center, and they helped the residents petition the government to donate land for a new village. Gordon and Teca solicited Habitat for Humanity International as well to help the families build their houses. All the pieces came together, and a new village, aptly named, was born: Bairro Liberdade, or Village of Liberty.

By the time we met them, the families had every reason to be upbeat, hopeful, and unified. The same could not be said for Dave and me. Our disagreements had begun when we started raising funds for the trip. Dave didn't agree with my efforts to raise money from corporate donors; he assumed that such contributions were made more for the publicity than for any humanitarian reason. He wasn't too keen on for-profit enterprises in general. That had been a flashpoint, but now we were arguing about how we would actually build the school. On the work site itself, I expected the community to provide volunteers, and I refused to pay for any labor, including skilled workers and translators. Dave argued that we needed to hire skilled workers such as masons to get the job done. I said no. I didn't want the organization to be a charity that swooped in, built a school, left behind a few pencils, and then moved on to the next village. We agreed that the local ministries of education should provide the teachers once we left, but I wanted the locals to put their own sweat equity into building the project. "We're all volunteers," I said. "It has to be pure." Dave relented, at least at the outset.

As Dave and I argued into the night, we sometimes forgot that the villagers might have their own ideas. We couldn't convince enough of them to volunteer, in large part because so many had to leave for their paying jobs as day laborers. An important early lesson: It would be easier to build with volunteers in rural areas, rather than urban, because subsistence farmers have far more control over their time. We were also stymied by language barriers, by our lack of access to materials, and by the local economy, which was reeling from hyperinflation. The rate had peaked in 1990 at a staggering 6,800 percent and was still out of control. We would convert dollars into the local currency, but if we couldn't buy materials that day, by the next day the prices had already gone up and the currency would be worth 20 percent less.

We also confronted our own ignorance. In the United States we had some experience framing houses but had never done construction of this sort. We didn't even know how to lay out the lines—creating right angles at the corners of the foundation is surprisingly difficult without some engineering expertise—and we would have been completely lost had Gordon not introduced us to an architect, or if Izary Lizias, the Habitat for Humanity official, hadn't joined us on the site to contribute his construction expertise. With their assistance, we laid the lines and began to dig the foundation and eventually got to mixing and pouring the concrete. We hired the right trucks to bring supplies from the city, but without sufficient manpower—we had about ten volunteers on any given day—our progress was slow. What we thought would take two and a half months soon stretched to four months, five months, and then six. Our frustrations mounted, but we were never tempted to abandon the project.

For all our struggles, Dave, Erik, and I developed close ties with the families who hosted us. Warm, expressive, and loving, the Brazilians gave us one of the new homes they had built with their own hands but had not yet occupied. Our neighbors included Elenese and Domingo, who had eight children. Elenese had a high voice and tight curly hair, and she worried about us incessantly; Domingo was shorter than his wife, quiet, always clean shaven (unusual in this community), and wore clothes that were impeccably clean. Two doors down were Edna and Alfonso, who had three children. Alfonso was an irrepressible spirit who loved to drink beer, smoke cigarettes, and play poker long into the night. And then there was Edna, a community leader whose emotions were always on display but whose long dark hair and dark eyes projected a kind of nobility.

These neighbors made us part of their own families. We bought our own food, but when we left in the morning for the work site, the girls from the neighborhood would come to the house, sweep the floors, straighten the rooms, and cook us rice and beans for lunch and chicken for dinner. They also shared with us *pão de queijo*, Brazilian cheese bread, whose rich aroma filled the streets. At night, Erik played his guitar for our neighbors. On one of our first days off, we hiked up to an abandoned church on a hilltop with some of the kids, checked out the view, and had a little picnic.

An odd kind of fatalism, as well as courage, defined the villagers. One day, for example, a coral snake slithered right over the hand of a little girl. Coral snakes are not aggressive, but they're quite deadly. In most places, if you see such a snake, you try to kill it. In this case, one of Elenese's sons, Jaiuto, captured the snake in a glass jar, poked holes in the metal top, and placed the jar on a shelf in the house. I couldn't understand why he'd want to do that. If the jar had tipped over, it would have broken on the tile floor, and an angry snake would be loose in the house.

I told Elenese I thought that was a strange place to keep a deadly snake. "Yes," she agreed, "it's the same kind of snake that bit and killed my dad." The family eventually released it into a swamp.

Though our Portuguese improved over time (mine was the worst), we didn't need language to communicate. Elenese and Domingo were always giving us hugs, and they set important examples for their own children. They were constantly on the work site—in Domingo's case, when he wasn't at one of his low-paying jobs in Belo Horizonte. That sent a clear message to their older kids, who did not have school the full day and were able to help us almost every afternoon.

Alfonso was a trained stonemason, and he volunteered to help us, initially a couple days a week. He was soon with us every day instead of working his paying jobs. Edna finally told us, "You have to talk to him because we've got no food."

We encouraged Alfonso to go to his day job and to join us when he could, but he kept coming every day. He loved the camaraderie, but he also understood the value of that school and wanted to do all he could for the community.

In many ways, the women in the village made even greater contributions. Organized by Teca, they formed a leadership committee, of which Elenese and Edna were copresidents. Their job, among other things, was to organize the volunteers, coordinate supplies, and bring food and water to the site. They seemed to understand the value of education more than many of the men.

As the months passed, we sent letters, photographs, and video footage back to the States, all of which was used to engage our volunteers and donors, who were continuing to raise money. Our three schools were also using the videos and photos to add students to the program and dramatize the impact of community service.

But we were fairly isolated, and frankly it was difficult to focus on America when so much was happening in and around Bairro Liberdade.

I had been reading *Brazil: The War on Children*, about the country's 8 million street kids, and I became keenly interested in them. I wanted to go out into the *favela* and see how the families and street kids lived. I thought they were the group we should really be helping, and if I could film them with my Hi8 video camera, I could show some eye-opening footage to the American students on how other young people around the world live.

But Gordon strongly discouraged me. He explained that there were frequent reports of theft, kidnapping, and murder. Elenese agreed. "*Jeem! Jeem!*" she would call to me in her high voice. "Do not go with the street children. They are very, very dangerous!"

I went anyway, and the street kids who took me around the slum weren't hostile at all. They scavenged for food, stole chickens, or maybe they wouldn't eat for the entire day. They weren't all orphans, but the other street children were essentially their family. One boy told me that they had three options to survive: they could beg, steal, or work, but there wasn't much work for them. I made several trips to visit them, and for all the warnings about my safety, I was surprisingly well received. When I photographed complete strangers, they would offer me a plate of rice and coffee. I wondered if my own neighbors in the States would be so generous to someone they had never met.

I didn't tell Gordon about these experiences, but we talked at length about the nexus of faith and social justice, and as a missionary these conversations came naturally to Gordon. I told him that I began our nonprofit because I wanted to live my faith, but he spelled out a larger vision of liberation theology, which interprets the goals of Christ as liberation from unjust social conditions. Just as Christ had called out the scribes and the Pharisees for their hypocrisy and pretentiousness, the job of Christians is to challenge authority when it has gone astray and to shake up the establishment when it serves its own interests—but to do so with courage, nonviolence, and forgiveness. I wasn't in position to challenge anyone in authority in Brazil, but at least I could stake out my own path.

Gordon introduced me to an outfit in Belo Horizonte called the National Center for Street Children, which ran a community center. There were thousands of street kids, and the center would drive a van into the streets, pick them up, and bring them back so they could wash up or receive food or medicine.

In addition to my work on the school, I started volunteering at the center, and I developed a deeper understanding of these children. They often traveled in gangs and lived under bridges or viaducts, in boxes, or wherever they could find shelter. They'd get high by dipping their shirts in gas, glue, or paint thinner, and then huffing the fumes. Many of the older kids, ages thirteen to fifteen, had already been in prison, and they bore scars from the guards' beatings. Armed policemen watched over the roads from towers, searching for child pickpockets and muggers to shoot like stray dogs. The kids sometimes robbed or endangered passersby or even other kids. I heard stories about the older boys raping the girls and exploiting the younger boys, and I heard about gang rapes as well. Teenage girls worked the streets as prostitutes, and pregnant teenagers sought out care at the community center. The streets took their toll: a mangled foot that was run over by a bus, or deep cuts across a kid's back from a bad fall. Some scars, I knew, would never heal.

The kids let me follow them around, film them, and even interview them. I befriended some—we developed elaborate handshakes that felt like a kind of secret code to our friendship—and came to believe that the perception of these kids was either exaggerated or outright wrong. True, some posed threats to the community, but most were not violent. Few were menacing. They were just trying to survive.

One night I was walking with Gordon and Teca in the downtown area of the city. About a dozen of the street kids I had been hanging out with saw us, and they ran toward me. The crowd on the street parted like the Red Sea; the adults were terrified. The kids and I exchanged our handshake, and we began trading barbs and goofing around, and I noticed that several dozen strangers had stopped and were watching us in fear and amazement.

The encounter blew my cover with Gordon and Teca, who now knew what I was doing in my spare time. They were surprised that I had forged such a strong bond with these kids. These experiences in the street made clear why the adults in Bairro Liberdade were so passionate about our efforts to build a school. Many of them had come from the *favela*; what they feared most was that their children would join the gangs and eventually be another statistic in some newspaper article. Our *crèche* would be a redeeming antidote, a humane alternative, to that possibility.

But as much as I loved the families in Bairro Liberdade, I real-ized they weren't the ones who needed our help the most. They had made it out of the slums, and a nearly triumphant mood drifted through the village. But the children who were trapped in the grime of São Gabrielle or who ran in the alleys of Belo Horizonte, they knew desperation. We couldn't even try to build a school in a *favela* because the *favelas* weren't permanent; a school there would someday be erased like everything else. I wanted to help the people who were living in the most extreme conditions. I had seen the extremes, and we weren't there.

I considered redirecting my efforts away from Building with Books and working instead with the street kids of Brazil. It seemed like the place where I could make the greatest difference. I was tempted, but I couldn't make that leap. I was too deeply invested in BwB, in the volunteers, the donors, the high schools, as well as two villages in Africa and Nepal that were waiting for us to build schools there. I had also made a commitment to Dave and Erik. We were going to complete what we started.

I continued on in Brazil, but after five months and with the school still not complete, I had to leave to work with the students in the States and to do more fundraising, and then to start up the next school ahead of Dave and Erik.

Before I left, I asked Edna to write a letter to the students in America. Their fundraising had contributed to the school, and I wanted them to hear directly from one of the beneficiaries. Edna wrote the letter, which I had translated right then and there. "Dear Friends," she wrote:

> *Full of thanks and my heart full of joy, I am writing to you. My name is Edna Lucia, and I have three children. . . . I dream of a better world for them. I dream of a place for the children of Bairro Liberdade. A gift of heaven, from Building with Books, brought to us by Jim, Dave and Erik, and you all. All you young people deserve the eternal pro-tection of God. Our children would never be so loved by our own*

government and authorities. Your help will always be remembered.
One day I will see children playing in the school. . . . We adore you.
May God give you twice as much as you give us. May God be with
you always, always, always.

On my last day in Bairro Liberdade, I was waiting to be picked
up by Gordon to go to the airport. I had said my good-byes the night
before, but now about forty people had come out, and we were all
hanging around, feeling sadder and sadder. Some of the girls began
to cry. Gordon finally arrived, and Elenese began to cry as I was giving my final hugs. It was emotional for me, but I was still holding
it together until I saw Domingo. He had a big tear running down
his cheek. I didn't realize how much these people cared about me,
about us. I didn't realize how much I loved them. I didn't know if
I'd ever see them again. I had never had that kind of bond with anyone outside my own family. I started sobbing. So did Domingo, and
we hugged. I got into the car, and a full twenty minutes later I was
still crying.

"Are you okay?" Dave asked.

"I don't know," I said.

CHAPTER 4

The Appalling Silence
of Good People

It took Dave and Erik two more months, but they finished the school, and its reach extended well beyond that one community. When I read Edna's letter to the American students and showed them the film footage and the photographs, they were amazed by the impact of that one project and were inspired to do even more in their own community—a perfect tribute, indeed, to the children of Bairro Liberdade, the Village of Liberty.

I was in the States for only a few weeks, but long enough to attend our second annual gala. This time I had far more to talk about. I did a slide show with my photos of the street children in Brazil and of the school construction, and I read Edna's letter as well. I also asked one of our students, Kim Mack, to address the crowd. Kim was one of our most motivated students—she recruited the teaching advisors herself—and I realized how powerful those first-person narratives are. I was glad that Jim Parke attended and could see our progress, and the event raised about $75,000—more than four times the amount from our first gala.

We had started our first after-school program in the South Bronx, at Morris High School, which the writer Jonathan Kozol had profiled in *Savage Inequalities* about the decaying schools in our inner cities. We were also receiving more assistance from corporate sponsors, which explains how I received a free ticket on Swiss Air to fly to Africa to start our next school. My destination was Malawi, but Swiss Air took me only as far as Cape Town, South Africa, nearly 1,700 miles away from where I needed to go. I was going to hitchhike the rest of the way and hadn't planned to spend any time in South Africa, but I got sidetracked. Apartheid will do that to you.

It was early summer of 1993, and South Africa's white minority government was still in power. The country was headed for free elections the following year, and tensions were as high as ever. What I witnessed—forced segregation, encampments surrounded by razor wire, government-sponsored terrorism—was completely new to me. Until then, my worldview had been focused on education and poverty. I now saw that social justice, intertwined with my own Christian faith, had to be front and center as well.

After landing in Cape Town, I needed one night to rest. Carrying my backpack and tent, I was picked up by a minibus at the airport, and the driver, Leonard, was the only other person in it. He had dark skin and was considered "colored," one of the racial classifications under apartheid, because his ancestors were from India and various African tribes. He seemed about my age.

"Where you going?" he asked me.

"I don't know," I said. "Malawi, ultimately." I asked him where backpackers and hitchhikers stay in Cape Town.

"I could take you to the bus station," he said.

I had a better idea. "Could I stay at your house for the night?" He seemed like a nice guy, and when traveling I often asked to stay at people's houses, as I was always trying to save what little (donated) money I had. "I could crash on the floor, and it would only be for one night."

Leonard slowed down, stopped the minibus, and turned and looked at me. "You want to stay at my house?"

"If it's okay," I said.

Aghast, Leonard repeated his question.

I thought I had breached some protocol, but we talked our way through it, and I slowly began to understand. It was unheard of in South Africa for a white person to stay with anyone of color. What's more, because I had blond hair and blue eyes, he initially thought I was an Afrikaner, part of the country's most militant supporters of apartheid.

I explained that I was an American, which put him more at ease. He took me to his house and, speaking in Afrikaans, immediately called someone on the phone. People started milling around outside the house, looking through the window. I was on display, and the children in particular seemed incredulous. It wasn't hard to figure out why: I was the only white person in this neighborhood and probably the only white person for miles. I had stood out somewhat in Brazil, but that country had no racial tension to speak of. In South Africa that tension was palpable. To the blacks who were now staring at me, I was not only an outsider, but, by virtue of my skin color, I was in the same category as their oppressors. For all I knew, I might have been violating some law to even be there.

They weren't angry, only curious. By now I had traveled all over the world and had never thought twice about introducing myself to strangers. I believe that if you show respect for others that they will do the right thing. I also liked the idea of breaking down racial barriers and showing the South Africans that not all whites were villains. My presence demolished a stereotype and demonstrated my own defiance against a morally bankrupt government.

A few minutes later, an intense black man named Charles Olkers arrived. "Where's the white guy?" he asked.

Charles was a member of the African National Congress, which for years had led the armed struggle against white rule. He embodied that spirit well: with fire in his eyes, a thick accent, and a deep scar across his leg from rubber bullets fired by a government soldier, he summoned gusts of energy when calling for the overthrow of apartheid and for freedom for the country's black population. He was a born-again Christian who didn't smoke, drink, or curse, and he spoke with an evangelical fury. That I was American was a huge point in my favor. Charles and his ANC cohorts idolized America because our economic sanctions against South Africa had weakened the government, and Charles peppered me with questions about my country. "Can you stay with black people in America?" he asked.

"Yes, if you want to," I said.

Did we have black politicians, lawyers, or doctors? What could I tell them about Martin Luther King Jr., Malcolm X, or Andrew Young? What about civil rights? I discovered that I needed to learn a lot more as well. Having just filmed the shantytowns in Brazil, I wanted to do the same in South Africa. I asked Charles if he would take me.

"Why?" he asked.

"I don't know," I said. "Maybe I can create an educational video about apartheid. Raise awareness among American youth. Educate them about the reality. It would be much more powerful than a textbook."

Charles needed no convincing. He took me to Crossroads, one of the country's largest and most notorious shantytowns and the site of several bloody riots in the 1980s. It still evoked a sense of imminent danger. Barefoot kids stood in garbage, fires blazed in trash cans, meat hung on sticks, and barbed wire shut the place in.

Then there were the huge yellow Casspirs. Used to transport troops in warfare, these four-wheel armored vehicles had been designed with a raised V-shaped body to withstand the explosion of land mines. Armed with machine guns and in some cases a cannon, they were lumbering, indestructible war machines on giant wheels, now deployed against blacks for crowd and riot control, for breaking down walls, and for sending an unmistakable message of intimidation and power.

I had seen profound hardship in several other countries, but this was altogether different. In South Africa suffering was enforced by the state; injustice, a matter of public policy. As I began to learn more, I knew I had to document what I saw. I needed to see it, hear it, feel it. My one-night stay at Leonard's house stretched into seven nights, as I slept on the floor and ate whatever they offered. Though they were a bit nervous at first, Leonard and his entire family were excited that I was staying with them. With Charles as my guide, I began meeting more black South Africans, who were surprised but gratified that a white person wanted to hear their stories about their beatings, arrests, and forced evacuations. I found reports from the country's Human Rights Commission, read newspaper articles, and conducted interviews. I learned about the laws that forced blacks to live and work in certain areas, subject to arrest if those boundaries were violated; the laws that segregated the schools, the drinking fountains, the libraries, and other public facilities; the laws that prohibited interracial dating; and the laws that turned the country's 33 million nonwhites, out of 38 million total residents, into an oppressed majority. I couldn't get enough information about the Sharpeville Massacre in 1960, in which the South African police opened fire on a crowd, killing sixty-nine. The grim statistics on death tolls and uprooted communities and imprisonments began piling up, and I recited those numbers into my video camera while filming the children in rags who lived in crumbling shacks amid the mounds of trash that littered the dirt roads.

In Brazil, Gordon Greathouse spoke at length about Martin Luther King Jr.'s philosophy of challenging corruption through nonviolent protest; so before I reached Africa I grabbed half a dozen books by or about him, and his words echoed the injustices I was witnessing and emboldened me to resist them. I read King's *Why We Can't Wait*, which focused on the civil rights movement in Birmingham, Alabama, in 1963 and included King's letter from a Birmingham jail. King threw into sharp relief how social injustice degrades us all and how nonviolence can spur social change. In his letter from jail, he said that patience is an enemy, which comes "from a tragic misconception of time, from the strangely irrational notion that there is something in the very flow of time that will inevitably cure all ills." But time itself was neutral. "More and more," he wrote, "I feel that the people of ill will have used time much more effectively than have the people of good will. We will have to repent in this generation not merely for the hateful words and actions of the bad people but for the appalling silence of the good people."

The appalling silence of the good people. Every day I was in South Africa, I saw that. In 1992, one year before I arrived, white South Africans held a referendum in which a "yes" vote would pave the way for a general election that would end apartheid. The result: 69 percent of white South Africans voted yes. A clear majority, in other words, favored ending a bankrupt political system that had been in place since 1948. If you included the nonvoting black residents of the country, as much as 97 percent of the population opposed the government. Where had they been? For that matter, where was the rest of the world? Why hadn't they ended apartheid earlier?

Until now, I had thought of social justice in terms of poverty and hunger, neglect and corruption and horrific conditions that were sometimes beyond human control. But apartheid was about intentional malice and systemic oppression. It was about evil, and it reset the stakes for my own actions.

If I had been fired up to make change before, now I was on rocket fuel. Nelson Mandela had been released from prison in 1990, the protests were becoming more organized, and the violence was only going to get worse. One day I was in Crossroads, and the next day I read that thirteen people had just been killed there. I was witnessing the historic transformation of a country, and though I couldn't take up arms, I had my cameras, and I could still do my part in exposing a decaying but dangerous regime.

After filming in and around Cape Town for about a week, I wanted to document what was happening in Johannesburg, about 870 miles north. Charles and Leonard wanted to go with me; they thought it would be a great adventure with their new American companion.

In Johannesburg, Charles introduced me to other ANC leaders, including Reggie September, a trade unionist who had been imprisoned with Mandela in the 1960s and had been in exile for many years thereafter. Charles also took me to Phola Park. One of South Africa's most violent settlements, it had thirty thousand residents, most unemployed and all living in one- or two-room shacks without electricity or running water. One year earlier, the police had cordoned off the entire camp with razor wire and then, backed by army troops and Angolan mercenaries, had ransacked or bulldozed many of the dwellings.

I hadn't realized that "black-on-black" violence was so prevalent, with tribes pitted against each other, often at the instigation of the white government. Such tribalism deterred unified opposition against white rule. I interviewed a black South African, Daniel Massamola, who told me that blacks from another tribe would enter Phola Park, singing a song while wielding axes and guns. As I filmed the conversation, he stood next to the ruins of a wooden shack, his emotions still raw. "The mother to this family is still alive," he said. "The father and two kids are passed. . . . They put the coffin right here. . . . It's what's happening now. Shot dead. So many people are shot dead, and what we will get [is just] another report. The one that carries the gun must drop it."

Daniel insisted on giving me his last name, which was unusual. Most of the people I interviewed wanted me to conceal their name out of fear of retribution. But Daniel wanted this massacre to be documented, and his name gave his testimony greater credibility. I admired his bravery, and his gut-wrenching account brought home the violence in a visceral way. I saw the shards of the burned-down hut, the ground where the children were murdered, and I felt the pain of the survivor.

When Charles and I were walking through the segregated townships, we often came across burly military fortresses. The first time I saw one, I asked Charles what it was. "A police station," he said. But it really seemed to be the opposite of a police station: instead of keeping the peace, it seemed to enforce oppression. To protect its position, it was fortified with barbed wire, sandbags, and snipers in towers. I wanted to film what was inside, and I finally got the opportunity when Charles and I, along with two or three others from the ANC, came across one of these police stations in Soweto, near Johannesburg. About two hundred feet away was a three-story building, and we climbed to the rooftop so I could get footage of the whole area. What I saw looked more like a military outpost, where the authorities parked their Casspirs, stored their weapons, and ran their jail. My filming ended quickly as four or five black soldiers, who probably came from Angola, saw us from behind their chain-link fence. Angry and volatile, they pointed their R1 rifles and began yelling at us. The building we were on was under construction, so we climbed down the scaffolding, jumped about six feet to the ground, and began to run. The soldiers, still shouting, were locked behind the fence, but we were within easy rifle range. We hadn't run far when one of our guys yelled, "Stop!" And we did.

Perhaps my whiteness protected me, but the soldiers didn't shoot. It may have protected my friends as well; later they said if I hadn't been there they would have been shot because they were black, and if the soldiers knew they were with the ANC, that would have earned them a bullet as well.

With our hands raised, we walked toward them, and I kept my video camera running. They spoke some English and demanded to know what I was doing. I told them I was filming the encampment, and I didn't apologize. In fact I was fairly defiant. They said that was illegal, and they asked if I was still filming. I lied and said no—a huge risk, obviously, but I wanted this on film; the reels moved so slowly and silently that the men couldn't tell the camera was on. They demanded to see my passport, which I gave them before realizing that if they kept it they could do anything they wanted with me.

We stood and waited, and the soldiers finally decided that we weren't a threat. They returned my passport and said that if they ever saw us again, they'd lock us up. It was the first time that I felt I knew what it was like to be truly vulnerable, without any rights or protections, completely at the mercy of authorities I didn't trust. The incident deepened my empathy for those who were being oppressed, enslaved, or discriminated against, and it caused me to want to learn more about what was going on.

Americans who opposed apartheid faced danger from all sides, threatened by white enforcers of the status quo as well as black militants fighting to overthrow the government. In the summer I was there, another white American, Amy Biehl, was in South Africa on a Fulbright scholarship. Amy was an anti-apartheid activist, but when she drove through a township outside of Cape Town, a mob of black youths threw stones at the vehicle, forced her to stop, dragged her from the car, and murdered her.

I read about the murder when it happened, but it didn't deter me. I wouldn't have stopped working in Detroit if I had read that someone there got shot. Fortunately, the black South Africans I had met had embraced me. I felt close to Charles and his friends and relatives. In Johannesburg his sister invited me to stay with her, even though that could have put her in jeopardy. Then my good fortune briefly ran out.

Charles and I were walking through a shantytown in Johannesburg when we saw hundreds of protesters from the Pan Africanist Congress (PAC) marching, fists in the air, hauling a banner, and chanting in Afrikaans. PAC was formed by a group that had broken away from the ANC in 1959; it advocated more hardline Africanist positions, such as denying equal rights to white people. Its leaders had organized the protest in Sharpeville that led to the massacre. I didn't understand their chants, nor could I read the banner, but I figured I had no reason to be concerned. I stood in plain sight about seventy-five feet away, shooting some photos and video, mesmerized by their fury. Suddenly Charles grabbed my arm and yelled for me to run. I had no idea why, but I took off after him. He was in a full sprint!

They didn't chase us, and when we were a safe distance away, we finally stopped. "They saw you," Charles explained, "and they were yelling, 'One Boer, one bullet.'"

They thought I was an Afrikaner, the enemy. I didn't realize that they were shaking their fists and yelling *at me*, and if I had stuck around, I could have been on the receiving end of that "one bullet." Besides relief, my main feeling was gratitude toward Charles. I didn't feel resentment toward the protesters; if I had been in that march and seen a white guy with blond hair, I might have yelled the same thing.

Despite the close calls, I was getting even more reckless. Part of it was my nature: I take a lot of risks in general, more if they're on behalf of a good cause. And the longer I stayed in South Africa, the more outraged I became and the more determined I was to document what I saw, even if that meant some ill-advised confrontations.

On one occasion I was outside a police encampment and noticed that the gates were open. No one was around, and even though Charles thought I was crazy, I walked in with my camera rolling. A Casspir was sitting on the lot, and I figured this would be a great chance to see the inside of it. Then I heard the drums: I didn't know where they were coming from or who was playing them, but a rhythmic beat could be heard loud and clear, and it became the eerie soundtrack for this segment of my video. I climbed right up into the truck, sat on one of the two benches that could hold ten soldiers, and peered through the bulletproof glass in the front. I was definitely behind enemy lines now. The footage would be great for the high school kids back home. Our students from the South Bronx thought the sight of police patrolling their neighborhoods in Chevy Impalas was ominous. These brooding tanks would give them a new perspective.

As I was climbing back out, I heard the voices. Two young white soldiers, thinking I was one of them, were talking to me in Afrikaans. They weren't angry or threatening, and I remained calm. I told them I was American and explained that I was taking pictures and video for high school kids in the United States. I didn't mention that my camera was still rolling. Despite my breach of security, they didn't seem too upset. I asked them about their guns and how often they used them. They said they fired only rubber bullets, which didn't hurt anyone. (When I edited the video later, I showed that was a lie, cutting to a shot of Charles's scars from the rubber bullets.)

The soldiers didn't see me as a threat and let me go. The riskiest chance I took with my video camera occurred inside a police station where it had been reported that ANC members had been tortured and killed. I was in Soweto with another friend from the ANC, filming this infamous jail from beyond a fence, experimenting with different angles, when a white guard approached us. He kept his gun in his holster, but he was angry. He told us that we were under arrest and the station commander wanted to see us. I asked why, and he said because we were taking pictures. I turned my video lens from zoom to wide and kept the camera running. What better way to see the face of apartheid than to film it from the inside?

I walked into the commander's office with the camera under my arm and placed it right on his desk, pointed at him. Terrified, I just concentrated on staying calm. I was even more afraid for my black friend. If the commander had discovered he was being filmed, I could have ended up in a prison cell for a very long time, and I have no idea what would have happened to my friend. But once again the Hi8's silent motor and slow-moving reels kept my cover.

With the arresting officer standing nearby, I gave my now standard explanation about taking photos for high school kids in America, but I also told the commander about some of the damning information I had gathered on police stations, including that twenty-five people had recently died in one month while in custody.

The commander flicked the ash from his cigarette. "This information you got is only from newspapers."

"I got it from the Human Rights Commission. When you do this kind of research, you get it from different sources, and this is just one source."

"Exactly," he said. "It's one-sided information."

"It is one-sided. I think that's why it's important for people like you to give me your side."

"I can't speak for someone else's problem at someone else's station, just anything that concerns my station."

"Do you guys get a lot of violence around this station area?"

"This is one of the quietest stations in all of Soweto that I know of."

If this was the face of apartheid, it was cold, detached, and, as Hannah Arendt famously said of Nazi officers, banal. Then the arresting officer walked over and picked up my video camera. I thought for sure I was finished. He looked right at it but appeared confused by how it worked. A red light showed that it was on, but the sunlight through the windows made the tiny light difficult to see. Incredibly, he put the camera right back on the desk, unaware that it was operating, the commander still in the frame.

With nothing better to do with us, the commander let us go. My ANC friend almost collapsed with relief when we were finally outside. I was just thankful that our interrogators were inept in video technology.

I would eventually bring home hundreds of photographs and many hours of video footage about apartheid that we used to teach American students who were in our program. When the government collapsed in 1994, I could say it didn't happen by accident or because time had run out on apartheid, but was due to the courageous work of many good people, some of whom had befriended me.

I understood, and indeed would devote myself to, the wisdom of Martin Luther King's words: "Human progress never rolls in on the wheels of inevitability; it comes through the tireless efforts of men willing to be coworkers with God."

It was time to leave South Africa. I had been there for nearly two weeks, but I was still on my journey to build a school in another country that was also in the midst of political turmoil.

Malawi is a landlocked squib of a country in the southeastern part of the continent; it is about the size of Pennsylvania but less than 0.5 percent of the land mass of Africa. Malawi hasn't suffered from rebel insurrections, famine, or other headline-grabbing calamities, but it's not a success story either. Unlike other African nations, it has no oil, few natural resources, and little industry. This former British colony is one of the world's poorest countries, and in 1993 just getting there was a major challenge.

From Johannesburg, I began hitching rides on the top of trucks. I crossed the border into Zimbabwe, made it to the capital city of Harare, and hitched another ride toward Mozambique, which was at the tail end of a long civil war. Crossing into the country, surrounded by farmland, I traveled atop a truck along the infamous Tete Corridor, or Gun Run (so-called because of pervasive violence on the road during the war). To keep the snipers back, the United Nations had burned the brush on either side of the road, which white UN trucks patrolled.

After five hot days on the road, I reached Blantyre, the commercial center of Malawi, and picked up my mountain bike, which had been shipped there from the States. I also met Kurt Fenske, an administrator with Habitat for Humanity. At 6 foot 1, he was about my size, but he had short, light brown hair and wore silver-rimmed glasses. Smart, soft-spoken, and with a dry sense of humor, he had married a Malawian woman and seemed to have totally immersed himself into the culture. He liked what we were trying to do and appreciated that I made conversation with the Malawians on his staff who worked as secretaries, bookkeepers, and managers. When you're an outsider in any country—and when you're a *nzungu*, or white man, in Malawi—you need to show a genuine interest in the people or else you'll be seen as an interloper out for personal gain.

Fenske gave me advice on where to buy materials, what foods to avoid, how to engage the community, and so much more. He thought my biggest problem would be transporting building materials to the desolate village to which I was headed. Frankly, I really hadn't thought about it.

I spent several days in Blantyre, which had the battered trappings of a modern city. The electricity was sporadic, the water murky, the sewage lines incomplete. A road would be paved for a little while and then suddenly wasn't paved anymore. The place was edgy and chaotic—the headquarters for most nongovernmental organizations were protected by high walls and guards—but at least it had a familiar urban feel.

Outside of the city everything was different, starting with the dirt roads that were deeply rutted, hazardous, and at times impassable. In the small trading towns, fabrics and used clothes were proudly displayed, "bottle stores" sold beer and soft drinks, coffin makers advertised their wares, and haggard goats sniffed for food. The countryside was beautiful in the rainy season, lush and green, a rolling agrarian tableau of small farms of corn, peanuts, and sugarcane and large plantations of tobacco and tea. But I was there in the dry season, when the hot winds covered everything in a fine, grainy sand.

Fenske arranged to have a British driver haul me, my tent, and my bike to the village of Misomali. To get there, we had to drive twenty-five miles around Mount Mechese, to the valley between two granite masses. It took three hours. Misomali is beyond remote, located in the Mulanje District, whose undulating plains are set off by Mount Mulanje, a massive rock mound whose peak of 9,800 feet is the highest point in the country and one of the highest on the continent. Next to it is the smaller Mount Mechese.

We rolled into the village and bounced to a stop in front of the chief's mud hut. I got out and, with the driver's help, retrieved my belongings from the payload. It was getting dark, so the driver jumped back in and without saying good-bye drove off. There I was, alone in my first African village. It was the most desolate place I had ever seen. And I thought to myself: There's no place I'd rather be.

CHAPTER 5

The Road Taken

was met by Chief Misomali, a short, muscular man with a shaved head, a gap between his front teeth, a penchant for black shirts, and a ready smile. He spoke little English, and I didn't know any Chichewa. With hand gestures mostly, the chief invited me to pitch my tent in his compound and to eat my meals with him. The tent itself was just big enough for my backpack and me; I couldn't even stand up in it. But it was now my home, and as I pitched it, the chief kept telling me, "Zikomo, zikomo," which I figured out meant "Thank you, thank you."

Misomali, a farming community, was really a collection of five small villages, with about six hundred families, many of which had seven or more children. If landowners could bulldoze villages in Brazil and the government could flatten shanties in South Africa, Mother Nature could wreak similar havoc in Malawi. Two years earlier, flash floods had swept off the mountains, killing more than a thousand people in the region and wiping out Misomali's mud huts. The villagers had rebuilt them with hand-molded mud bricks and leaking thatch roofs. Each hut was about twenty by twenty feet, the size of a one-car garage, and often housed ten or more people across three generations. Though the huts had no chimneys, the women used open fires to cook meals, the smoke from which was a hazard, particularly for children.

Flying to Africa, I had to move the hands on my watch forward six hours. But in Misomali I felt like I was stepping back five hundred years. Though Habitat for Humanity had sent me the fax about how excited the village was for a new school, there was no celebration upon my arrival—they were surprised I was even there. Because others had made similar promises to them in the past, they never really believed we'd come to their village and build a school. Dave and Erik would join me in about a month, but for the moment I was by myself. That Chichewa is one of the most difficult dialects in Africa complicated my ability to assimilate. I never did learn how to speak it. I was an alien to the children. They looked at me wide-eyed and ran away screaming, *"Nzungu! Nzungu!"* Some of the adults, I suspect, felt the same way.

The villagers suffered a level of material deprivation that I had never imagined. I had seen shacks and huts without electricity, but Misomali was different. There was no access to electricity for many miles. There was no running water, few bicycles, no beds or even chairs. A toothbrush was considered a luxury item. So was soap. Most of the children didn't have shoes, many of the adults didn't have teeth, and the nearest clinic was in Chiringa, a seven-mile walk. Even if you got there, the clinic might not be staffed that day. Women gave birth on dirt floors. A broken bone healed naturally or didn't heal at all. Herbs and roots were used to fend off disease.

The village had one latrine, for the chief, but it was treacherous. A dark shadow covered it during the day, creating a false sense of comfort. At night, I once shone my head lamp down the hole and saw thousands of moving things: insects, maggots, roaches, who knows what else. The timbers over the pit didn't seem sturdy, and I had heard the story of a Peace Corps volunteer who once used a latrine just like this one at night, fell into the pit, and didn't get out until the next day. Whether that story was true or not, most villagers didn't even have access to a latrine

One of the first things I noticed was how much time and effort were devoted to problems that didn't exist in less impoverished countries. I was amazed, for instance, at how villagers cut planks from a fallen tree. This could be easily done with an industrial circular saw used in Western lumber mills, but the locals didn't have the money for that type of equipment, never mind for the gas to operate it. Instead they used a long saw with handles on either end, with one man standing on top of the massive trunk and another standing in a ditch beneath it. Back and forth, back and forth, they would saw all day long, all to create perhaps a single eight-foot plank. I now had great respect for the wood that we used for our boards and trusses. One night a hut caught fire and went up in flames, and once I knew the family was okay, all I could think was: Man, that's some valuable wood that just went up in smoke.

Even getting drinkable water was a problem. We got it mostly from a pump, occasionally from a river, and though I used iodine tablets and boiled the water when possible, it was never really clean. I waged a constant battle against the amoebas, and the amoebas usually won. I battled dysentery pretty much constantly. That was bad enough, but the resulting dehydration was exacerbated by the scorching sun, and the combination of dysentery, dehydration, and heat left me light-headed.

In other countries, I equated the night with peace, a time of rest and reflection, and enjoyed sleeping beneath the stars that seemed flung across the sky. Not so in Misomali, where nighttime never seemed so dark. I slept mainly in my tent, but sometimes I crashed on the floor of a family's mud hut. One night I felt something crawl across my feet. I turned on my head lamp to discover that it was a tarantula, but as I wrote in my journal, "I was neither surprised nor alarmed—guess I'm getting used to Africa."

Nighttime brought the chanting of traditional healers performing their *juju*, a kind of voodoo, to exorcise the spirits from the ill or the lame. The pounding drums that seemed to follow me from South Africa now accompanied the vigils for the dead; the raucous chorus of animals and insects—frogs, crickets, jackals, monkeys, and probably hyenas—gave some nights an even more ominous soundtrack. Cornfields surrounded the village like a buffer against the world, providing sustenance but little else. The villagers also grew peanuts and sugarcane. The main food, prepared every day, was *nsima*, a thick corn-based porridge that was essentially tasteless but could be mixed with vegetables or hot sauces. The sauces, labeled "Dynamite Hot!" or "Friends Beware!" would make your scalp sweat. Boiled cassava roots offered another bland option for carbohydrates. The better-off families raised thin chickens or coaxed greens from vegetable gardens. Lake Malawi yielded mounds of tiny, pathetic fish. Some families ate minnows, and when it rained, villagers speared mice, cooked them over an open fire, and sold them on sticks—a delicacy.

Every day I saw children with distended bellies, the effect of widespread malnourishment and protein deficiencies. I also saw goiters for the first time, a swelling of the thyroid gland brought about by insufficient iodine in the diet. In the States, we take for granted that even the poorest among us will have enough iodine—salt—to fend off such conditions, but nothing could be taken for granted in Misomali.

The community had little recourse against disease, and I was struck by the banality of death. On one occasion, I was near a girl who had a bad hacking cough, and a villager barked at her to go away. I looked again, and her eyes were glazed over, her nose was running, and she was urinating on herself. I touched her forehead, and she was burning up. One villager thought she had malaria; another guessed tuberculosis. Whatever she had, the locals couldn't help her and, for that matter, barely even noticed her. I had no idea where her parents were. I felt terrible, but all I could do was give her older sister some money to take her to the clinic in Chiringa. Some villagers were surprised at my concern.

For all of its cruel medical history, the country in the early 1990s was facing an even more devastating threat from AIDS and the HIV virus. One-third of the adult population was estimated to have been infected, and as I first noticed in Blantyre, the victims were not hard to identify. They seemed to retract physically, their eyes shrinking back into their sockets, their cheeks sagging, their jaws and mouths protruding. They sweated all the time, even at night. For an isolated village like Misomali, lacking the most basic information on health care and disease prevention, AIDS was a deadly plague with no name.

In that first month, my closest company was the books I had brought with me, again on Gordon Greathouse's recommendation. I read that Mahatma Gandhi had spent the years from 1893 to 1913 in South Africa, and that his philosophy of *ashima*, or nonviolence, and civil disobedience had been molded there. His crusade against government tyranny in Africa was a precursor to his role as the father of India's independence.

Gandhi's message had inspired me before, but reading about him in Misomali showed me that I needed to completely immerse myself in this daunting culture if I wanted to make a lasting difference. In a discussion about politics, Gandhi said that India's leaders were too far removed from the masses. "We must share their sorrows, understand their difficulties and anticipate their wants," he wrote, adding that the problem was even greater in representing the pariahs.

> *We must identify ourselves with the villagers who toil under the hot sun beating down on their bent backs and see how we would like to drink water from the pool in which the villagers bathe, wash their clothes and pots and in which their cattle drink and roll. Then and not till then shall we truly represent the masses, and they will . . . respond to every call.*

That was how I felt. Unless I ate the same food, drank the same water, and toiled under the same hot sun beating down on bent backs, I was unworthy of support from these villagers. I had to walk in their shoes.

Early on, I made an effort to break through the gender barrier and connect with the women. I pounded the maize with a mallet, which the men never did, and tried to walk with a water bucket on my head. I usually dropped it. The women made a distinctive high-pitched noise that reminded me of an Apache war cry in an old western movie; the noise communicated welcome or appreciation, and it seemed to replace applause. I tried to make the same sound, which they thought was hysterical.

The children who initially scattered when they saw me soon overcame their fear. After a few days they moved closer to me, began following me around, and were like my giggling shadow. They were immensely curious about everything I did—brushing my teeth, for example, was a source of endless fascination—and they saw that I was harmless.

For all my reading and socializing, I never lost sight of the fact that I was in Malawi to build a school. I had a stalwart supporter in Chief Misomali, who was far-sighted about education. The village was similar to virtually all subsistence farming communities in Africa; many adults didn't understand why literacy was relevant when they had survived so long without it. Chichewa was probably not even a written language until the British colonized the area in 1891. Some worried that Misomali could even be hurt by a new school if it enabled newly educated youngsters to move to a city.

Moreover, in many African villages girls were refused education as part of a larger system of gender discrimination. To keep the village afloat, the women had responsibilities that far exceeded those of the men. They woke up before dawn to gather the firewood and make the morning fire. They pounded the maize, cooked the meals, worked in the fields, and hauled buckets of heavy water on their head. Teenage girls were often forced to marry older men in the village, and the women cared for the children, feeding them, bathing them, and carrying them on their backs. Keeping women ignorant was a patriarchal weapon: if they couldn't read, write, or count money, they would be financially dependent on husbands, fathers, or brothers.

Our new school in Misomali could change all that—indeed, that was one of its most important functions. Starting in this village, it was clear that if our organization was going to tackle poverty in developing countries, gender equality would have to be required for any effort in any community. Chief Misomali himself recognized that education levels, for boys as well as girls, had to be raised. Just three years earlier, he had reached out to a Catholic church for assistance in building the village's first school. The flimsy hut was destroyed in the flood and then rebuilt; large enough for about seventy-five children, it packed in 150. Now the chief wanted a permanent structure, with brick walls and concrete mortar, a secure roof, and pit latrines. He had already found a plot of land. We just needed the workers.

The day after I got there, the chief called our first meeting to recruit volunteers, and several hundred people showed up, which was promising. In Brazil we never attracted more than two or three dozen. The chief introduced me and explained what I was trying to do. I got the gist of his comments, that we wanted to build this school and needed everyone's help. Then I addressed the group, and with a struggling local translator by my side, I tried to convey my excitement in short, straightforward sentences.

"I am honored to be here, and I look forward to learning from all of you," I said. "We all have something to offer. Everyone has an opportunity to help with this project. This school is for your children. You will be able to lead the project and build the school with your own hands. And this may be the first step in breaking the cycle of poverty."

The reaction was enthusiastic. It appeared everyone was on board. Then a man raised his hand and asked, "How much will you pay us?"

"Nothing," I said, repeating that the school was for their children. "We're all volunteers, and everybody contributes." The villagers suddenly looked deflated and upset, and their attitude would not be changed by my paeans to education and community service.

Within a day or so, I began to realize why the locals had assumed that I would be paying them. As I wandered through the village and was invited into some of the huts, I noticed fifty-kilo sacks of rice stacked high and gathering dust. "What are these for?" I asked one of the locals.

"The flash floods," he said.

Through a translator, he explained that after the flood, the U.S. Agency for International Development had brought in food and money and helped with the rebuilding, which included restoring the crops.

"When was the flood?" I asked.

"Two years ago," he said.

"How long did it take to rebuild the huts?"

"A couple of months."

"How long to restore the crops?"

"A season."

But the aid kept coming! Not only did the handouts deter farmers from returning to the fields, but they nurtured an entitlement mentality that made recruiting volunteers more difficult. I think this type of aid also destroyed the community's pride and sense of self-determination.

My recruitment efforts encountered other difficulties. I went hut to hut, village to village, with the chief and with a local named Andrew Gatoma, a lean, charismatic family man who had learned passable English as a miner in South Africa. As my translator, Gatoma brought an evangelical zeal to the cause. One day a villager told us he wouldn't join us because we were withholding money.

"I'm not getting paid," I told him. "The chief is not getting paid, and Gatoma's not getting paid. We're here in solidarity as volunteers."

It was then that I learned about the political hornet's nest we had walked into.

Malawi was in the midst of a heated political transition, as its first president had recently been forced to leave the country at the point of a gun. Hastings Banda had run Malawi as a corrupt, eccentric strongman whose edicts included outlawing speculation about his age, banning all television, and requiring every business, school, and government building to hang a picture of him on the wall. But a referendum had recently ended his one-party rule, and Banda had now been forced into exile. Fair and free elections would take place throughout the country the following year, and that meant, on a local level, that Chief Misomali would have to face the voters in his village.

According to the villager we spoke with, one of the chief's main political rivals, Mr. McCrory, was sabotaging our recruitment efforts. He followed us and told the locals that I was secretly paying the chief or that the chief was keeping money that was intended for the workers.

I was infuriated and wanted to confront this Mr. McCrory, but he was like a phantom, impossible to locate but haunting my every move. When I finally tracked him down, I found a man who looked like a cross between a politician and a used-car salesman. Tall and balding, he wore a polyester suit, spoke unusually good English, and was always shaking hands. He reeked of affability.

I introduced myself and told him that we knew what he was telling people behind our backs. "Why are you trying to sabotage this project?" I demanded.

"I'm not sabotaging this project," he said. "But thank you for being here."

"Oh, come on, we know what you're doing. You're telling lies. Nobody is getting paid."

He denied saying any such thing, and he told me what a good job I was doing.

I told him that the school was being built for his children and grandchildren. In fact his son was one of the kids who followed me everywhere. I asked him if he would come to the work site and help us.

"Yes, I'll do that," he said.

I asked if he would join me in recruiting villagers to the work site. He said yes to that as well. He insisted that he only wanted what was best for Misomali.

I thought the problem was solved and that our nemesis would now be on our side. But nothing ever happened. Mr. McCrory never came to the work site and never helped me recruit volunteers. He remained a phantom, rarely visible to me, and continued to spread lies about us so he could advance his own political ambitions.

Mr. McCrory's actions ensured that we never had the same regular volunteer base that I had experienced in Brazil, but we did have a wonderful core group of committed volunteers whose work was supplemented by the rest of the community occasionally.

In some ways, Andrew Gatoma was the most unusual of the volunteers. A man who bore a look of success, he wore short-sleeve shirts with collars, nice trousers, shoes, and a wristwatch that actually worked. Because of his experience mining in South Africa, he had a sense of his own importance. When I first met him, he said he wanted a job as a construction supervisor and asked if I could pay him.

"No," I told him, "but I'd love to have you with me, and I'd be happy to share my food with you."

That was good enough for him, and he became part of my core group.

Then there was Steven Tenthani, an irrepressible spirit who chatted on the work site as much as I did. "You talk too much," I once told him. "We have work to do."

He stopped in his tracks, looked right at me, laughed, and said, "If I talk too much, you talk *three* much!"

Even though his English was choppy, Steven became my closest friend in Misomali. He was the first one on the work site each day and always watched out for my well-being. When I planned to go camping by myself on Mount Mulanje, he insisted that he come with me. He was worried that I would run afoul of the mountain's evil spirits; he himself was petrified of them and would never have considered climbing up there, but he wanted to protect me. I don't believe Steven influenced any otherworldly bodies, but he did shield me from very real snakes. We saw several puff adders, which are slow, fat, ugly creatures, responsible for more deaths than any other snake in Africa. I almost stepped on one by accident, but Steven pushed me away.

Our core group of volunteers included three other men: Mr. Joseph, whose shaved head accentuated his age difference (he was ten years older than I); he laughed often, loved to tease me, and spoke some English that he too had learned while working in South African mines. There was Mr. Gamma, tall and thin, a skilled and steady hand who was on loan to us from the government and whose most distinctive feature was a bright red jump suit he wore every day. Also on the site was Frackson, a quiet, conscientious local who had a wonderful smile and worked without complaint.

Few villagers made a deeper impression on me than Mahata, who stopped by my tent on my very first morning. He was about eighty years old, an age nearly unheard of in Misomali. He had deep wrinkles across his face and a look of warmth in his eyes. His clothes were rags, but he carried himself with dignity. An old soul, I thought. He came bearing a gift, a single egg, which I thought odd. Maybe two eggs would be a meal, but one egg? I thanked him for the egg—he spoke no English—and then he left, until the next morning, when he once again brought me a single egg. And he kept doing that, several times a week.

I was grateful, but I was also hungry, and after a couple weeks I asked the chief if we could get more eggs so we could actually have a meal. But the chief explained that eggs were in very short supply. I should have known, as I hadn't noticed many chickens, and that made Mahata's gift to me all the more precious. One evening he invited me to his threadbare hut for dinner (not eggs), and I saw how little he had. He was one of the poorest among the poor, his generosity an act of grace. Here I had been reading about Martin Luther King Jr. and Gandhi, but I had the perfect role model in Mr. Mahata. And he also showed up on the work site every day and did all he could to help us out.

In the first phase of building the school, we dug the foundation, which may have been the toughest part. The foundation itself was a series of trenches, three feet deep and three feet wide, which were filled with cement mortar and brick. But in the dry season, the ground was a stubborn mix of hard adobe clay and rock. In the States, we'd be using a backhoe, a dump truck, and maybe a bulldozer. Here we had a single shovel, a pickax, and a hoe.

On one of those early days, I was walking with the chief when we came across a kiln that, he explained, was built specifically to make the school bricks. The villagers had to dig pits in the adobe, flood the pits to soften the clay, and then hand-pack the mud into single brick molds. They let them dry out for a few days and then stacked thousands of them into the shape of a large kiln with three main tunnels. They sealed the kiln in a layer of adobe to contain the heat, then packed each tunnel with firewood and maintained the flames for about thirty-six hours until the bricks were burned. They had made forty thousand bricks in this fashion, still stacked in the shape of the giant kiln.

I was awestruck—then worried. The bricks were more than a half mile from the work site, and all we had to transport them were two old wheelbarrows. How were we going to move all those bricks? When I asked the chief, he laughed and told me not to worry. When I asked again in the days ahead, he always gave me the same shrug and assumed a look of total unconcern, even serenity. I had expected to finish the foundation in two days. But the soil was like concrete, so we were already more than a week behind. I did not share his peace of mind.

We finally completed the digging for the foundation. I had my small crew waiting, and all we needed were the bricks to start constructing the walls. I again asked the chief, and again he told me they were coming. I wondered if he had lost his mind, and I feared the project would die.

Then, about fifteen minutes later, I heard some singing: "*Chimwehweh, chimwehweh, chimwehweh.*" I looked up, and through the trees I saw several women walking toward me, then several more, a dozen, two dozen, fifty in all. Each woman had six to eight bricks balanced on her head, some carrying babies on their backs just below the stack of bricks! Others were carrying quarry stones as well. Behind them came the boys, who carried the bricks in their arms, and the girls, who had piled them on their heads. Two hundred kids in all. The women and children understood the value of that school, and they hauled forty thousand bricks in one day. Not one was dropped in transit.

With the foundation dug and the bricks in hand, we still needed cement, which I'd have to get in Blantyre. Now it was my turn to step up.

To travel between Misomali and Blantyre, I usually took a bus, the equivalent of a thirty-year-old, bucket-of-bolts American school bus; it left once or twice a day. The trip took a slow and wobbly eight or nine hours, and the bus was so overcrowded that I often had to ride on the roof with the luggage.

But the bus would be no help with the cement, as I needed at least 150 sacks, each weighing a hundred pounds. Even before I could worry about transport, though, I had to find the actual product. In Blantyre I went to hardware stores, where cement was supposed to be sold, and visited other vendors, but they said they were all out. I was skeptical, believing they were just angling for a higher price. But then I visited the country's one cement manufacturer, and the manager said he was out as well and the factory had been down for a while, owing to some missing ingredient. He said he thought that the district education manager might have sacks of cement in the town of Zomba, about forty miles farther by bus. So I rode over there, and the manager did indeed have more than a hundred bags in storage. (The mix is used for government-built schools.) I offered to pay for the bags, but he said I could just replace them when more became available.

I still had to transport them all, but the small trucks in Blantyre were typically unwilling to drive out to Misomali. They didn't want to travel such a great distance over lousy roads and broken bridges. I finally convinced the cement maker to let me borrow one of his trucks, and he even gave me a driver. From there we went back to Zomba, loaded the bags, and made the long drive to Misomali, rumbling in around 10 p.m. Several dozen villagers came out to greet me, quite surprised that I had found the cement and a way to bring it home. It was an exhilarating experience, for it showed the community that the depth of my commitment matched their own.

As the school walls began to climb, Dave and Erik arrived. They had been to the States but were not involved in our high school programs or fundraising. Their passion had always centered on building the schools. I had had no contact with them since I had left Brazil, and they told me the good news that the school there was completed. I was elated to have them with me again, my partners in this enterprise—they were smart and fearless, and they spoke English.

Not long after Dave and Erik got to the village, our father decided to visit us. Dave and I were surprised. It's a brutal trip for anyone at any age, but my dad made it when he was in his sixties, while his friends were skiing in Vail or relaxing at beach-side resorts. He made the trek with his cousin Dick, and they spent several nights in tents in Misomali. The Malawians show great respect to visitors and to elders in particular, so my dad was treated accordingly. The group village headman, Chief Nazombe, had shown no interest in Dave, Erik, or me, but when my dad rolled in, the man in charge of the entire valley requested that we visit him.

Because we were all so thinned out, my dad seemed even larger and more robust than usual. The chief was in awe, and so was his adult daughter. When she first saw him, she immediately bent down on one knee to shake his hand. She was careful not to look him in the eye since that would be a sign of disrespect. Instead she caught my eye and exclaimed, "Jim, your father is a great fat man!"

Confused, my dad leaned over and said, "That doesn't seem very polite to me."

I explained that in Malawi, size is correlated with wealth and wisdom, a sign that you've had the resources and savvy to fill your table and live well, so her words were a compliment. He looked me in the eye and slowly asked, "Jim, are you bullshitting me?"

Though I was serious, it was hard for him to believe me because we had always poked fun at my dad's girth by playfully referring to him as "the big guy." Now he sat back in his chair, crossed his arms, and said with some satisfaction, "This is my kind of place!"

Under her father's orders, the daughter later brought in a live duck and placed it squarely in my dad's lap. Again he looked confused. "What am I supposed to do with this duck?" he asked.

"We eat it, Dad."

I explained that this signaled the chief's great respect for him. My dad wasn't so easily convinced. "Are you sure you're not bullshitting me, Jim?" he asked.

Dave backed me up this time. "No, Dad, we're serious."

My dad once again sat back in his chair and chuckled to himself. "This really is my kind of place!"

My father stayed in Malawi for two weeks. He made the trip to show his love and support for Dave and me, like any parent who would visit a child in some new city or on a new job. But this was different. Even though a hot, tribal, underdeveloped country in southeast Africa was not the natural destination for a fiscally conservative, white Catholic businessman from Michigan, he came to Malawi because he knew that *we* were living what *he* believed in. When he visited Misomali, he was aghast, as we all were, by the poverty, and part of him couldn't believe I had actually been living there for a couple of months. But the school walls were now five feet high, and he beamed with pride when he told Dave and me how much he loved us.

Not long after my father left, both Dave and Erik contracted malaria. Both cases were severe.

A mosquito-borne disease that is pervasive through sub-Saharan Africa, malaria has rightfully attracted global attention. It highlights the tragic connection between poverty and health: a mosquito net costs less than a dollar, but that's prohibitive for many families. In Malawi alone in the early 1990s, more than a hundred people died of malaria each day. Once symptoms present themselves—the strain affecting Dave and Erik brought high fever, vomiting, and diarrhea—victims are in a race to get to a hospital before rapid dehydration, possible brain damage, and ultimately death. Children are particularly vulnerable. Only the strong survive.

Dave and Erik were in that category. At the Seventh Day Adventist Hospital in Blantyre, one of perhaps two hospitals in Malawi in those days, Dave was given a heavy dose of quinine. It kept him awake for four nights straight, dulled his senses, and, in his words, "trashed every antibody in my body." It took him a couple years to fully recover from the effects of the drug, but it did save him.

Erik's experience was even more traumatic. He had been stricken in the game park while he was in a tent with his parents. He also had shigella, a water-borne disease that causes dysentery, and was running a 105-degree temperature. His parents put him in a truck and sped off for Blantyre, but Erik soon became delirious, telling his mom that he wasn't afraid to die. They found a medical outpost, where Erik received an IV drip, and when he reached the hospital in Blantyre, the doctor said he had come within one hour of losing his life.

Every Peace Corps volunteer I knew working in this country had contracted malaria. Some strains were more serious than others. It came with the territory, and it wasn't something I worried about, even after my own brother and friend had been laid low.

I had attributed the malaria to the mosquitoes. Then I had a conversation with Kurt Fenske, the administrator with Habitat for Humanity, and he said that the locals believed our run of bad luck might have been caused by evil spirits.

Misomali villagers were highly superstitious, certain that their ancestors were still present, walking among us but in the spirit world. They believed these mountains were haunted with evil spirits that could terrorize mortal souls and perform *juju*, and those same evil spirits could bring sickness to those of us trying to build a school.

I couldn't tell if Fenske was serious or joking, but it seemed that he was not dismissing the possibility out of hand. Then, a month or so later, I met a European named Dieter who worked at an NGO in Blantyre. Like Fenske, he was an educated Westerner, with an advanced degree, doing serious development work, and he too had some ideas about the evil spirits in our midst. But his view was personal. Dieter told me that his brother had mysteriously disappeared on Mount Mulanje, and helicopter teams from Europe never found the body. He believed this tragedy was somehow connected to Malawi's many traditional healers, whom he identified as "witch doctors." When performing a healing, he said, they had a habit of frothing at the mouth, and they may have put a hex on his brother. He also told me that the Mulanje District had the most concentrated practice of *juju* in the country.

Both Fenske and Dieter were Christians. I knew they believed that Jesus Christ was more powerful than any evil spirit. I certainly didn't believe in *juju*, but it was unsettling that they considered its possibility.

Then there was Sister Irene, a Catholic nun who worked at the health clinic in Chiringa. She told me that a comatose relative of Chief Nazombe had been committed to a sanatorium and was then cured by the faith healers, who made her drink chicken blood. That she gave any credibility to this type of faith healer was also disquieting.

The longer I was in Misomali, the more I realized how deeply these beliefs were ingrained in the culture. I once saw a large community meeting with about two hundred villagers who were engaged in what could only be called a witch hunt. I was with a friend who spoke some English and could translate what was happening, but I didn't need any translator to see the fury that was directed toward one man. They were angrily accusing him of "stealing the rain." We were in the midst of a drought, and if he didn't return the rain, he could go to jail. In the eyes of his emphatic accusers, there was no doubt this man was guilty. I'm not sure what happened to him. All I know is that there wasn't a cloud in the sky.

The belief in traditional healers, in hexes and *juju*, in people controlling the weather—these were all symptoms of a larger problem: the lack of education, and only through education could Malawians feel some control over their lives and take real steps toward better health, improved irrigation, and even economic self-sufficiency.

Dave survived malaria, but our relationship was suffering. A few days after he arrived in Misomali, he told me that they ended up paying for skilled labor in Brazil, despite my objections. He now wanted to do the same here, but I was still adamant that we not pay anyone. We remained at an impasse. We had been best friends for most of our lives, but now we argued bitterly over expenses, operations, strategy, and the very goals of the organization. Even though paying for skilled labor had been necessary to complete the first school in Brazil, I stubbornly refused to concede the point. Often when we finished an argument, I would hold onto it for days—that really bothered me—and our haggling reached absurd levels. I was often to blame. For instance, Dave had spent $1,500 on his plane ticket to Africa, which was more than we had budgeted, and he agreed to reimburse BwB $750 from his own savings. But I didn't think that was enough and wanted him to pay $850. I was nickel-and-diming my own brother when he was every bit as dedicated to the cause as I was.

Erik was able to get along with both of us but not able to forge a truce. On a trip to Blantyre to buy supplies, after one of these tense days between us, Dave and I were spending the night on the floor of the Habitat for Humanity office. He told me he was happy just working in the field and thought I could handle the fundraising and administrative work, but I wasn't up for dividing our responsibilities in that way. I told him that I couldn't argue with him anymore. "We're brothers, but I think this partnership is destroying us," I said in a moment of calm. "I don't think this can work anymore."

Dave thought otherwise, or maybe just didn't want to hear it.

"Look," I said, "if you want Building with Books, go with it, and I'll find something else after we finish the third school. Your call."

Dave asked me why I wanted to end the partnership.

I realized the answer as I said it. "Because I'd rather have you as a brother and best friend than a business partner."

The following day, Dave told me I should take over BwB. He didn't like fundraising and hated organization and hierarchy, so he probably knew that running BwB was not the best fit for him. Our plan all along was to build three schools, and Dave would stay on until our third one was built, in Nepal. I really had no idea what I would do next.

Still not fully recovered from their illnesses, and about seven weeks after they had arrived, both Dave and Erik planned to return to the States while I finished the school in Misomali. Several days before they were to depart, we were back in Blantyre, staying in a concrete hostel whose quarters were a cross between a dorm room and a prison cell. On my last night before heading back to Misomali, I got some takeout food and was walking on the crowded streets when everything seemed to slow down. I felt very much at peace, but movements around me had an odd, eerie quality. The city's blaring noise and chaos seemed to recede, as if I were in an altered state. Someone would wave, and a trail of colorful molecules would seem to follow. The fever was coming.

I got to my chamber and lay down on the hard cot. Dave was there, sleeping. I knew I was addled but didn't know how badly. The room was dark and damp, and the electricity was out (as usual), so I had my head lamp on. After nodding off, I got up in a fog and staggered to the bathroom, a rectangular space about four feet wide and eight feet deep. I had to squeeze around the crude sink to get to the seat-less toilet. It was so cramped that once I sat on the can, I could lean forward and vomit into the sink. I had diarrhea as well. I stumbled back to bed, woke up again, and went back to the toilet. The world faded and disappeared. The next thing I knew, I woke up on the floor with my head pounding. I had no idea what had happened.

I crawled back to the cot, but there was no relief. Unknown to me, the virus was coursing through my blood, turning over my stomach, spiking my temperature, and convulsing my body. I was soon back on the toilet.

If I die right now, I thought, *I'd be okay with that. Go ahead, God. Take me. I'm at peace.*

The fog lifted enough for me to walk over to Dave and tell

him what happened, but he was still swimming in quinine and not entirely lucid himself. "Wake me up next time," he said.

Soaked in perspiration, I reached my cot, but I was soon up again, heading to the toilet. The next thing I knew, Dave was standing over me, eyes bulging. He had a straggly beard, long hair, and in that moment looked like Jesus Christ Himself. He told me that I had passed out.

"For how long?" I asked.

"I don't know," Dave said. "Your eyes never closed and your body seized."

I had convulsed, but my eyes stayed open until the darkness lifted and a very hazy world came back into focus.

"It was the freakiest thing," Dave said.

I also had a cut and some bruises on my forehead, which must have hit either the sink or the ground. I had never felt so helpless, and I prayed for courage. I kept telling myself, "Fear is useless." Then a disturbing thought occurred to me. "I might not make it," I told Dave, "and I'm not sure I'm going to make it to heaven."

"If anyone makes it," he said, "you will."

Even in that delirious state, his words went straight to my heart. Neither of us was saying very kind things to the other at the time, but my love and respect for Dave were still boundless. I was reminded that he loved me and would do whatever was humanly possible to keep me alive. But I knew I was very ill and close to death, and Dave's words ironically gave me peace with the possibility of death.

I have no memory of what happened next, but somehow Dave got me to the hospital. When I awoke, I felt as though I was floating in ether, still removed from reality. Then I heard Dave yelling. I gradually focused on my surroundings. It was daytime, and I recognized that I was in a hospital. I had no idea how much time had passed. I had an IV tube coming out of my arm, and Dave was scolding the nurse because the tube was filled with blood, which was flowing back into the IV bag. The bag itself was supposed to have quinine but was now empty except for the dripping of my blood. Thanks to Dave, the nurse soon attached a new tube to a fresh bag of the medication.

Both of my forearms were badly bruised and punctured. When I saw the doctor, he explained that my veins had collapsed from dehydration, complicating their efforts to insert the needle that delivered the quinine. He soberly explained that had I been away from the hospital another couple of hours, I would be dead. He treated me for shigella as well as malaria, though he couldn't immediately diagnose it. To do so, a blood sample must be taken when your fever is spiking, but that was impossible with my damaged veins. I was alive, but hardly encouraged. I was in a barely functional city, in an African hospital, in a country with sky-high HIV infection rates, and my arms were punctured with needle holes.

Recovery rates vary with malaria depending on the strain, and I was fortunate to rebound quickly. I was out of the hospital in two days. The cost: about $30, which was manageable for me but prohibitive for most Malawians. I felt stronger than I had anticipated, and I now had a decision to make: to return home with Dave and Erik, or return to Misomali and finish the school.

"It's your call," Dave told me, "but I think you should definitely come back home."

The smart decision, the *obvious* decision, was to do just that. To rest, recover, and not tempt the African savannah again. In another eight weeks or so, we'd be traveling to Nepal to build our last school. So what if we didn't complete this one? Two would still be a success, and I was alive.

"I'm going back to the village," I told Dave. "Just don't tell Dad I got malaria."

After Dave was back in the States, he sent me a letter that discussed our complex relationship. "I want to let you know, despite our differences, I have a lot of respect for you," he wrote. "I think you are very good at what you do. You have an incredible future in front of you." Then he said:

I agree with you that it would be best if we took separate paths in the near future. However, I do not feel that our working together has been without merit. Although we have had many differences and heated arguments . . . I still love you! . . . I wonder sometimes why we have been placed together when it can be so painful. I think it is so that we learn from each other and I believe I have learned a lot from you. . . . I sincerely hope someday that you and I can be at peace with one another.

His letter touched me and gave me hope about our relationship. Moreover, his vote of confidence helped me in my own time of need, as I was once again by myself.

I went back to Misomali. The school needed to be built, and if I quit halfway through the project, that wouldn't happen. I knew how much the chief had invested in the project and how many false accusations he had already endured because of it. I didn't want to let him down, or Steven Tenthani, or any of the other volunteers who had committed themselves for the good of the children. Steven would never give up, so neither could I.

I don't like to lose, but deep down I was also trying to fulfill Martin Luther King's injunction about embracing adversity: "The ultimate measure of a man is not where he stands in moments of comfort and convenience, but where he stands at times of challenge and controversy."

To return to the village, I took a crowded bus to the town of Chiringa and walked the last seven miles on a dirt road. To the east were open plains that led to Mozambique, where gunshots from the civil war could sometimes be heard; to the west were the beautiful forested slopes of Mount Mechese and Mount Mulanje, whose peaks would often jut above the mist.

The long walk gave me time for further reflection. I had thought that by living in the village, I could immerse myself in the daily struggles of its residents, the better to understand their suffering. It was my application of Gandhi's goal for "complete harmony of thought and word and deed." To walk in the shoes of those who suffer was an act of solidarity, and in that solidarity to help alleviate the hardship, disparity, and discrimination.

But the villagers were living on the dirt floors. They were living the political corruption and the dysfunctional aid and the long hungry nights. They were living on less than 50 cents a day, exposed, without information and without health care. When their children got malaria, they didn't have a near-death experience; they died. So even as I became part of the community, even contracting the same harrowing diseases, I realized that the gulf between them and me was too wide. When I got malaria, I had the money for medical care, I had a safety net, I lived.

I now understood my mission on a more personal level. How can health information be distributed if the people can't read? How can they buy mosquito nets if they lack the skills to earn the extra income? The pieces fell into place. Misomali was living in a different century, and education—literacy, numeracy, knowledge of geography, history, science—was the first step out of the darkness. It would bring dignity, opportunity, and economic self-sufficiency. It would be an equalizing force for girls and women, and it was essential to combat disease, to lower child mortality rates, and to improve living conditions. It could save lives.

I had wondered if, in addition to building schools, we should be involved in providing direct relief, giving villagers mosquito nets or medicine. That too could save lives. But Gandhi told the story of how he had to distance himself from his British friends when he was leading India's liberation movement. He told the Brits that he loved them, but they could not help him anymore, or else the outside world would believe they were responsible for any success the freedom movement might attain, and India's own people would think the same. To Gandhi, it had to be a purely Indian revolution, something for which they took pride of ownership.

I realized our efforts had to be the same thing. We were not a relief organization or a charity. We couldn't rescue villagers; we had to empower them through education to break the cycle of poverty, illiteracy, and low expectations. That lay at the heart of my argument against paying the villagers: for the enterprise to succeed, it couldn't be a paying job for them. It had to be a cause.

All of these ideas were coming together during my seven-mile walk, and when I finally arrived in Misomali, I pledged to myself that I would finish the school, but then I was not going to "return to life" after the three years to which I had originally committed myself. I would have to keep going, not only building more schools abroad but also expanding our afterschool programs at home. With the help of our donors and volunteers, we had added two more schools in the South Bronx, increasing our total to six, and now that we had a system in place, we could surely multiply that number in the years to come.

The reasons behind my decision were painfully validated shortly after I returned to Misomali. Andrew Gatoma was one of my closest friends, and though he lived in another village, he was at the work site every day and was a joy to be around. Only weeks away from finishing the school, he approached me one morning and said he needed to take a day or two off. His wife had a fever, and he needed to care for his two little boys. I said of course.

A week later, he returned. "How's your wife?" I asked.

"She died," he said. "I don't know. She got a fever and she died."

I was shocked and told him how sorry I was. Gatoma simply accepted it. He attended the funeral and returned to his work. Like so many Malawians, he seemed almost desensitized to death, even the death of his spouse.

A few days later, Rachel, a friend from the Volunteer Service Overseas (VSO), which is akin to the Peace Corps in the United Kingdom, stopped by. She had never come to Misomali before, so I knew something was wrong. "Where's Gatoma?" she asked. I told her he wasn't here.

Rachel said the health clinic at which she worked had been taking blood tests of Gatoma's wife, as she had been pregnant. "The tests came back," she said, "and she was HIV-positive." Rachel asked me if I would explain to Gatoma what happened to her and what that meant for him.

"Me? I can't do that. That's your job. Can't you come back to talk to him?"

Rachel said Gatoma had to be told, and I had to do it.

"I'm not really qualified," I insisted.

"He needs to know now."

Gatoma's fate, and that of his wife, was all too predictable. Sister Irene had told me that the HIV infection rate in this region was estimated to be 50 percent. Many Malawians were in denial, and basic information on safe sex was useless when so many were illiterate.

When I next saw Gatoma, I sat him down and tried to explain. "I have something to tell you, and it's very serious. It's about your wife." I told him about Rachel's visit and his wife's blood tests. "She was HIV-positive," I said. "She died from AIDS."

He stared at me blankly.

"It's very likely," I continued, "that you're HIV-positive. You need to get tested."

"I'm sure she didn't die of AIDS," he said, "and I do not have it."

Gatoma had spoken about his casual sexual encounters while working in South Africa, but he couldn't understand or wouldn't believe that having sex with a woman seven years ago could have led to his wife's death.

I was in Malawi for about six more weeks, and I witnessed Gatoma's gradual decline. He had always been a dynamic presence with a sparkle in his eye. But he began to weaken on the work site, a low fever dragging him down. His clothes started to hang on him. He missed a few days. He never admitted that he was sick, at least not to me. He was determined to keep working on the school. He was about 5 foot 7, and his weight dropped from about 150 pounds to 120. But even in his compromised state, he never stopped trying.

His two sons would be orphans, and he was dying, literally, to build that school for them.

His decline shook me. I felt helpless that I couldn't do more. The longer I was there, the more sickness and death that I saw, the more isolated I felt. The nights were not getting any shorter. Everything about the school, the village, and the country seemed darker and more tenuous.

One evening, just after sundown, lightning flashed across the sky, so I went into my tent in anticipation of a storm. I turned on an incandescent lamp to read by, and I soon heard the drops pelting the rain sleeve. But after several minutes, I realized those weren't raindrops but large insects, probably locusts, attracted to my lamp and now aimlessly bouncing off the walls of my dome tent. Then I heard something burrowing just beneath the tent's fabric floor. I looked over and could see the silhouette of this thing moving toward me. I wasn't sure if it was a small rat or a maybe a snake that had just eaten a rat. I couldn't decide if I should smash it, coax it out from underneath, or maybe just move my tent entirely. Exhausted from the day and with the rain coming, I just rolled over and fell asleep.

About three weeks before I was to return home, with the school nearing completion, I hopped on my mountain bike and headed across a mountain pass between Mount Mulanje and Mount Mechese to the town of Phalombe. I had to use a telephone, and Phalombe, about two hours away on the bike, was the nearest town. I made the trip once every two or three weeks, but on this particular ride, I was on the downhill, moving so fast and quietly that I surprised a pack of monkeys congregating on the dirt path. I swerved but lost control of the bike, flew over the handle bars, and skidded on the gravel for a good ten yards. It was a classic "digger."

I suffered some nasty scrapes, but they didn't prevent me from reaching Phalombe, riding back to Misomali, or finishing my work on the project. I figured it was just one more close call. But after I returned to Stamford, my ankle began to swell up, to the point that

I couldn't put my foot in a shoe and had to wear Birkenstocks in the snow on New Year's Eve. I went to a clinic the next day and discovered that my ankle was infected and had begun to turn gangrene. A doctor named David Reed said the infection was too advanced for antibiotics, and he would need to drain it surgically. I had neither the insurance nor the money to cover such an operation and asked if he would reconsider. He said that without the surgery, the infection would spread, and my foot would eventually need to be amputated. He somehow convinced Stamford Hospital to let him do the procedure for free. He drilled a tunnel through the swollen tissue in my ankle to drain it—quite painful, despite the anesthesia—but he saved the limb. (He later joined our board in Connecticut.) Had I been in Misomali at the time, my ankle would have been treated with mud packs, and I would have lost a foot.

In my final weeks in Misomali, as the school's latrine pits were dug and the tin roof took shape, I started thinking that I wanted to leave behind something special. I wanted the school to be part of a beautiful, even reverential setting, a gathering spot not just for children but for the entire community. A solution came when I was on a brief camping trip up on Mount Mulanje, and I ran across a rudimentary tree farm. Perfect. I bought about fifty eucalyptus saplings, about ten inches high, and planted them near the school. My friend Rachel gently reprimanded me for planting this kind of tree, whose roots draw considerable water and whose leaves are acidic. Too late; they were already in the ground.

Steven Tenthani joined me on the trip that yielded the saplings, and on the day we returned, he was told that his wife had just delivered a baby girl. Ruthie was their first child. I knew why Steven came with me; he feared for my safety. Had I known that his wife was expecting, I would have insisted he stay behind.

His return to his family was joyous and emotional. He proudly held the baby in his arms, and she had that toothless smile that melts the heart of any new dad. I held the baby as well, and the moment was a powerful reminder of why Steven was giving so much of himself to this school. He was there for her.

Our small but hearty band of volunteers had laid down the lines, dug the foundation, filled it with bricks and concrete, constructed the brick walls, reinforced them with pillars, laid down the floor made of concrete, built the trusses, and attached a corrugated tin roof. I was there on the opening day, when the structure was formally named: the Thambe FB School.

I was surprised by the turnout. We had government officials, village headmen from all over the district, and many local chiefs. But what made the event unforgettable were the children, hundreds of them, who sang and danced to celebrate the opening. We presented certificates to our most dedicated volunteers, most of whom couldn't read or write or even sign their own name. As I wrote in my journal, "It was the biggest day of their lives."

Mr. McCrory didn't attend. Neither did Gatoma, but Chief Misomali, smiling broadly, gave a brief speech. My only regret was that Dave and Erik weren't there to see it.

For all the hoopla, I was worried about the future of Thambe FB School. Would the community support it? Would another flood wipe it out? Would it even be there five, ten, or twenty years from now?

Five months had passed since I had arrived in Misomali. It was now December of 1993. The hot dry season was ending, and a sweet cool dampness hung in the air. After the school's inauguration, I hugged the chief and Steven, and I walked to Gatoma's village, met him in his hut, and, fighting back the tears, embraced him. I told each of my friends, "God bless you." I wasn't sure that I'd ever return to Misomali or see my friends again. Habitat for Humanity had lent me a truck, and I threw my backpack and tent into the payload, started the engine, took one more look at the school, and was gone. The rains were coming.

CHAPTER 6

Harlem

Dave, Erik, and I connected back in the States. They were healthy again, and we were going to head to Nepal for our third and final project together. Then my ankle got infected. So we decided that they should go, and I would join them once I could walk again. After Nepal, Dave and Erik would continue with their humanitarian efforts, though along somewhat more conventional lines. Dave joined Teach for America and taught high school in the Rio Grande Valley, while Erik enrolled in medical school.

But I was grateful to them. The first three schools would have never been built without their dedication, grit, and enormous effort, and before they left for Nepal, they took the lead on developing a more structured approach to working in the villages. In our first two schools, we had failed to secure the commitment of the locals in what contributions they would make, and generic promises weren't good enough. We needed something far more concrete. In America we could draw up a legal contract, but we couldn't do that in developing countries. We found a way, however, to achieve the same end.

Starting with our first school after Misomali, in the village of Hau Pur in Nepal, we asked the community to elect a leadership committee of six women and six men, which ensured that women would be in decision-making roles for the entire project. In Hau Pur and in virtually all the villages we served thereafter, this gender equality was a departure from how things usually worked. We then sat down with the committee to draft a covenant that explained our responsibilities while spelling out what the villagers would provide in unskilled labor and local material. The covenant was written in the local language and then translated into English. We were specific in requesting the number of volunteers we needed each day and how local materials and land must be contributed. The leadership committee would organize the volunteers, lead the project, manage the finished school, and ensure that as many girls as boys attended. We also outlined the materials that we would contribute: cement, rebar, trusses, roofing, bricks, doors, windows, and so on. We would pay for skilled labor—Dave had been right on this score. My lofty goal of all-volunteer workers motivated by their commitment to the cause was unrealistic, given the difficult task of actually building a school. We were also responsible for engineering and construction supervision, but the locals would provide more than two thousand volunteer workdays.

In other words, we proposed a true partnership, not charity. To guarantee that we had everyone's support, we asked all the adults in the village to sign the covenant. Because so many adults were illiterate, many signed with a thumbprint. This was done at all the villages thereafter and still happens today.

With this new clarity and accountability, we built the school in Hau Pur in only three months, even though it was twice the size of the school in Misomali. With six rooms and a reinforced concrete roof instead of corrugated tin, we were convinced that it would last a hundred years, and I still believe it will. What's more, the methodology could be transferred across cultures and continents, and I did just that.

I spent the next three years overseas, building more schools in Brazil and Nepal, as well as in Bolivia. The challenges always varied, but I was willing to adapt until nothing really fazed me.

In Goje Village of Nepal, for example, a distant speck of a community in the majestic Himalayas, hard against a rugged 3,000-foot drop, I found myself with a water buffalo for a roommate. There were actually four of us: me, the buffalo, and two Nepalese guys in a fifteen-by-twenty-foot mud-and-stone hut. It had two levels: the humans on a top slat, the animal on the dirt floor. We slept under the same flimsy roof for months, and, as a bovine roommate goes, he wasn't half bad. The buffalo stayed out of my way, didn't eat my food, and didn't keep me up at night. He did stink up the place a bit, but no one's perfect.

This was 1994, and I wanted to continue to immerse myself completely in the lives of those I was trying to help. Goje was one example, though it would seem quite tame compared to the improbable living conditions I would later experience in America.

By the end of 1997, I realized I was far more in tune with villagers from Africa, South America, and South Asia than I was with teenagers in my own country. I felt that we were making more progress overseas than at home. No wonder—I was the leader of the organization, and I was hardly ever there. We had nearly a dozen afterschool programs, and I wanted to expand that. We were in middle- and low-income neighborhoods, but I wanted to go deeper and work in our neediest schools like those in the Bronx, where we had already made inroads. I also wanted to put more emphasis on what we do best: working people-to-people. Painting murals or cleaning parks is valuable, but the most transformational aspect of what we do occurs when a student develops a relationship with an elder in a nursing home or a homeless woman in a shelter or a child who's hungry.

So I hired our first program coordinator, and I also recruited Marc Friedman to head up fundraising and to be the number-two person in the organization. Even as a volunteer, Marc was a key advisor as well as my closest friend, committed to the organization like few others. When I was in Misomali, he was my main contact to the States through telephone calls. To save me money, he would place the call from our GE office to Phalombe. Sometimes it would take an hour for the call to get through, and if it didn't get through,

Marc would call me the same time the next day. At the end of the conversation, we would set the next day and time that he would call. Here's the amazing part: because of the time difference, Marc had to drive to the GE office at four o'clock in the morning so I could take the call in the afternoon. He then went to his day job as the COO of his uncle's electrical wire and cable business. The company was actually a defense contractor that sold its products to the navy, and Marc would go on sales calls to nuclear submarines, aircraft carriers, and battleships. So the decision to join our organization was a big move, but Marc loved working with us, even if he did so at considerable cost: he took a pay cut from $160,000 per year to $40,000.

I had received no compensation until 1995, when my savings were depleted and the board approved an annual salary of $25,000. (The board consisted of eight members, including Jim Parke; Joe Dionne of McGraw-Hill; Missy Kiernan, the attorney who incorporated us; the principal of one of our Bronx schools; and several other executives.) When Marc joined two years later, he insisted we make the same salary, so mine was bumped to $40,000.

I thought we could double or even triple our domestic youth programs within a couple years, but I was concerned about my own lack of experience in America's inner cities. I wondered if the teenagers would think I was fit for my job. I had traveled widely, but in this country I had always been fairly sheltered, growing up in a small town in Michigan and now living in a suburban, blue-collar neighborhood in Stamford. Though in 1997 I was only in the States three or four months, I often worked with high school students in the South Bronx, and I saw the drugs, the gangs, the prostitution, and the poverty. But then I'd drive home and leave the students behind. How could I walk in their shoes if I didn't even step on their pavement? I couldn't identify with them in a meaningful way. If the kids in our program thought I was unqualified to lead them, I wouldn't blame them.

So I decided to move to Harlem.

Long the center of black culture in America, Harlem also had a certain allure for those who enjoyed its music, restaurants, and nightlife. But I didn't want to be another white voyeur. I wanted to live it and experience it. Harlem had some trendy parts, around 125th Street, but that wasn't what I was looking for. I found an ad in the *Village Voice* for an apartment on the corner of 140th and Hamilton Place, between Broadway and Amsterdam, next to an abandoned lot and down the street from an Evangelical church. If the ad made any desirable claims about the dwelling, I don't recall. The building itself was an old brownstone; the second-story apartment had two bedrooms and, as I discovered on my first visit, was a pretty good size. But the carpet was soiled, moist, and smelly. The paint was peeling and probably contained lead. The appliances were ancient; the bathroom, musty; and the only furniture was two folding chairs and a small kitchen table.

I was hoping for a roommate and approached two guys I knew who worked with Teach for America in the South Bronx. They looked at the place but said it was a dump and the neighborhood wasn't safe. They preferred their apartment in the Village, so I lived alone.

My landlords, a married couple from Ghana, Ellen and Jaffet, lived on the first floor. Ellen was a large, dynamic woman with a huge laugh, while Jaffet was a skinny, mild-mannered accountant with glasses. Ellen did all the talking. She said she'd rent the apartment for $1,100 a month, including utilities. I offered $800 and asked for a new carpet and a paint job.

She agreed quickly, perhaps because she knew I hadn't investigated the building that carefully. Half of it was boarded up, or maybe bombed-out is a better description, and occupied by at least one squatter. Ellen might also have given me a discounted rate because I was a preferred client. This I discovered in the winter when my apartment lost its heat and hot water. I woke up and could see my breath. Showers felt like the Arctic Ocean. My fingers were numb. When I complained to Ellen, she said the boiler was broken. "You better get it fixed because it's freezing," I told her.

But a full month passed, and still she didn't fix it. When I only gave her $250 for rent, she started screaming at me. I took out the lease and showed her that utilities were supposed to be included.

She was both angry and surprised. "You're white!" she said. "I brought you in here because you could pay the rent in full and on time."

I couldn't believe it. I started laughing at the irony, and so did Ellen's twelve-year-old daughter. Being white carries privileges even in Harlem, I guess. This was one of many times I got a glimpse of how much more difficult African Americans have it in this country, even in black communities. But Ellen eventually repaired the boiler.

A friend of mine, Kenny Krayeske, a journalist who later became a lawyer and was a dedicated volunteer for our organization, helped me move in. When he first got to the apartment, he looked out the window and surveyed my block. On one corner were two or three cops, a paddy wagon, a cruiser, and flood lights. On the other corner stood five or six Dominican drug dealers warily doing business with passing cars.

"Dude," he said, "you just moved to the front lines of the drug wars."

While I was living there, the *New York Times* published a story about the drug trade in the city, and a photograph of my very building was splashed on the front page. The corner of Hamilton and 140th, it turned out, was the drug-dealing mecca of New York, ideally suited for clients on the go. Broadway was two blocks from the Henry Hudson Parkway, and sometimes it appeared as if there was one long exit ramp into the neighborhood. The cars came from New Jersey and beyond, Lincoln Navigators, Cadillac Escalades, and other SUVs with large spinning hubcaps, the kind favored by homies as well as suburban dealers. The transactions were nothing if not efficient. Kids on their BMX bikes would ride up to the drivers, ask "What do you want?," hand over the goods, take the money, and pedal off. The cars never came to a complete stop. The drivers would cruise in, peel away, reach the highway, and merge into a thousand other stories.

The drug dealers ran the neighborhood. I couldn't park in front of my building because they would use my car as a table for their meals or take a leak on the tires. The street corner was their office. In those first few weeks, they constantly approached me and asked what I wanted.

"I'm not looking for drugs," I told them.

"What are you doing here, man?"

"I live here."

They didn't believe me and assumed, because I was white, that I was a cop, so instead of approaching me when I appeared on foot or in my car, they scattered.

The cops also noticed me, and they asked the same question: What was I doing there? And I told them the same thing: I lived there. They didn't believe me either and assumed I was there to buy drugs. That first month, the cops pulled me over four times. They were a bigger nuisance than the dealers.

My passion for music gave me early entrance into Harlem's culture. Café Largo was a short walk from my apartment on Broadway and featured excellent Dominican food and poetry slams on Tuesday nights. What I loved most, however, was AfroMantra, a band that played there every week. Its leader, the drummer Alex Garcia, drew upon his personal background from Chile, Peru, and Cuba to create an Afro-Cuban jazz blend. I tried to catch the band live several times a month, and listening to the rich, complex rhythms put me in another world.

Then there was the historic St. Nick's Pub, in the Sugar Hill District on St. Nicholas Avenue, where Billie Holliday, Miles Davis, and Sonny Rollins once played and where nothing worthwhile happened until midnight. A smoky, dim room, it drew a cross-section of the community: establishment types with dark suits and fedoras who breathed tradition and experience, and the younger hip crowd who were still learning about the depth and power of jazz. The club was about a fifteen-minute walk for me, and I was the only white person there unless I brought some friends. I went there most weekends when I wasn't overseas, and I got to know the bartender, Boogie, a large, gregarious woman who always took good care of me.

One night I was there with some friends, and a Brazilian guy invited us to an after-hours club that didn't open until 3 a.m. (To be honest, he was inviting one of the women at our table, but we were a package deal.) I felt like I was stepping into the Harlem underworld. At the base of an old brownstone, we descended a staircase, about ten steps below the sidewalk. At the bottom of the stairs we had to knock on a thick metal door, look through a two-way mirror, wait, and knock some more. Someone finally responded. The proprietors were two guys named Pumpkin and Slim, and they wouldn't let us in without the password.

We entered a darkish room that had the feel of a speakeasy, and maybe it was at one time. We immediately felt everyone's eyes on us. They probably thought we were the cops. But once they saw us belly up to the bar, they returned to their business of drinking from short glasses and snorting lines of coke. I stayed clear of the drugs, but I settled into a chair with a shot and a beer, and I listened to a trio with a guy playing a dazzling electric bass. He had a goatee, a skull cap, and a six-inch "fatty" in his mouth; that joint never left his lips, and after about twenty minutes it was gone. The music had a different texture than at St. Nick's, a grittier, electronic sound. I returned enough times that Pumpkin and Slim stopped asking me for the password.

Though I had found a few regular haunts, my time in Harlem was also a series of confrontations with my own naïveté. I lived near a place that was a diner during the day but a quasi–Latin disco at night, with strobe lights and loud Dominican music. I stopped by one evening for a beer, and sitting next to me was a young woman who seemed to be sixteen or seventeen years old. She had a pierced tongue, nose, and ear. We chatted for a while (she also thought I was a cop, until I told her otherwise), and at one point she brought out some photographs of her kids. The oldest may have been three. I was surprised that someone so young would have a child that age. "Are you married?" I asked.

She gave me a cold stare. "Do you have to be married to have a child?"

It was a dumb question but a revealing conversation. I honestly didn't realize how many unmarried teenage girls were also mothers, a huge factor of inner-city poverty. Asking the question showed how little I knew about this community. But that's why I had come to Harlem, to see it firsthand and to understand the disorder that so many of our students faced. The open crack vials on the sidewalk. The addicts with needles hanging out of their arms. The pit bulls tugging at their leashes, leaving behind messes that no one picked up. The gunshots at night.

Crime was prevalent, but I also saw how the community was vulnerable to overzealous police. I drove a red Volkswagen GTI, with a sixteen-valve head, 123 horsepower, low-profile wheels, and round European headlights. It was nothing special, but it was fast, and the homies and gangbangers loved it. I'd be at a stop light, and guys would come up to me and say, "Hey, you want to sell that car?" Unfortunately, they liked it too much. I had a club on the steering wheel, but one night some thieves broke in, hacksawed the steering wheel, and stole the car. I reported the crime to the police but figured the car was gone for good. Then, a month later, a tow pound sent me a notice that the police had recovered my VW and dropped it off at the pound, where it had been sitting for four weeks. I called immediately and asked if the speakers and stereo were still there. I had an after-market system with a powerful amplifier. The guy said yes, the car was intact. I was relieved, until I went there and saw that the car had been stripped. Gone were the headlights, the grill, parts of the dashboard, the VW logo, and, of course, the stereo and speakers. I suspect that the guys at the pound stripped the car themselves after I opened my mouth; the pound also collected a huge check for holding my car for a month at $75 a day.

I was angry at everyone, but my problems had just begun. On Halloween night, I was driving south in the VW on the Henry Hudson Parkway between 155th and 125th Streets when I noticed a police car with a flashing red light behind me, and a police car next to me, and then one in front of me. I'd gotten many speeding tickets over the years—in my youth, driving too fast was one of my worst habits—and I may have been speeding then, but that wouldn't account for all the flashing red lights. I pulled over, and one of the cops walked up to me, pointed his gun in my face, and yelled, "Put your hands on the wheel." The end of the barrel was three inches from my face, and I could see his finger nervously resting on the trigger. Not a good place to be.

I asked the officer what the problem was.

"Do you know you're driving a stolen a car?"

"A what?"

I tried to explain what had happened—that the car had been stolen from me, but now I had it back. He wouldn't hear it. He told me to get out. I did. He frisked me, slapped on handcuffs, and shoved me into the patrol car.

Then one of the other cops got into my VW, cranked up the stereo, and red-lined it, leaving a patch of burned rubber.

It was clear that I was part of their entertainment for the evening. When we got to the station, one of them tried to taunt me, getting in my face and singing "Busted in a stolen car" while snapping his fingers. With my hands still cuffed behind my back, I looked up to the station commander, who sat on a podium and witnessed the whole thing. "Are you watching this?" I asked.

"Yes, I am," he said. "Throw his ass in the tank."

They walked me over to the jail, pushed me inside, and slammed the metal door.

I was hardly the first person to be hassled, taunted, and roughed up by the cops. This was during Rudolph Giuliani's reign as the city's law-and-order mayor. To crack down on street crime, he advocated intimidating tactics, even after those tactics went too far. I knew that New Yorkers of color experienced more unlawful arrests, not to mention police brutality, than white residents. But that gave me little comfort on the night of my arrest. Once in the jail, I sat there on a bench fuming until I finally looked up and noticed another guy, a Hispanic dude, sitting on a second bench. He didn't seem angry. He was relaxed, and once I cooled off a bit and surveyed my situation, I knew there was a question I had to ask. So I caught his attention, nodded, and said, "So, what are you in for?"

The man rattled off a list of drug-related charges. Ten grams of this, thirteen ounces of that. Animated and engaging, he continued with his list until he finally stopped, and I thought the conversation was over. Then he asked, "Hey, what about you? What are you in for?"

"I am innocent."

"Me too, man!" he cried. "We'll be out of here in no time!"

I had to chuckle, and he laughed too. He thought I was crazy because I said I was innocent, and I thought the same about him. Only one of us was right.

After three or four hours, the cops verified that I was telling the truth. They let me go, with no apology, and I told the station commander that I wanted to file a report. He pulled me into a back office and began telling me all the great things that the New York City Police Department was doing, about how Mayor Giuliani had ramped up enforcement against drug peddlers and street thugs but how officers themselves still faced abuse, and he said the officers were doing great work for the youth in these communities. I wouldn't budge. I still wanted to file the complaint.

Then, in a judgmental and condescending tone, he asked me what I was doing to help people in "these kinds of neighborhoods."

So I told him. "I develop afterschool programs in the South Bronx and Harlem, in some of the toughest high schools in the city and the country. We're trying to break the cycle of poverty and low expectations, and we do that by getting the kids involved in intensive community service programs. We work in the classrooms, we work in the community, and we work with the kids."

He tried to get me to soften my stance against the officers. "This could really hurt their careers."

"You know what," I said, "I'm a white guy. If I was a black kid or any of the kids I work with, as bad as it went for me, it would have been much worse for them. Much worse. I want to file a report immediately."

The station had an electric typewriter, but the commander said I couldn't use it and had to wait for an officer to come in who could type. I told him I could type, but he refused. He was stonewalling me so that I would give up and leave. But I waited several more hours and finally filed my report well after midnight. I called to follow up, but no one knew anything. I assume the report died in some bureaucratic graveyard, and I never again wondered why many of the kids in our programs don't trust the cops.

I have no illusions about how much damage drugs do in our society, particularly among young people. I see it when I'm working in our schools. But I wasn't in Harlem to fight the drug wars or pass judgment on the dealers. For all I knew, those dealers were the brothers or sisters of the kids in our programs. I needed to better understand the circumstances that drove them to dealing so we could develop alternatives to the drugs and the gangs. And as fellow human beings, they deserved to be treated with respect. As the months passed, I came to know some of the dealers and even had one of them, Francisco, up for a beer. My brownstone's front door was often left unlocked, but he and his friends looked out for me and my apartment while I was abroad. In fact, I never had anything stolen from me when I was in Harlem (my car was ripped off in the East Village).

On another occasion, after a trip to the Laundromat one summer night, I pulled up in front of my building so I could drop off my laundry before parking the car. While I was in my apartment, I heard Francisco and the guys shouting through my open window to warn me that a cop was giving me a $100 parking ticket. The officer was riding one of those three-wheel buggies, and I raced after him in my Birkenstocks. It took me four blocks to catch him. Trying to catch my breath, I explained, "I was just taking my laundry up. Aren't you allowed to double-park to unload your stuff?"

"What? You live there?"

"Yeah. You can come up and see my apartment if you'd like, but can you do something about this ticket?"

He seemed flabbergasted but was accommodating. "Okay," he said. "But you've got big balls to live here."

He ripped up the ticket, and I had Francisco to thank for it.

By the end of my first year in Harlem, I found that I was able to connect better with our students. I was no longer the white guy who drove in from Connecticut. Unlike many other white teachers and administrators, I didn't live the urban/suburban double life. The students knew where I lived and knew about some of my experiences there, such as the time some guys climbed onto the roof and tapped my telephone wire so they could make $1,600 worth of calls to Haiti. The kids respected that I walked to some of their schools and that I took the subway and buses to get around. I saw the same homeless people sleeping on the park benches that they did, knew the same children who were hungry and hanging out on the corner, dodged the same women pushing shopping carts on the street in search of food or clothes. I had spent a night in the Missionaries of Charity homeless shelter in the South Bronx, serving dinner, playing dominoes, and sleeping on a cot in a room with about thirty other men. I got to know some of those guys and now had a much better idea what they did during the day.

To our students, these experiences gave me credibility; I could now see the world through their eyes. They would often tell me that their own families were one step away from a shelter or a soup kitchen, or they had received food from the very kitchen we were now assisting. Sometimes they told me these things with a feeling of shame, and I told them about the compassion of the people I had met at the shelters and the kitchens, how many of them went on to become volunteers, and that there was no shame in using their services.

Our organization had begun to fill a void in these students' lives. I remember talking to a high school student in the South Bronx named Chris who was being heavily recruited by the Bloods, a notorious gang, and was ready to join when we reached out to him. At six foot four and about 270 pounds, more muscle than fat, Chris was a man child. Yes, the Bloods would have loved to have had him. But he joined our organization instead and never looked back. I asked him why he even considered rolling with the Bloods in the first place, and he said, "I wanted to be part of something bigger. I wanted to feel that I'd be missed if I was gone." I've met many others who quit their gangs and joined our group for exactly the same reason.

Our goal was not simply to expand these programs in number. I also wanted to deepen our involvement in the schools and use traditional business measurements to determine our success. So we developed Key Performance Indicators (KPIs) to track student engagement, service hours, and their fundraising. (Every dime they raised was used for constructing schools.) We also gave the students more responsibility to choose their own service projects, run their own meetings, and elect their own officers (president, vice president of service, vice president of recruiting, vice president of sponsorship, treasurer, and so on). We made a stronger pitch to reach kids who were falling through the cracks and were in jeopardy of dropping out. We ran training workshops in the summer for our teacher advisors and expanded our presence in the classroom with a global education curriculum, delivered by the teachers and by our staff.

Our most ambitious effort, by far, began in 1999 when we started taking students overseas to build schools. Travel abroad rightly connotes excitement and adventure, but these are demanding trips, lasting two weeks, with the students living in village huts with host families, completely shorn of all modern amenities. To be selected, the kids go through a rigorous application and interview process, in part because they are expected to contribute hard labor on the work site. We also see the program as an investment. We expect the students to return to their community; share their experience through lectures, slide presentations, and essays; and inspire others to service.

We began by running several "treks" a year, with about fifteen kids on each one—a huge commitment of resources by us, but certainly one of the most transformational things we do.

For all its chaos, Harlem was also a community in which I felt very much at home, and my apartment became an unlikely oasis of tranquility and peace. I owe that to a Tibetan Buddhist monk who briefly became my roommate.

I had met Lobzang Tsetan while scoping out possible school sites in the mountains of Ladakh in northern India. The region borders Tibet and is sacred to Buddhists who went into exile there after the Chinese invaded Tibet in 1950. Lobzang is actually a *geshe*, a highly educated and respected teacher of Buddhist theology. Always gracious, always smiling, Geshe was the community leader who convinced us to build a school in his idyllic mountain village. Afterward I stayed in touch with him, so I knew he had come to teach at a Buddhist learning center in New Jersey. Marc Friedman and I decided to visit him for a couple days, and when we were packing our bags to leave, Geshe asked if he could get a ride to New York. We said of course, and he soon met us at our car with a satchel the size of a small day-pack.

"Where are you going?" I asked.

"I don't know. Where should I go?" he asked. "Maybe I should go to the bus station. I hear you can sleep there."

Only monks like Geshe roll like that: not a big planner, living in the moment and completely trusting the *dharma,* the teachings of Buddha. I suggested that he stay at my place for a week or two while he figured things out. He moved in and provided quite a contrast in the hood: the shaved head, the flowing gold and maroon robes, the *mala* (prayer beads) wrapped around his wrist. He turned his room into a meditation space, where he chanted for hours in the morning, and sometimes I meditated with him at night. He walked me out the door every morning, waved to Francisco, and then headed back up for more prayers. I showed him around the neighborhood, introduced him to the homies, and took him to the bodegas where he could find fruit, vegetables, and rice. He spoke broken English and took walks by himself, his hands folded behind his back, quietly chanting mantras, always smiling. People stopped in their tracks, but everyone loved Geshe.

He did some teaching at Columbia and New York University, but after three months he had to return to India. I was sad to see him leave, but he needed to go back to Ladakh to expand the school we had helped him build. Geshe's teachings spread so that a few years later, the Dalai Lama identified him as a *rinpoche*, the highest ranking teacher or incarnation. Now when he comes to the States to teach, we'll meet in New York for lunch, and I've noticed that other Buddhists bow to him respectfully.

As he did in Malawi, my father visited me in Harlem. Staying five nights at the apartment, he came in part to make sure I was safe but also because he wanted to see my work and to be part of my life. With all its street life, Harlem was his kind of neighborhood. He strolled right up to Francisco and the other drug dealers and introduced himself as if he was still back in our small town in Michigan: "Hi, how are you? I'm Jim's dad." He assumed everyone in the neighborhood knew everyone, and therefore they would all know me. Francisco welcomed him to the hood. My dad later saw the cops put some of the guys in the paddy wagon. "What'd they do wrong?" he asked.

"They're drug dealers, Dad."

The visit once again validated for my dad what I was doing with my career and my life. He saw how experiencing the turmoil of the neighborhood was all part of my own effort to live my faith, and his only real complaint was the noise: the sirens, the loud music, the bottles breaking, and the occasional gunshot.

My mom stayed home, and when she asked my dad about my place, he chose his words carefully. "It's adequate and clean," he said. "There are no roaches or bugs."

At the time my dad visited, I had not yet found a Catholic niche in Harlem. The closest spiritual connection I had made was with a black Baptist church, St. Luke, on Morningside Avenue, where I was enthralled by the Reverend J. G. McCann Sr. I don't recall how I heard about the church, but one morning I walked in with some friends, and Reverend McCann saw us and yelled, "We got visitors! What's your name?" I told him, and after that, whenever I walked in, he loudly declared, "There's Jim Ziolkowski! Thank you for coming, Brother Ziolkowski!"

Services at St. Luke were an *event.* Unlike most Catholic churches, where the parishioners dress casually, the congregants at St. Luke wore their finest clothes, with men in dark suits and women in elegant dresses, hats, and gloves. They welcomed me with hugs and handshakes, and I was always in for a ride. Reverend McCann had a magnificent baritone, and with a towel around his neck and droplets of sweat streaming down his forehead, he would start softly, build momentum, gradually raise his voice, and then cry out the lessons from the Gospels in a grand, rhythmic cadence, with the congregants responding in equal force. *Hallelujah!* The crowd was whipped into a frenzy, and a choir of about eighteen would then appear in robes, accompanied by a drummer, a bass player, a guitarist, and a guy pounding a Hammond B3 organ. The parishioners then filled the aisles and danced, shaking the walls of the large storefront church. Services lasted four hours, and even if you stayed for only two or three, you'd come out of there invigorated and wondering, "Oh my God, what just happened?"

I went to St. Luke about once a month and loved it, but it wasn't my church. I had not gone to Sunday Mass at a Catholic church in Connecticut because I didn't feel connected to any church community. Much of Fairfield County is wealthy, and I felt that most of the parishioners didn't understand my life choices. Nor could I reconcile my progressive beliefs with the messages of some of the churches I attended. I was a misfit. I preferred smaller chapels and attended Mass only during the week at a chapel near our office in Stamford. When my dad was in town, he reminded me that going to church on the weekdays doesn't fulfill our obligation to attend Mass on Sundays. The Third Commandment is to keep holy on the Sabbath, and for us, Sabbath is Sunday. He seemed very concerned.

As we were walking along, having this conversation, we happened upon the Church of the Annunciation on Convent Avenue and West 131st Street, which was founded in 1854. Though he was a complete stranger to the church, my dad swung open the doors and introduced himself, and me, to the pastor, Father Felix. We started talking, and I was immediately drawn to him. An immigrant from Spain, he was in his sixties, warm and welcoming, but also brilliant, progressive, and charismatic. In our first conversation he spoke eloquently about the poor and the needs of the community. The church had eight Masses on the weekend, seven in Spanish, one in English, and my dad and I decided to attend.

Though he was small in size, Father Felix thundered about social justice in a way that made him larger than life. He engaged the congregation and made his sermons relevant. Around Christmas, he reminded us that Christ was born into poverty, on the dirt floor of a stable, and he remained humble for the rest of his time on earth. Father Felix connected that to the poverty in our neighborhood, reminding us to find meaning in every circumstance and to exercise compassion at every turn.

Father Felix brought further clarity and light to complex moral issues. I had trouble, for example, with the church's position on the exclusion of gay people, on not allowing women to be ordained as priests, and on priests not being allowed to marry. Father Felix taught me that you don't have to agree with every church position to be strong in your faith. He himself thought that there should be female priests. He welcomed gays in his church, and he often preached that we must have respect for all faiths. In our conversations, he even got me to soften my view of the New York police, noting that without them, "the gangs would rule completely."

At the time, I was having heated debates with a close friend about abortion; he was adamantly opposed. I also believed abortion is wrong but was conflicted about whether you should vote for a political candidate only because he is pro-life. Is abortion a matter of legislation or conscience? Father Felix told me that the question of when life begins is highly personal. He believed abortion was a sin, but he did not believe that government should legislate the matter. The question is between you and your God and is indeed a matter of conscience—yours, not the government's. I found the answer reasonable and reassuring.

I wondered how pro-life candidates could be in favor of capital punishment, and Father Felix too was confused by the contradiction and pointed out that Christ was a victim of capital punishment. He said he always votes for the candidates who "do the most for the poor."

Geshe. Reverend McCann. Father Felix. I felt as if God had put me in Harlem to stretch and deepen my own faith.

I had found my circuit of clubs and churches, disparate venues to be sure, but they had one thing in common: I always knew I was in the right place. I was reading Alex Haley's *Autobiography of Malcolm X* and James Baldwin's *The Fire Next Time*, both of which captured our country's racial inequities in angry, searing prose. That made me all the more sensitive to the community's historical slights, more understanding of its challenges, and more appreciative of the warmth and generosity that it so often extended me.

Unfortunately, Harlem did not serve my social life well. I dated many women who, upon hearing where I lived, didn't want to see me again. It was just one more obstacle: the constant travels to isolated countries, the erratic schedule, the total focus on my work. I wanted to settle down, but I couldn't find a woman with whom I connected on a spiritual, intellectual, and emotional level. I was in my early thirties and became uncomfortable seeing women who I enjoyed hanging out with but to whom I could not make a bigger commitment. It didn't seem right or fair to them. So I established a one-year threshold: I would not date a woman for more than a year unless I was willing to spend the rest of my life with her. But since I had moved to Harlem, even getting a second date was a challenge.

I wasn't thinking about my personal life at all in October 1998, when I returned from six weeks in Nepal and Ladakh, India, where I was scouting a possible school for Tibetan nomads. To keep costs down, I flew a roundabout route from Kathmandu to Delhi to Singapore and then across continental Europe and finally to New York. Forty hours in all, a brutal trip. I got to my apartment on a Friday night, knowing that Building with Books had a service project in Stamford the following day. Our high school students were painting an outdoor mural over graffiti in a tough part of town. Exhausted, I didn't want to go, but Marc pushed me hard to participate.

Shortly after I arrived in Stamford the next morning, I noticed a young teacher who must have been a new advisor for the BwB program at Stamford High School. She had short dark hair and was wearing a T-shirt, an old pair of Levis with holes in the knees, and no makeup. Totally engaged with the kids and our project, she had a certain way about her—peaceful, dedicated, and confident with all the students. She had dimples, grayish blue eyes, and a dazzling smile. She was beautiful. She was also oblivious to me.

I finally approached her and struck up a conversation. Her name was Jenny Freres, and in the course of a five-minute conversation, I was amazed to discover the parallel nature of our lives. Just as I had quit GE, she had quit her marketing job at Nestlé to get her master's degree in teaching because she believed that's where she could make the most impact. This was her first year at the high school, and she preferred working with youth in high-risk situations. Like me, she had also lived in Colorado and loved to ski.

I was probably breaking some sort of rule, but I asked one of our staff members to schedule me to do a series of talks and slide shows in her class. I brought my slides from Nepal and talked to the students about joining our movement, but Jenny was the reason I was there. I intended to ask her out, but every time I was about to, another teacher or student interrupted us. I left without asking, but now I really couldn't get her out of my mind. A few days later, while sitting in my apartment, I summoned the courage to call her. "I'm not calling for Building with Books," I said. "I'm calling to see if you'd like to grab some dinner sometime."

She said yes, though she seemed reluctant.

She lived in a blue-collar section of Cos Cob, Connecticut, and shared a small house with two other women. When I picked her up, I didn't have much of a plan, which one of her friends later told me is "a fatal mistake for a first date. You never pick a girl up without a plan." At Jenny's suggestion, we started out at a dive bar, where she promptly ordered a pint of Guinness and a shot of Maker's Mark. A woman with her own whiskey. I knew there was something special about her.

Some first dates feel right from the get-go, and this was one of them. She told me that she believed her ambitions could be fulfilled at Stamford High School, which had about two thousand students, with a significant percentage of those receiving free lunches (meaning they were living below the poverty line). It was a raucous, polyglot community. Some kids had parents who were top executives and were bound for the Ivy League; other kids were homeless. "I like working with all kids," Jenny told me, "but my preference is the kids with ankle bracelets." Those were the students who were in and out of jail.

She wrote poetry, read voraciously, and loved music, nature, and travel. She was candid, telling me about a ten-year relationship that had just ended. We went to another bar, one that I knew, and we shot some pool and drank some more beer and Maker's Mark.

It wasn't long before I started calling her Sunshine because of her radiant smile. We spent our first Christmas together, huddled around the open door of my cranked-up oven, as the broken boiler had left me without heat. Jenny didn't care that our first gifts were exchanged in my frigid moldy apartment. She embraced Geshe and any other visitor or friend, no matter how unconventional. She traveled with me to Haiti—we had already built one school there and in 1999 were looking to build a second one in the Central Plateau. (We had built thirty-one in all by then.) When we couldn't get a four-wheel-drive truck, Jenny was willing to ride on the back of a motor-cycle to climb muddy mountain trails in the rain while searching for building sites. We stayed in huts that had tarantulas hanging from the ceiling, but she never complained.

Early in our relationship, my dad pulled Jenny aside and told her, "Don't get too attached to him. He moves around a lot and will never settle down. I don't want you to get hurt."

"Dad," I later told him, "you're not helping my cause."

Six months into our relationship, I realized this was the longest I had been with someone for nearly a decade. At nine months, it occurred to me that my twelve-month deadline was approaching. I knew that I loved Jenny very much, and I couldn't see myself with anyone else. Her thirtieth birthday cleared up any doubts I may have had.

Jenny didn't want a party and just asked that we go away. "Surprise me," she said. So over Labor Day Weekend, we decided to drive up the coast to Portland, Maine, pulling an old catamaran on a trailer. My dad and I had bought the boat years ago, and I had recently fixed it up. The idea was to reach Portland and then sail to a small island I had mapped out, where we'd pitch a tent and spend a couple days. But about ten miles from Portland, I looked into my side-view mirror and saw smoke coming out of the trailer wheel. The bearings were shot. We limped into Portland and were lucky to find a Napa auto parts store. A guy there looked at the problem and said I had to repack the bearings. I'm no mechanic, but I bought the parts and a lube gun and spent two hours in the parking lot teaching myself how to repack the bearings and put the wheel back on.

We had to stop at a grocery store for food and wine, and instead of reaching the boat ramp at noon, we got there at 3. I could see the island a mile and a half off the coast, but soon the clouds came in, and then the fog. By the time the boat was rigged and we had packed our supplies—two hours after we had arrived—the island was no longer visible.

Then it started to rain.

Jenny and I had on our wet suits, and I thought we were ready to shove off. Then, incredibly, the boom-pin snapped, and the boom disconnected from the mast, disabling the sail. I sprinted back up to the car and grabbed a pair of Vise-Grip pliers, but when I returned, Jenny was holding the boat in the water, in tears.

"Do you still want to do this?" I asked.

"Yes," she said.

I used the Vise-Grips to clamp the boom back onto the mast, and we finally shoved off in the rain and wind. The fog had really closed in, and we had only twenty feet of visibility. Should we continue on? We decided to keep a close eye on my compass bearings and give it a try. I figured it would take us fifteen minutes to reach the island.

But fifteen minutes passed, and we still weren't at the island, and the fog had now gotten worse. Jenny didn't know that we were lost. All I had was my compass, and I began to wonder if we were going to end up in the North Atlantic. Then a light appeared, on a boat, and we sailed right up to it. The guys on board asked what the hell we were doing. I told them we were looking for the island, and they said it was only a few hundred yards away.

It rained pretty steadily for two days, giving us only a few overcast hours to sail. We mostly had to stay in the tent. But we had plenty of wine. On Monday, Labor Day, we sailed safely back to shore and figured the drama was over. We hopped back on the highway, heading south, but just after we passed Kennebunkport, my car lost all power. Everything, gone. I had manual transmission, so we were able to coast to a rest stop with a gas station. But because it was Labor Day, the station had no mechanic, just a kid working the cash register. I needed a new V-belt, and Jenny waited patiently, grading English papers, while the cashier and I took four long hours to install a new one. By the time we were back on the road, it was almost midnight, so after a half hour we pulled over and spent the night in a crummy motel. Worse, Jenny had to call in absent for work on Tuesday, which is a cardinal sin for a teacher after a three-day weekend.

So for Jenny's thirtieth birthday, about everything that could go wrong did go wrong. It was a complete disaster. And yet I would have to say it was the most beautiful weekend of my life. And Jenny said it was one of the best birthdays that she'd ever had. Why? Because we were together.

Maine confirmed that I wanted to spend the rest of my life with Jenny. Without ever discussing marriage or even saying the word aloud, I started looking for a ring. A few days before the one-year anniversary of our first date, I found one and bought it. I put it in a silver box with purple enameling that I had bought in Ladakh, but I didn't have "a plan." Though it was early November, I decided to pull together a picnic and take Jenny to the Cloisters, the museum of medieval art surrounded by beautiful gardens overlooking the Hudson River. I brought the wine and white roses with assorted purple flowers, purple being Jenny's favorite color. I found some nice cheeses and fruit and then spread out a blanket beneath an unusually bright November sun. But I was nervous. I honestly had no idea what she was going to say.

I opened the wine, but before I could ask the question, she had something on her mind. "You know," she said, "I swore to God I would never tell you this unless we were getting married or breaking up."

I didn't know what was coming next.

"The first time I saw you," she said, "I had this vision that we were going to spend the rest of our lives together."

All my anxieties melted away. I got out my silver box, and I wanted her to open it. But she put it aside, thinking the "pretty little box" was an anniversary gift. I couldn't get her to open it, so I finally picked it up myself, lifted the top, and said, "Jenny, I love you with all my mind, all my heart, and all my soul. I want to spend the rest of my life and all of eternity with you. Will you marry me?"

She just started laughing. I was in tears, but she didn't answer me because she was laughing so hard.

"Well, will you marry me?"

"I didn't answer?"

"No."

"Of course!"

I was exuberant, relieved, and somewhat in disbelief.

We returned to my apartment and called our parents. Jenny spoke to hers first, and then I called mine. I assumed they'd be thrilled because they loved Jenny. Then again, they doubted I was ever going to settle down. My mom picked up the phone, and I told her that Jenny and I had gone on a picnic to celebrate our one-year anniversary. I told her about the cheese, the grapes, the wine, the purple flowers. I told her about the whole setup. Then I said, "I asked Jenny to marry me, and she said yes."

There was silence.

There was more silence.

"Jim," she finally said, "it's really not a good idea to pull your mother's leg."

"No, I'm serious."

"Jim, come on now. Can I talk to Jenny?"

I handed over the phone, and my mom began her interrogation. "Did Jim really take you on a picnic?"

"Yes," Jenny said.

"Did he really get you wine and cheese and flowers?"

"Yes."

"Did he really ask you to get married?"

"Yes."

"And you said yes?"

"Yes! I did."

She chuckled and handed the phone back to me, but all I could hear was the dial tone. Jenny explained that after her final "yes," Mom shouted joyfully "Sweet Jesus!" and hung up the receiver. When I called her right back, I asked to speak with Dad. He was next door at Uncle Bob's house, so Mom had to get him. When he got on the phone, I went through the whole story again. Silence.

"Jim," he finally said, "are you bullshitting me again?" He didn't believe me and also demanded to speak to Jenny for confirmation.

Sweet Jesus indeed.

Jenny's family lived near Stamford in Darien, but we decided to get married in Harlem by Father Felix. My mom asked me if such an event would be safe in Harlem, but that was the whole point. I wanted our family and friends to experience the Harlem that we knew and loved, not the Harlem that they may have read about in the paper or seen stereotyped in gangbanger movies. The weekend began with Alex Garcia jamming with AfroMantra at Café Largo for our rehearsal dinner, which everyone was invited to. When I saw our guests spilling out into the street and celebrating with the locals, I knew we had made the right decision.

We wanted to find ways to make the ceremony itself special, and Jenny had a great idea for lighting. She sent me out to get two hundred Catholic prayer candles that are popular in Latino communities; the candles come in a durable glass jar about twelve inches in height. They burn for many hours, so we lined them up along the aisles and on the altar. At the dinner afterwards, Jenny and I put a favorite book on each of the eighteen tables and asked the guests to sign the one at their table. My father, quoting from *The Little Prince*, wrote, "'What is essential is invisible to the eye for it is only with the heart that one sees rightly,' and that is with love."

I was in charge of music, and I asked Reverend McCann if we could hire the Baptist choir at his church. They were traveling, but he connected me to another black Baptist choir in the Bronx, which agreed to come. The singers wanted me to bring in speakers and a sound system, even though that was, shall we say, unorthodox for a traditional Catholic ceremony. But Father Felix didn't care, and the choir blew the roof off. My sister, Mari, who has a doctorate in ancient goddess traditions and has rejected Catholicism as too patriarchal, read a poem in honor of Jenny and me. Marc Friedman, meanwhile, was my best man. So too was Dave, at a time when his own career had taken an interesting twist. He was teaching poor students in the Rio Grande Valley, with Teach for America, but he had also begun developing residential real estate—and he was good at it. At the wedding, his heartfelt toast to Jenny and me was much appreciated.

Early in my relationship with Jenny, one of our favorite downtown musicians was Dana Fuchs. At about six foot one, she was stunning, and her music was a blend of blues and funk. She had a soulful voice, a combination of Aretha Franklin and Janis Joplin. We had seen her many times in the Village, and I was shocked when she agreed to play at our wedding reception at a midtown restaurant. She overheard me call Jenny "Sunshine" and immediately let loose with a rendition of Bill Withers's "Ain't No Sunshine (When She's Gone)" followed by the classic Temptations song "My Girl."

After we were married, Jenny agreed to move into my apartment, and her father helped her. A senior partner at PricewaterhouseCoopers, Ron had grown up on the South Side of Chicago, and now he looked around at the pit bulls, the garbage, and the shady characters. He shook his head, and I asked him what was on his mind. "I spent the first half of my life working to get out of the ghetto," he said, "and now I'm moving my eldest daughter back into the ghetto."

Some months after we settled in, I was driving Marc's Jeep Cherokee down a street when I got distracted and bumped into a car. It was winter, and five guys, dressed in enormous North Face down parkas over hoodies, got out. They looked angry, and I was sure at least some of them had guns inside their parkas.

"Stay cool," I said. "I've got insurance. I'll be able to cover all repair costs."

"You better," one of them barked.

"The first thing we got to do," I said, "is call the police and fill out a report."

"Police! You ain't calling the fuckin' police." They got in my face and things became tense, but I wasn't intimidated. They were just like the kids we worked with every day in the schools.

"Okay," I said, "but without a police report, you can't get any insurance money. There's probably a thousand dollars in damages."

"But what can you do for us?"

"I can write you a check for a couple hundred dollars." That would have been my deductible anyway.

"What's in your pocket?"

"I don't know. Maybe about $90. But I could write you a check."

"What do you mean, 'a check'?"

I explained what a check was. I think some of them knew, some didn't.

"Okay, let's do that check," someone said.

The problem was that none of them had bank accounts, so a check would work only if we went to a check-cashing place in the South Bronx, and I'd have to go as well. They didn't quite believe the whole check thing, and they didn't trust that I would follow them, so one of the guys drove with me.

He appeared to be Dominican, probably had a gun, but couldn't have been more than sixteen. I started talking with him as I would with any kid in our programs—with respect. "What school do you go to?" I asked.

"I don't go to school."

"Okay, what school *did* you go to?"

"Kennedy," he said.

"John F. Kennedy in the Bronx?"

"Yeah. How do you know about that?"

"We run a program there. Do you know Miss Santoro?" She was one of our teacher advisors.

"Yeah! I know Miss Santoro. I liked her. I had her for history."

So we connected over Miss Santoro, talked some more, and after a while the kid dropped his gangbanger façade and became just a kid. We talked about his choices, and I encouraged him to go back to school and join our program. He shrugged me off, but I had to try.

When we reached the check-cashing store, he jumped out of the car and said to his friends, "Hey, man, he's okay." After I gave them their $200, the kid handed me his phone number and said, "If you need anything, snow, whatever, just let me know, and I'll take care of you."

I said "No thanks" and told him we'd be looking for him to join BwB once he came back to school. He half-grinned, and they drove off.

It was a telling experience. I knew they were capable of killing me, but I also saw that they were no different from the kids I had met all over the world. From the South Bronx to sub-Saharan Africa, children are subjected to abject conditions, but they still have hope, and for our mission, that's all the fuel we need.

I know we can't inspire every kid, but I also know that if we can provide alternatives—namely, the opportunity to truly change the world through service and education—we can help many teenagers regain control over their lives. They don't want to escape from Harlem or the South Bronx or whatever city they're in. They want to transform their neighborhoods and lift up their communities. In doing so, they will chart a better future for their cities *and* themselves.

As for Harlem and me, well, I wasn't able to stay. Jenny's commute to Stamford was long. I traveled a lot, and Jenny didn't feel safe staying there by herself. She would often stay with her parents. I understood. Less than a year after we got married, we packed up a U-Haul and moved into a house in a blue-collar neighborhood in Stamford. We still live there today.

I won't deny Harlem's many shortcomings, but I didn't go there to judge or rescue. I was there to inhale and to experience, and everything about Harlem, especially the people, enriched my life, enlightened our mission, and exhilarated my faith. Christ turned his beliefs into action, and I tried to do that in Harlem, by going to a place where they said I shouldn't go and finding grace amid mayhem.

CHAPTER 7

Your Will Be Done

At first glance, my brother John does not look like someone who'd want to spend time in the slums of Calcutta. He is a true *fashionista* who loves designer brands like Armani and Prada, drives a Mercedes, and, with his blue eyes and wavy dark hair, always looks immaculate. Five years older than I, John worked for years in the financial services industry, so he had the income to indulge his tastes. But he is also highly spiritual and compassionate, which led him to his sojourn in Calcutta. In 1996, he lived there for three months as a volunteer at the Missionaries of Charity, the religious order created by Mother Teresa.

I certainly admired that, and I decided to visit John on one of my trips to Nepal. When I told some high school students in America about my plans, they suggested questions that they wanted me to ask Mother Teresa. I explained that such a meeting was highly unlikely. Devoted to the poor and driven by her faith, Mother Teresa was a role model to the world for her compassion, a winner of the Nobel Peace Prize who was hailed as a living saint, the founder of a religious order that now operated in more than a hundred countries. You just don't show up in Calcutta, knock on her door, and begin an interview. Nonetheless the students persisted, so I told them to write out their questions just in case.

I reached Calcutta by plane and left the airport on a tuk-tuk. At first the city reminded me of New Delhi—the whirl of color and noise, the beauty of the temples and palaces, the swarm of humanity—but everything was amped up. The streets were more crowded, the cars louder, the sun hotter. I rode to the Kalighat neighborhood, where my brother was living in a boardinghouse. One of the most congested areas in the city, Kalighat was a cauldron, with orphans begging for food, the homeless using bed sheets for shelter, the trash piled high on the street and in abandoned lots. It was the worst urban poverty I had ever seen.

It was also where the Mother House was located, where Mother Teresa and her Sisters lived. After I settled in with my brother, I attended early morning Mass in a chapel attached to the Mother House. There were no comforts, no frills. You sat or kneeled on a hard tile floor beneath fluorescent lights and before the altar and a single crucifix. The nuns went every morning, all wearing the same blue-and-white sari, a sign of solidarity in their commitment to God. The priest was there. So were John and I and a few other volunteers, maybe thirty-five people in all. It felt as if we were all on a pilgrimage. And then, on that first morning, Mother Teresa walked in, wearing the same habit as the Sisters. She sat on the floor like everyone else and prayed.

I admired the other nuns as much as I admired her. They had all made the same vow of poverty; each day, they ate rice, drank tea, shunned every modern amenity, and devoted themselves to the destitute and the ill. After each Mass, they sang beautiful hymns like a heavenly choir, unaccompanied by any instruments, just their voices celebrating God and connecting us more directly to Him. In the Mass itself I noticed the Sisters used slightly different language for the Lord's Prayer. The prayer itself had always been a favorite of my father's, and mine, but we had recited the beginning in this fashion:

> *Our Father, who art in heaven,*
> *Hallowed be thy name*
> *Thy Kingdom come*
> *Thy Will be done*

At the Mass in Calcutta, they said *your* instead of *thy*.

> *Our Father, who art in heaven,*
> *Hallowed be your name*
> *Your Kingdom come*
> *Your will be done*

It may seem like a minor difference, but I thought the less formal language conveyed a more personal relationship with God. It made Him more accessible to us, more familiar, and I loved it.

Though I was able to pray with Mother Teresa, I still had no expectation that I would meet her. John, however, had developed a good relationship with the nun who effectively served as her chief of staff. Sister Priscilla, by reputation, was stern and protective, all the more so since Christopher Hitchens had written his scathing book about Mother Teresa, *The Missionary Position*. But when I spoke to Sister Priscilla after Mass one day, she was quite nice. John had explained to her the work I was doing, and I figured I had nothing to lose, so I asked if I could interview Mother Teresa.

"I'll think about it," she said.

During the day, I walked through the city amid the garbage and sewage, where "the poorest of the poor," as Mother Teresa called them, scavenged. I saw the streets where the Missionaries collected the terminally ill and brought them to the Home for the Destitute and the Dying. I visited the orphaned children and held the babies who were left on the Missionaries' steps or in trash cans, and I toured its facility for lepers and talked with them about their lives. I was overwhelmed not by despair or even the tragic circumstances but rather by the compassion of the sisters and the joy it brought to those who suffered. Mother Teresa's organization had clinics, orphanages, soup kitchens, refugee centers, and homes for the poor, the sick, and the dying all around the world, but the problems of this city alone seemed overwhelming.

The next morning, after Mass, I was standing with John outside the chapel on a white stone veranda, and Sister Priscilla approached me. "Do you still want to do the interview?" she asked.

"Sure," I said. "When?"

"I'll let you know."

She left, but then moments later, I turned around and there she was—Mother Teresa. She walked toward me, hunched over, a figure so slight and frail that she hardly seemed capable of shouldering her own burdens let alone those of the poor. Her head was tilted downward, so the first thing she saw were my Birkenstock sandals. Then she slowly looked up until she caught my eyes, and at that moment I felt her hand on my forehead. Her eyes were peaceful, glowing, and warm. I immediately felt I was with someone who loved me immensely and unconditionally.

"God bless you," she said, and she smiled. "Would you like to sit down?"

"Sure," I said. "Thank you."

We sat on a bench. Fortunately, I always traveled with my video camera, and I had my notebook with all the questions from the high school kids, but I didn't have a tripod or a microphone. I had to sit close to her and held the camera in my right hand; I wasn't even sure if she was in the frame, and indeed she sometimes fell out of it. Nonetheless, during the interview, with the nuns' hymns providing a background harmony, Mother Teresa's spirit shone through. I told her that I had brought questions from high school kids in the United States who wanted to know more about her. She invariably invoked God or Jesus as the source of her strength. When I asked who had influenced her as a child, she said, "Jesus. It's a vocation, no?" Asked how she would handle violence, she said, "By praying. How can we have peace if we do not have peace in our own heart?"

She stressed the importance of family. When I asked how we can overcome selfishness, she said, "By sharing small things with great love at home. If we can bring peace, unity, joy, and love into the family, the whole world will change. Love begins at home."

She acknowledged the hardships of the poor, but she said that material poverty was not our only threat. "Everywhere there are peo-ple," she said, "they may not be hungry for bread, but they are hun-gry for love. And that is much more difficult to satisfy."

Beyond prayer, Mother Teresa's message was about "love in action," those gestures, however small, that might alleviate human suffering. "The other day," she said, "I got a letter from a child in America, and he wrote to me in big writing, 'MOTHER TERESA, I LOVE YOU SO MUCH,' and he underlines 'SO MUCH,' and 'I'm sending you my pocket money.' And inside the letter there was a check for three dollars. All a beautiful gift from God. It was a check for three dollars, but to me it looked like three thousand!"

The most meaningful part of the interview occurred when I asked what she would like to be remembered for. "Serving the poor," she said, "and in serving the poor, remember what Jesus said: 'What-ever you did to the least, you did for me. If you serve a glass of water in my name, you give it to me. If you receive a little child, you receive for me.' When we die and go home to God, again we will hear Jesus say, 'Come, you blessed by my father, possess the kingdom prepared for you, because I was hungry and you gave me to eat, I was thirsty and you gave me drink, I was naked and you clothed me, I was sick and you visited me. Come.'" As she quoted the gospel of Matthew, she explained, "This is exactly what happens when you do something for someone." Then she turned her head, looked straight into the camera, and spoke slowly and loudly, "You did that to me."

You did that to me. Those words echoed in my heart, capturing the very essence of what I was trying to do: when we help the poor, we help Christ. That was the foundation of social justice. That is our calling! I drew upon other passages from the Gospels for strength, such as "Fear is useless," but the passage that Mother Teresa quoted had been my motivation.

This is what Christ is asking of us.

This is what we are responsible for.

"That's why our work is so beautiful," she told me. "We have the poorest, the unwanted, the unloved, the sick, the dying, the crippled, the leper, and now all over the place, we have many houses for [people suffering from] AIDS. Nobody wants them, but we want them and help them."

After the interview, she placed a rosary and a Miraculous Medal in the palm of my hand. She closed her hand over mine and blessed me again.

I was blessed indeed. The interview, I thought, was a gift from God, and I believed that even more strongly the following year, when Mother Teresa died at age eighty-seven. I have one of her last extended taped interviews, and I've shared it with as many groups as possible.

Just after the interview finished, Sister Priscilla handed me a small piece of paper. It was a typewritten permission slip that allowed me to take photos and film the various facilities run by the Missionaries of Charity in Calcutta, and Mother Teresa signed it herself and wrote, "God bless you." I knew how rare it was to receive such permission, and I understood the responsibility they had given me to document and share the beauty of it all. I was also touched by their stationery, which had a line printed at the top: "As long as you did it to one of these My least brethren, you did it to Me."

In Calcutta I visited the Home for the Destitute and the Dying. John worked there; he and the other volunteers washed and cleaned the patients, massaged their sore limbs, fed them, and spent time with them. It was all about compassion. But as I walked through the ward with John and Sister Delores, what struck me was that the facility was so clean and cheerful. I thought it would be depressing, but the people on their deathbeds were smiling. I asked Sister Delores why they were so happy.

"Because the greatest fear that any human being can have," she said, "is to be alone when they die. These people know they will not be alone when God calls them. They are with us."

Sister Delores's words would soon strike me in a much more personal way.

★ ★ ★

In the early months of 2003, I had just returned from overseas—we had now built 100 schools, including in Mali and Nicaragua—and I called my mom to check in. She casually explained that Dad had some kind of growth or bulge in his stomach, and his physician asked him to check into the local hospital the next day for some tests. I spoke to my dad, and he assured me it was nothing serious. But I had a strange feeling, so I decided to fly to Detroit and drive to Jackson so I could be with him when he got the test results. My dad was happily surprised when I showed up in his hospital room, joking that my trip wasn't necessary. A few hours later, his physician came into the room and gently explained that he had cancer. It was probably pancreatic, but more tests would have to be conducted. My dad was peaceful and unconcerned.

My brother John, however, had a friend who was an oncologist, and he had reviewed the tests and had a more complete diagnosis.

I was in my office in Stamford when the call came, and the oncologist explained that my dad had pancreatic cancer and was not going to beat it. "Bullshit," I said, hanging up the phone. Then I broke down and cried. I made it through the afternoon, but when I got home, I was nearly inconsolable. Jenny sat with me for hours, holding my hand, helping me through.

Several days later, I flew back to Michigan so I could accompany my parents on my dad's next doctor's visit. He was going to meet with a leading oncologist at the University of Michigan for another opinion. When I got there, my parents were in their bedroom. I said hello, embraced them, and was keeping my emotions under control. Then my dad said, "Hey, I've got some stuff I want to give you." He showed me his skis and some other gear he thought I would want, and that's when I lost it. "Dad, I can't talk to you about this. It's not over. We aren't giving up."

The next day we went to the oncologist, joined by my older brother Pete. Pete is about six feet tall, wears glasses, and, with his MBA and a master's in theology, is quite smart.

The doctor, in his late forties, had a gentle manner. He was Polish, which my dad liked, and an easy rapport developed between them. When they spoke, each man looked the other in the eye. The doctor confirmed that my dad had pancreatic cancer. He said there was no need for chemotherapy, as there was no cure. Some palliative measures could be taken, but the cancer was too far advanced.

"So it's terminal?" my dad asked.

"Yes," the doctor said.

My dad appeared perfectly calm. "How much time do I have?"

"Three months at most."

That news would shock most people. Or make them angry. Or terrified. Or something. My mom seemed to be in denial, asking the doctor, "What makes you so sure?" But my dad just sat there. It was as if someone told him he had a cavity and it needed to be filled. The news seemed almost incidental to him. I thought I must have been in an alternate universe. I told my dad that we had to fight, but he just slowly shook his head.

He loved life but was living to meet God, and there was no doubt that was the next step in his own journey.

Though no conventional therapy was in order, Pete found an NIH trial for an alternative treatment being run at Columbia University. My dad was actually too old, but he was so fit for his age, seventy-two, that he was allowed to participate. He had to swallow thirty pills every six hours to replace the enzymes that the pancreas was failing to produce and go on a strict macrobiotic diet: no meat, some fish, a half-gallon of raw carrot juice every day. Four organic coffee enemas every twenty-four hours were meant to cleanse the lower intestine and stimulate the pancreas. I know, because I did them once a week as well as a form of solidarity with my dad. He thought I was crazy. I'd call him on the phone from the bathroom, and we'd laugh at the absurdity of it all.

He didn't want any special therapy, but he did so to humor us. And the treatment actually worked, as he was walking or biking every day.

My dad wasn't always at peace before his diagnosis, but he was afterward. It seemed to unleash a spiritual calm. I often thought he was living in an enlightened state during those months, and the bond between us deepened further. During one of my visits, I picked up his Bible and turned to the Gospel of Mark, where Jesus says, "Fear is useless, what is needed is trust." To my surprise, my dad had highlighted that very passage! I showed it to my dad and told him how important it had been to me over the years. "It's one of my favorite passages."

"Mine too," he said.

At Christmas he wanted to take the family back to Marathon Key in Florida. We had driven there when we were young, and my dad wanted to go back to the same motel. The place hadn't been updated since we were last there thirty years earlier. It was a dump, but no one cared.

Jenny was pregnant with our first child, and about a week earlier we had learned that it was going to be a boy. So once on the Keys, we asked my parents if they'd go on a walk with us. We walked a long time and decided to rest on a beach. We all sat on a wooden bench, watching the late afternoon sun beginning its descent, an idyllic setting for a man who so loved the water.

"Dad," I said, "we have some news. We just found out that Jenny is going to have a baby boy. And we have decided that we're going to name him after you. His name is going to be John Daniel, and we will always think of you when we call our little boy's name."

Through his tears, my dad said how happy he was to hear that, how honored he was.

"No, Dad. The honor is ours. It will be an honor for this little boy to carry your name for his entire life."

John Daniel "Jack" Ziolkowski was born on May 2, 2004, and in one of my most treasured photographs, the newborn, swaddled in his blanket, is held in the strong arms of his adoring grandfather.

We asked Father Felix to baptize Jack at the Annunciation Church in Harlem. My parents joined us, as did Jenny's parents and sister.

We had also asked my dad to be Jack's godfather; a friend of Jenny's, Patsy, who joined us as well, was his godmother. The church was otherwise empty. The baptism, Jack's first and most important sacrament, brought so much of my life into full circle. My son was being baptized by my spiritual mentor, whom I met only because of an introduction from my father. And now my father was standing in the very church that he found for me, the church where Jenny and I were married and where his namesake grandson and godson was about to be baptized. It was a truly amazing circle.

That miracle did not beget another. My dad stayed on his treatment for thirteen or fourteen months, then stopped. The swallowing was too painful, and his stomach was kicking back with acid reflux; maybe the cancer was attacking his stomach as well. Once the treatment ended, his health began to deteriorate, and he prepared for the "home stretch," as he called it. He brought the family together and reconciled past rifts. He began discarding his possessions and sold his boat. He carried with him a small book titled *Golden Counsels of Saint Francis de Sales*, in which he discusses death:

> *The words "We must die" are harsh, but they are followed by words of great sweetness: "in order to be united with God through death."* . . . *We ought not to think about death with worry.* . . . *Let's leave this concern to divine providence. It's enough for us to belong entirely to him, not only through duty but also in love. Why should we care about the rest except to abandon ourselves to this sweet providence which will never be lacking to us in life or in death.*

That's how Dad saw his own death, and though he could talk about life, death, and his faith for hours, he often distilled his philosophy into a few succinct words. "I love God, and God loves me," he would say, "and that's all you need to know."

He and my uncle had remained very close over the years, and one day Uncle Bob said to him, "You haven't had any time to grieve."

"I have nothing to grieve about," Dad said. "I've had ninety years of good living, and I'm only seventy-two!"

One of my dad's favorite books was Victor Frankl's *Man's Search for Meaning*, which tries to make sense of the author's experiences in Nazi death camps. Many of his insights spoke directly to my father in the final stages of his own life. Frankl wrote:

> *We must never forget that we may also find meaning in life even when confronted with a hopeless situation, when facing a fate that cannot be changed. For what then matters is to bear witness to the uniquely human potential at its best, which is to transform a personal tragedy into a triumph, to turn one's predicament into a human achievement. When we are no longer able to change a situation—just think of an incurable disease such as inoperable cancer—we are challenged to change ourselves. . . . In some ways, suffering ceases to be suffering at the moment it finds a meaning.*

I believe that's what my dad tried to do. He taught us about life through his own death, showed us courage in the face of despair, demonstrated the very faith that he had spent his entire life talking about. He never cried, except when he saw someone in our family cry. Before he stopped his treatment, and before I had given up on his beating the cancer, I began interviewing him on videotape to create a time capsule. I ultimately collected two full hours. At one point, I asked if he was afraid.

"No," he said, "I am never afraid. Sometimes I am sad but never afraid. It makes me sad because I would like to live longer. I would like to be part of your life. I don't look at this as hardship or adversity, though. I look at it as God's will. It has drawn our family together and helped us to understand our own mortality. I think this is all God's will, and with my remaining time I am supposed to show you how to die. Every living creature eventually dies. This is part of life."

★　★　★

For well over a year, I was traveling back to Michigan at least twice a month on weekends, sometimes three or four times, and with each week I could see Dad's increasing weight loss. One day he was lying on the couch looking out our large windows at the lake on a crisp autumn day.

"What are you thinking about?" I asked him.

"The moment I die," he said.

"What does it look like?" I asked. "How do you want it to be?"

"Nothing special," he said. "I just want all my family to be around me when I pass."

The hospice nurse began coming to our house regularly to check in on us. My dad did not take any pain medication, which mystified the nurses. They offered him anxiety pills, but he rejected those as well. He either had a high tolerance for pain, or he just wasn't suffering. On some nights, Uncle Bob brought home communion from the church. At my dad's house, he lit candles, passed the saucer around, and had a little service. "I'm not big on the rosary," Uncle Bob later said, "but it seemed like something you could do. We'd ask John if he had any thoughts, and every time he had something beautiful to say."

In my dad's final days, I helped bathe him and brush his teeth. Nineteen months had passed since his diagnosis. One night he started to cough up blood and vomit. My mom, exhausted physically and emotionally, had to leave the bedroom, and she asked me if I would sleep there. I said of course, and I went in around 10 p.m. The room itself had large symmetrical windows overlooking the lake, which was my father's favorite place, and the moon was out on a cold winter night. It was so peaceful.

Once he began vomiting blood, my dad could no longer speak, and it occurred to me that I may have already heard his last words. After his first prolonged coughing spasm, he didn't have the strength to sit up. I gently took off his pajama top, cleaned him, and put on a new top. This happened again about an hour later, and then again, and each time I cleaned him, each time put on a new top. No words passed between us. He was normally such a big, robust man, but now his body was shriveled, his eyes buried in their sockets, a skeletal figure except that his stomach was swollen from the cancer. It was a privilege to serve him, to be there for him, because he had always been there for me. Then around 4 a.m. he began to cough again, but this time he motioned for me to help sit him up. So I propped him up and lifted a bucket, and he bent over and vomited more blood. I put the bucket down, but my dad wanted to stay upright. So I took his hand and began to quietly pray the Our Father. I was astonished to hear him speak the words aloud with me.

> *Our Father who art in heaven,*
> *Hallowed be your name.*
> *Your Kingdom come,*
> *Your will be done*
> *On earth as it is in heaven.*
> *Give us this day our daily bread,*
> *And forgive us our trespasses*
> *As we forgive those who trespass against us*
> *And lead us not into temptation*
> *But deliver us from evil.*
> *Amen.*

My dad put special emphasis on "Your will be done."

At the end of the prayer, I looked up and said, "I love you, Dad."

And he said, "I love you, my son." Then I helped him lie down for the rest of the night. He never spoke another word.

The morning light poured through the window the following day. We were waiting for two of my siblings, Pete and Mari, to arrive, so we sat my dad up in a recliner. He could no longer see or speak, but Mom was by his side, holding his hand and singing quietly to him. Still, he was holding on, waiting for all his children to be there, until he was finally surrounded by his family and his brother, just as he wanted it.

At 3 the next morning, Pete woke me and said he thought that Dad was close. I went into the room with Jenny, and he was still resting on the recliner. As I held his hand, I took his wrist to feel his pulse. It was slow, each heart beat about five seconds apart, then ten seconds, then twenty, until finally his pulse had stopped. He was gone.

If Sister Delores was right—that dying patients were at peace because they knew they were not alone—then surely my father was at peace. We were all with him in his final moments, and God never left his side.

It was only fitting that seven priests presided at his funeral at St. Rita's Parish. My dad had always befriended clergymen, and now they were there in force.

"As you can all see," I said during my eulogy, "my dad was a good Catholic."

Everyone smiled knowingly.

I had been close to death several times, and in those moments I had not been afraid. But when I saw the physical devastation of my dad's body and just how disposable it had become, it shook me. I didn't think I could ever summon that type of courage and grace. Over time I realized that I was just in awe of my father—how relentless he was in his devotion, so sure that nothing, including his own death, could faze him. I came to see that his faith, far from being unapproachable, was a model for us all.

I still dream about my father. I dream that he is alive and is with me and Jenny and our boys, watching over us. And I pray for him each day, and I think of him and honor him when I say the Lord's Prayer.

Your will be done.

CHAPTER 8

Rayia's Smile

With the birth of Jack and my father's long illness, I could no longer work sixty to seventy hours a week or travel across the globe for months at a time. I couldn't devote as much time to the organization as I once did. My responsibilities as a father and son caused me to set different priorities.

At the same time our organization continued to grow. We had achieved a fundraising breakthrough in 2000 with the help of some familiar allies—executives at GE. Geoffrey Norman was a longtime executive at GE Asset Management who supported our organization early on and became a trusted friend, even flying to Michigan to attend my father's funeral. Norman introduced me to John Myers, the president of GE Asset Management. At the time, we were still holding fundraising dinners in Stamford, raising several hundred thousand dollars in any one evening. But Myers had a lot of friends on Wall Street, so we decided to have a fundraiser that honored him, and we held it at the New York Hilton. Instead of a fancy dinner, we had the event in the morning and just served breakfast—attendees could be in and out before their day started, and our costs would be kept down. The event drew representatives from the city's top investment firms, banks, and law firms, reaching a community well beyond our Stamford base, and we raised an astounding $1.3 million—more than three times what we had ever raised from a single fundraiser.

We now had a new donor base, which helped us expand nationally and grow all parts of the organization. By 2006, fifteen years had passed since its founding, and we had now built 194 schools abroad. We were also operating programs in ninety schools in the States and were stretched across the continent, from New York and Detroit to Oakland and San Francisco.

When my father became ill, I began expanding our leadership team, not merely to fill in any gaps when I wasn't there but, more important, to make us stronger and to accelerate our growth. I thought we had people in our organization who could manage different aspects of our mission more effectively than I. They would also be able to invest 100 percent of their time in their area of responsibility, whereas I was stretched across the entire organization, and this would give others a chance to lead.

Running highly effective programs in American high schools was far more challenging than building schools abroad. When we went overseas, the villagers wanted us to be there and were united around the common goal of building that school. Though they suffered from extreme poverty, the communities were tight-knit and stable. But in the States, we often worked in communities beset by family disorder, violence, drugs, crime, and, in some schools, apathy among teachers and dysfunction among administrators. Many of the schools we chose were failing: we wanted to engage the kids that so many others had left behind. The students themselves have always loved what we do, but sometimes it takes great effort to make it work.

When it did work, the students researched their own community and drew maps that outlined the most pressing needs. Then they tried to find solutions through service and advocacy. They worked with physically and developmentally disabled children or with the elderly; they prepared meals for those with HIV, cancer, or other terminal illnesses. Because their neighborhoods were often "food deserts" with no access to fresh produce, they helped plant and harvest community gardens. They organized festivals or other activities that gave younger kids an alternative to gang life. They also mentored younger children in local elementary schools, cleaned up parks, painted murals over graffiti, and helped out at libraries or play-grounds. This approach was influenced by my years in Harlem and my realization that kids don't want to escape from their communities but want to stay and make them better.

While I was satisfied with the goals we had set for our programs, I wanted to improve the quality of our work and to be in more communities. I also wanted to reach the most neglected neighbor-hoods. I had always faced resistance on that count, either from my colleagues, from some board members, or even from the educa-tional bureaucracies themselves. Too dangerous, too difficult, I was told. We can't reach enough students in these distressed schools to make it worth our while; they are too far gone, they said. So I created a new position, vice president of U.S. programs, and pro-moted Abby Hurst, a steady and caring colleague who did not rattle easily. As a nineteen-year-old pilot, she once had to cut the tiny engine of her ultra-light aircraft at 10,000 feet, glide it back down to earth, and land it without power. Abby had grit, and she also shared my passion for wanting to help the most disadvantaged students. She had been with Building with Books since 2000, though I almost didn't hire her because she's married to my cousin Joe, and I was wary of nepotism. But she quickly proved herself, won my trust, and opened a new phase of growth for us. Abby focused on met-rics, initiating independent evaluations and improving the quality of our programs. She took us into Philadelphia and Chicago, added forty schools in two years, and moved us deeper into the inner city of Detroit.

That's where I met Rayia Gaddy, at the Detroit Veterans Center. I never know what I'm going to learn when I meet one of our stu-dents, but I'm rarely disappointed.

The Detroit Veterans Center is in a square brick building near the "Cass Corridor," one of the city's toughest stretches of pavement.

The center itself stays busy, as Detroit has one of the highest populations of homeless vets in the country. With more than a hundred beds for transitional housing, a soup kitchen, and various counseling, job training, and health services, it assists men and women who served in Afghanistan, Iraq, and Vietnam, many of whom are still battling old wounds, both physical and emotional. Our students are always humbled by both the strength and the vulnerability of these individuals; so am I.

In the fall of 2009 I accompanied a group of our students from several Detroit high schools to the center. By now our organization had a new name—"Building with Books" had led to confusion as American kids thought we were a book club, and some villagers would ask if we used real books to build our schools. But with the help of Suzie Ivelich, a branding expert who later joined our national board, the organization was renamed "buildOn" in 2008 to more accurately reflect our mission: we build on to communities; we build on to education; we build on to lives.

At the Veterans Center on that fall day, I was standing next to one of our students while serving meals. Rayia Gaddy, a sophomore in high school, wore a white apron, had her black hair pulled off her face, and cheerfully scooped the rice and mashed potatoes. I asked her why she volunteered for this particular service event.

"I like working with the vets," she said, "because I can connect with them."

I was skeptical. How does a fifteen-year-old girl connect with battle-hardened vets who may be suffering from posttraumatic stress disorder or depression, or who may now be alone or penniless? But Rayia was clearly comfortable with these men. She had a big smile, was charming, and loved talking to them; they responded in kind. After we served the meal, one of the vets, Charles, pulled her aside. He appeared to be in his sixties. He wore glasses, a dark brown beret, and an olive sweater, and his face had a serious, intense expression.

Charles was homeless and told Rayia that he was a street artist, and, after he saw her smile, he asked if he could sketch her portrait. She agreed. She sat down, and as Charles got out his pencils, she began asking him questions about his life. Where was he from? When did he serve in the military? Did he ever see combat? Charles answered the questions, at first mechanically but then with more spirit and life. He told Rayia that he had served in Vietnam and had fought in the Tet Offensive. I just listened. As Charles slowly opened up, he flashed a playful grin, told some harmless jokes, and by the end, both he and Rayia were smiling and laughing. He drew a pretty good portrait of her as well.

Afterward, as we were walking out, Rayia asked me, "Did you see him smiling?"

"Yes, I did."

"That's what it's all about," she said. "Helping them smile gave me my smile back."

"What do you mean? You've got the biggest smile in the world. Did you lose it?"

"Yes, I did," she said, "and I lost a lot more than that."

Rayia invited me to stop by her house in Highland Park, an incorporated community inside the city limits of Detroit. Once at the heart of America's car industry, Highland Park is now known for barren lots, crumbling houses, and seamless stretches of urban blight. Rayia's family lived on a block with several condemned houses, including one right next door, the gutter, unhinged, drooping across the front windows like a flourish from a Salvador Dali painting. The street reminded me of the boarded-up brownstones in my old Harlem neighborhood, though this place may have been worse: furniture on front lawns, porches in disrepair, gaping holes in the ground where street lamps once stood. Highland Park ripped them out because they were too expensive to operate, leaving the road in darkness at night and on winter mornings, when Rayia had walked to Cortland Elementary School. She had to pass abandoned buildings, outside of which men would be taking drugs. The bus stop was no safer. Rayia said that a girl had been raped there. Her mother later told me, "I asked the Holy Angels to guide her all the way to school."

Broken families are common in the inner city, but that wasn't the case with Rayia's; she was raised by two parents who were loving and, in their unique ways, unforgettable. Over the course of several visits, I spoke at length to her father, Arnaz, and her mother, Rachel, often on the front porch next to a ripped screen door. What emerged from those conversations, and from those with Rayia, was a story of random violence and unspeakable sadness, but also of redemption, forgiveness, and faith.

Arnaz was fifty-one when I met him, but with a couple of teeth missing, deep lines across his face, and a thin frame, he appeared older—and not without reason. He had been a drug addict for much of his life. When he was thirteen, he said, he had been put in a mental hospital and prescribed Valium, which put him on a narcotic path for years to come.

"You want to know the truth?" he asked me. "I'll tell you like I tell everyone else. I was a crack-head, alcoholic, dope-fiend, weed-smoking, pill-popping, glue-sniffing son of a gun. I've had hash. I've had Asian dust. I've had heroin. I've had purple haze. Morphine. I used to work in a bar. I would start right there and drink all the way across."

He said he had been a "functional addict," able to hold down temporary jobs to make ends meet. "No matter what I did, I took care of my family," he said. "I paid my bills, I fed my family, I made sure they had food before I got high." He had one son out of wedlock, Vandell, then he married Rachel, who also already had a child, Nickia. Arnaz and Rachel then had four children, Rayia being the second youngest.

A role model, Arnaz wasn't. He sometimes stole money from Rachel's purse to pay for his drugs. But his life came to a crossroads when he was thirty-seven, one night in an empty parking lot, sitting in his car, holding a bottle of wine. He looked into the mirror and was unnerved by what he saw, or, as he told me, "It's what I didn't see. For more than twenty years, I was using drugs and stuff. I had a wife, kids, women, alcohol, I had all that stuff. But there was one thing I did not have. I did not have Arnaz."

He checked himself into a rehab center, the SHAR House, on January 5, 1996, and stayed there for three months. When he returned home, he knew he wasn't ready to face his own demons, so he returned to the center each day for two more months. He's been clean ever since, and he's made sure that his children did not make the same mistakes. As Rayia told me, "I was like four years old when I knew the twelve steps to recovery."

Arnaz takes a philosophical approach to his checkered history. "I have to live *with* my past," he said, "but I don't have to live *in* my past."

He now works as a counselor at the SHAR House, trying to save one life at a time. "I'm not educated at all," he told me, "but I am wise." The job has some uplifting moments. "I saw a guy who I had helped, and he had been clean for six years. He told me, 'I owe it all to you.' But it's not about the person you help. It's about how he helps himself."

His first son, Vandell, was raised by his mother, but she died of cystic fibrosis when he was a teenager. Vandell was then raised by his maternal grandmother. Arnaz made it clear to me that Vandell was no saint; he smoked some weed, had his girlfriends—"Like father, like son," he said. But he was a good kid. Vandell spent time with his father, stepmother, and four half-siblings on a regular basis, eating meals with them, driving the kids around town, and offering them encouragement and guidance.

Vandell was not without ambition. Encouraged by his parents, he picked up application forms to a community college in the fall of 2008 and was going to apply for the next school year. He was a solid student and had scholarship money to go to college, but when he was in high school he had his own daughter out of wedlock. He stayed home, got a job at Red Lobster, and helped support his child. A photograph of Vandell shows a lean, baby-faced, handsome young man, his left arm around his daughter, who's wearing a pretty white dress.

If Arnaz was a survivor from the streets, Rachel was a romantic, a robust woman with large dramatic eyes and a love for nature, poetry, and music. As a child, she was raised as a Seventh Day Adventist and went to church four times a week, and her spiritual core saved her from adversity. She said she was raped by her grandfather when she was nine years old, a fact that she shared with her own children. When they asked how she got through it, she told them, "A lot of prayer."

Her mother was a homemaker, her father an auto worker and heroin addict. "As a girl," she told me, "I would sing church songs in my head, and I'd look up at the sky and see the stars and just wonder at how beautiful they are." Rachel wanted to be a doctor. That didn't work out, but she stayed in the helping professions, and by the time I met her she was working in a VA hospital, making sure patients got their proper medications before leaving. Those human connections, and her faith, sustain her. "I hug and kiss my children all the time," she said. "I love that closeness. A lot of kids don't have no one to hug them."

All of Rachel's children were compassionate, because that's how she brought them up, but Rayia could still surprise her. One winter they were walking out of a drug store when they happened upon a homeless man without a coat. Rayia gave him hers, and the man wept with joy.

"You already got a cold," Rachel later told her. "What made you do that?"

"Mamma, I got another coat at home, and that man's got nothing."

Rayia was quiet and timid; Rachel called her an "observer." She felt overshadowed by her older siblings, Malia and Ryan, who were more athletic, social, and confident. Always a good student, Rayia attended University Preparatory Academy for middle school; that meant following her sister and brother, and some of the students expected her to be like them. She couldn't, at least not socially, but that didn't stop kids from teasing her. It didn't help that she was overweight. She thrived in the classroom, but her self-esteem suffered.

Rayia leaned on Vandell for support. In our first conversation, at the Veterans Center, she told me that she was closer to Vandell than to anyone, even though he was ten years older than she. In addition to his usual visits to the house and his driving her around town, he made it a point to take her out on her birthday. That was really important, making her birthday special.

By the time she was a freshman in high school in 2008, Vandell was more heavily involved in her life, attending her classroom presentations, driving her to activities, and sending a very direct message: *Do not make the same mistakes I made that kept me from going to college.*

Rayia and Vandell bonded over something else, buildOn, which she joined her freshman year. Vandell believed that community service would help keep her on the right path. He drove Rayia to and from service projects. Those were special times. "When he took us home from school, there would be other people in the car," Rayia told me. "When he took me to service, it was just me, and we could talk one-on-one. That was my favorite part."

Vandell encouraged all of his half-siblings. "I want you all to be the best," he'd say, "because I'm very proud of you." Rachel, his stepmom, said, "When he hung around us, his softness came out." He told her he didn't know what he wanted to do with his life, but he wanted to make his daughter proud.

"Get back to school," Rachel told him.

"I'm too old for that," he said.

"You're never too old for that," she replied.

One night, they were all in the same car, and Vandell said the oddest thing. He talked about being loyal to his family, and then he said, "Whatever may happen to me, I don't want anybody crying. I want everybody to be strong."

"Why are you saying that," asked Jaylin, his youngest half sibling.

"It could happen to any of us," he said, "so don't get angry and don't be crying on me. Just remember—faith and loyalty."

His words scared Rachel, who told her husband, "Keep an eye on Vandell."

★ ★ ★

The following morning, on December 15, 2008, Arnaz was at his house when his cell phone rang.

"Pops?"

It was Vandell's voice, but his breathing was labored, and Arnaz knew something was terribly wrong. "Vandell," he said, "you've been shot."

"Yeah."

"Where are you?"

"At your job," the SHAR House. He was sitting in his car.

Vandell had been driving his beige Honda Accord with his window rolled down. He was on I-96 when a van drove up beside him and a gunman open fired with an AK-47. The side of the car was riddled with bullets, but one went through Vandell's spine and hit his lung. Incredibly, he was able to drive about a mile more, making his way off the highway and to his father's place of work.

After Arnaz spoke to him, he called his son Ryan, who was with his younger siblings, Rayia and Jaylin, at the dentist's office. Arnaz explained what happened. Ryan could reach Vandell faster, so he told his sister and brother that he had to leave and rushed out without explaining. He raced to Vandell and was holding him in his arms when their father arrived. Vandell was still alive, and his father rode with him in an ambulance, assuring his son that he would be okay.

Arnaz then picked up Rayia and Jaylin at the dentist's office, and when they asked their father what was happening, he told them that Vandell had been shot but didn't say anything about his condition. Rayia didn't think it was that serious; people got shot in Detroit all the time. It wasn't until that night, when her parents told her that Vandell had stopped breathing and that one of his lungs had collapsed, that Rayia realized how serious his condition was. Then, at 4 a.m., Ryan woke her up and said Vandell may not make it, and they needed to get to the hospital.

There they stayed, the entire family, eating their meals, sleeping on the floor, and waiting. The days passed, and they hoped and prayed for Vandell's recovery. Finally the doctors explained that Vandell was brain-dead; a ventilator was breathing for him, and he would never be able to know or speak to them again. They had to make a decision: either keep Vandell on the ventilator for the rest of his life or allow him to die now, peacefully. Rachel said she didn't want to pull the plug, at least not yet. The Lord would give them a sign when they should end his life. A day or so later, the doctors reported that Vandell's "brain had fallen back." They didn't know what that meant, except that his life was imperiled even more. It was, for Rachel, the sign she needed. As she later told me, "I kept thinking about those words that Vandell had just used—*loyalty* and *faith*—and I had to figure those words out. I had to be loyal to my son and I had to have enough faith that the Lord would take care of everything."

Rayia saw him one last time in the hospital. "At first I was scared," she said. "I had spoken to him the day before he was shot, and he was supposed to pick me up the day after. Now he had tubes in him, and he was all 'blown up' and swelled." She said good-bye.

Arnaz had one final moment with his son. He took his hand and said, "Your body won't be here, but you'll be here." He kissed his forehead and left.

When the crowd gathered at the funeral home that Saturday, the funeral director told Arnaz that the cost would be $22,000. Arnaz said he was short $1,500 but could have the rest by Monday. The director replied that the burial would have to wait. Arnaz explained his predicament to the attendees, and they reached into their wallets and purses, and in twenty minutes donated the remaining sum. The burial was held that day.

On the afternoon of the shooting, Arnaz told one of Vandell's friends, "You know I left the streets in ninety-six, but I want to know what happened to my son, or else there's going to be a lot more shit than you've ever seen."

The friend told him the name of the suspected shooter, which Arnaz passed along to the police. He later said to me, "If I told you that revenge didn't come to my mind at that time, I'd be lying. I wanted to go grab a pistol and find out everybody involved, which I could have done. But what kind of example would I be setting? I had already lost a son. My children already lost their sibling, but then they would lose their father by going to jail."

Vandell's friends may not have been as forgiving. The empty house of the suspected gunman was burned down several nights later. No one was injured.

The police arrested a young man named Timothy, and Rachel and Arnaz were stunned to see him at the trial; only then did they recognize Timothy as a kid from the neighborhood whom Vandell had known for most of his life. Timothy's mother was also a familiar face; Rachel had known her since she was in kindergarten.

At his trial, Timothy acknowledged that he shot Vandell, who was collateral damage in a feud between Timothy and a friend of Vandell's. Timothy testified that he couldn't find the friend, so he shot Vandell to send the message that he was looking for him. That was it: a schoolyard bully who happened to own an AK-47.

According to Arnaz and Rachel, Timothy had a smirk on his face during the trial. "He showed no remorse," Rachel told me. "He was just big and bad sitting up there. 'Yeah, I did it. I wanted to show this boy that this was going to happen if things don't be right.' His mother and father are looking at him, like, 'What are you saying?' And the judge said, 'Get him out of here.'"

After the trial, Rachel "was fighting with bitterness and hurt at the same time," she recalled. "I was crying, and a coworker said, 'I understand about your son.' And I said, 'I wasn't crying for my son. I was crying for Timothy.' She said 'What? You crying for that boy who killed your son?' I said 'Yeah. I don't know why.'

"I don't care how much pain and anger I felt, that love was still in my heart. That forgiveness. That's what it was. That forgiveness is what I had for him, and I couldn't figure that out. I had to talk to the Lord about that. It was really powerful that day because the hurt was so bad. . . . [But] I figured it out later. Beyond all the anger that I had, that hurt came from watching his mother. That's the only child she has. She didn't ask him to go that route. He made that choice."

Rachel did not go to the sentencing, but Arnaz did, and this time he found a very different defendant. Timothy would receive a sentence of thirty years, and perhaps the enormity of his offense had settled in. He turned to Arnaz and said, "I'm sorry, sir. I apologize for what happened. Will you forgive me?"

"Son," he said, "you've already been forgiven."

Arnaz later told me, "You have to realize that through my addictions, I have been forgiven many times. If the Lord can forgive me, why can't I forgive him?"

If someone had killed one of my sons, could I forgive? I could not say for sure, but I did know that this couple had set a powerful example for me. My dad set the bar for faith and courage, and Arnaz and Rachel did the same for forgiveness. I'm grateful to all of them.

Whenever they get into their car, they say a prayer before they turn the key. Arnaz says he feels Vandell's presence more tangibly in death than in life, and Rachel still looks at the stars at night. "It's so peaceful," she said. "That's why I like to write. I think about things that I want out of life for me and my family, and how to go about getting that. Sometimes things don't come as fast as I'd like, like getting another house, but I know He hears us, and I know He understands. I know things will come in time, and the Lord is setting things up for us."

After Vandell's death, Rayia's struggle was long and difficult. He died only weeks before her fifteenth birthday, and she retreated into a shell, trying to block the events from her mind but remembering everything all too vividly. She didn't want to talk to her family, didn't want to see a counselor. "They're just getting paid to hear you," she told me. No one else in the family wanted to talk about it either. Rayia wondered if they were even still a family. She became increasingly despondent. She returned to school, but she rarely spoke in class and could not focus on her work.

She knew that her birthday, January 17, the day that Vandell had always made special, was going to be brutal. It would be impossible to celebrate, so when it finally arrived, she decided to do a day of service and dedicate it to her brother instead. Since Vandell's death, she hadn't been able to bring herself to participate in any buildOn activities, but on that day she joined a group of students and went to the Detroit Veterans Center. The group was there to organize and clean out some rooms, and taking a break midday, some of the students went to the cafeteria to speak with the vets. It was odd for Rayia because her parents had always told her not to talk to strangers, but she sat down with two men. She wanted to make conversation and smiled, but one of the vets—he wore a black coat and had graying hair and a goatee—noticed something. "I can see right through that," he said. "That's a fake smile."

Rayia thought she was a good actress and was surprised she hadn't fooled him.

"Cheer up," he said. "You're beautiful. Why are you even sad?"

"I had a tragic loss in my life," she said. She didn't mention it was her brother.

The vet said he had lost someone too, many years ago when he was in the army, and he had felt bad that he wasn't there with that person. Rayia just listened as the man told her what he tried to do to overcome his loss. He was a stranger, but he knew how Rayia felt. He wasn't judging her but talking to her sincerely, as an equal. Rayia opened up and told her about Vandell, and the vet listened carefully. "You go through hard times," he said, "but if you believe in God, anything is possible."

He also told jokes and made her laugh. This time, she gave him a real smile. The other vet told her about his life, how he had served in combat, been shot at, and had almost died. "I went through that," he said. "I almost gave my life for my country. But I served for my family and friends."

The conversation was a turning point for Rayia. The vets, as she told me the first time we met, gave her back her smile. "Even though

146

they didn't know me," she said, "they were able to break down a barrier." It was the start of her healing.

For all of Rayia's challenges, or perhaps because of them, she became one of buildOn's most impressive leaders. She helped build a school in Nicaragua and spearheaded many programs at home, including one with the Detroit Health Department that tested teenagers for HIV.

In February 2010 I was going to Nicaragua on a two-week trip with other students from Detroit. Because Rayia had been there the previous year, I called her to see if she had any advice for the students who were going. "I almost didn't go," she told me.

"Really? Why not?"

"I had a meltdown a couple weeks before I was supposed to send in the application," she said. This was during the fall of her freshman year, when she first joined buildOn. "I was too scared." The village that she was to go to, El Rodeo, was nestled on a steep mountain near the border with Honduras, and she feared the trails would be too difficult to walk or that the actual building of the school, under a hot sun, would be more than she could handle. She also didn't know whether she would connect with her host family.

I asked Rayia how she got over her fears. She said she had talked to Vandell. "I went to him and told him flat out, 'I can't do it, I can't do it.'"

He had never been out of the country, but it was always his dream to travel. Now he wanted his sister to. He told her, "In life, you're going to be scared of certain things, but those are the things worth going for. That's how you know they're worth it. You can't expect to have a good ending with anything unless you go through the challenges to get there."

"I don't think I can do it," Rayia repeated.

Vandell responded lovingly but firmly, "Oh yes you can, Rayia."

And she did, but Vandell himself did not live long enough to see it.

Rayia told me there were times in the village when she felt over-whelmed by all the demands: the physical work, the mountain trails, the primitive conditions. But in those moments she looked in the sky and into her heart, and she knew Vandell was there.

I have no doubt he was. Rayia is representative of so many of the kids in our program. Yes, they live in difficult, even dangerous, conditions. But they are able to transcend them, and they do that by serving others. While Arnaz and Rachel inspired me by their ability to forgive, Rayia uplifted me with her courage and resilience. But best of all, in her darkest hours, she opened her heart to others, believed in herself, and smiled proudly.

In 1989, I had no real desire to make money or to save the world. I was looking for adventure, and I found it in places like Imja Tse in the Himalayas. Along my travels, I encountered poverty and beauty unlike anything I had seen before, and the direction of my life began to change. Two years later, my brother Dave and I founded a nonprofit to build schools in developing countries and to get American kids involved in intensive public service.

In 1992, I quit my job at GE Capital to focus on the nonprofit that became buildOn. We had no experience and no funding— and no way to make good on the promises we had made to American high schools or impoverished villages abroad. But thanks to the generosity and guidance of Jim Parke (left) and Marc Friedman (right) and many other supporters, our first gala in Stamford, Connecticut, raised enough money to keep us afloat and build our first school.

I met Steven Tenthani (left) in Misomali village, Malawi—the site of the second school we built, in 1993. Steven was the first volunteer on the work site every morning. When his daughter was born a few weeks before the school was completed, I realized why he had invested so much: he was building it for her.

Another dedicated volunteer, Andrew Gatoma (left, with his two sons), lost his wife to AIDS while we were building the school in Misomali and soon succumbed to the disease himself. The two boys later passed away. In the early 1990s the AIDS/HIV infection rate in his area was estimated at 50 percent.

By 1997, I realized I was more in tune with villagers from Africa, South America, and South Asia than with teenagers in my home country. How could I walk in their shoes if I didn't even step on their pavement? I moved to this brownstone in Harlem, on the corner of 140th Street and Hamilton Place, to develop programs that would engage inner-city students.

While living in Harlem, I met a young teacher named Jenny Freres at a service project in the South End of Stamford. It wasn't long before I started calling her Sunshine because of her radiant smile, and we married in 2000. Photo by Jay Savulich

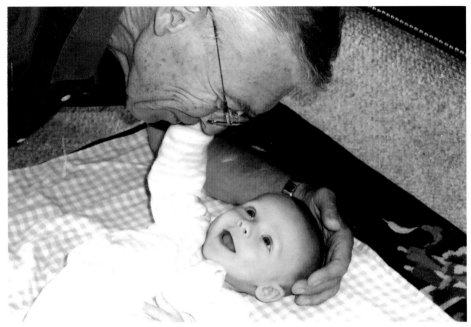

In 2004, our son John Daniel "Jack" Ziolkowski was born. We named him for my father, who had always urged me to deepen my faith and test my limits. This photo was taken a few months before my dad passed away. Three years later, Jack's brother, Quinn, joined our family.

Many of our students live in difficult or even dangerous conditions. But they are able to transcend them, and they do it by serving others. Rayia Gaddy "got her smile back" by working at the Detroit Veterans Center with vets like Charles. Photo by Wendy Hu

Komba Dumbia's two granddaughters attended a school constructed by buildOn in Masablah, Mali. Before the school, Komba said she was living in the "darkness of illiteracy," but now she is living in the light. Komba's sign says *Awnice yeelen kola* in Bambara, Mali's native language, or "Thank you for bringing the light!"

Jack and Quinn on the first day of school in 2010. Later that day, Jack was rushed to the hospital after an unexplained seizure, and our family began a difficult odyssey with an inexplicable illness. I had realized long ago that I could never truly walk in the shoes of the people I wanted to help, but when Jack was stricken, we learned what it was like to walk for a few steps with those who feel they've lost control over their lives.

Ram Dulari Chaudhary passes concrete to Brooklyn student Dalmar Nation while building a school in Pakariya, Nepal. Ram is a member of the Tharus, an ethnic group that have been historically discriminated against or held in a forced-labor system called Kamaiya. Ram said that those who enslaved her people "would not let us see the inside of a school." She was building the school so that "no one will ever enslave our children the way we were enslaved."

Meeting the Dalai Lama in 1997 and interviewing Mother Teresa in 1996 are among the high points of my life. I took this picture of the Dalai Lama in Dharamsala, where I encountered his poem "Never Give Up," which had become my mantra. You're going to have setbacks almost every day; you're going to encounter skeptics; you will fail. But that's when you must summon the courage to keep going.

I returned to Misomali village in 2012, excited to see my old friend Steven again. Nineteen years later, our work together had paid off in exactly the way we had dreamed. Steven told me that our first school had been the "ignition" that led the community to build four more schools, which now educated 1,055 students, of whom 533 were girls.
Photo by Esther Havens

Steven's daughter Ruth, now a teacher in Misomali, attended the primary school we had built. Steven told me, "I'm an illiterate man. But my daughter attended all of these schools, and she is a teacher, and she will lift up our family name for generations."
Photo by Esther Havens

Since 1991, buildOn has partnered with rural villages to construct more than 550 schools that educate equal numbers of boys and girls in some of the economically poorest countries on the planet, and buildOn students have contributed more than 1.2 million hours of service to seniors, young children, and the homeless in their communities in America. Above, Rahni Davis, Jonathan Ramos, Gimy Arzu, and I mix concrete for the foundation of a school in Kankhumbwa, Malawi, and below, Jesus Marques works with a child and a volunteer from New York's KEEN (Kids Enjoy Exercise Now) program, in which buildOn students help disabled children play and get exercise.

Photos by Esther Havens (top) and Srijan Tamraker (bottom)

CHAPTER 9

From Darkness to Light

I've learned that to break the cycle of poverty through education, you have to build a true partnership with everyone in the community. That means living in the village or city and experiencing it fully. Plenty of social entrepreneurs and nonprofit organizers are compassionate from afar: they raise money, they launch marketing campaigns, they write checks. Those efforts, if carried out properly, are important and have tremendous reach. But that is not what we do. I advocate boots on the ground because only when you live in a community do you begin to understand its history, capabilities, and aspirations—whether it's in America or a foreign village. That lesson was reinforced early on, in Nepal, in the mountain village of Goje, when I had the water buffalo for a roommate, and when the donkeys saved my ass.

I was working with the Gurung people. Though not physically large, they were said to be among the strongest and most resilient people in the world, and I was going to test that theory on this Himalayan project. The school needed to be built on the side of a steep, rugged mountain, and we needed to carve a massive hunk of earth out of the mountain without machines, modern equipment, or explosives. Our only tools were pickaxes, sledgehammers, and strong backs. The locals and I pounded on one ill-positioned boulder for ten days, and it took more than two weeks to complete the excavation. As the villagers began preparing for the foundation, I needed to figure out how to bring the cement to this remote locale. The first load would be 3,500 pounds, and there were no roads to Goje. Perched 12,000 feet above sea level, it was accessible only by foot, and the nearest road was a two-day hike.

You might think we were ill prepared, or even reckless, but that was the nature of this work. It is also true that we completed every school that we began. I believe in action. Taking the first step after you've decided to do something is the hardest part. But once you take that first step, anything becomes possible.

I spoke with Ashramji, a smiling, gap-toothed village leader who seemed to have tree trunks for legs and almost always wore shorts, even in cold weather. We devised a plan for the cement. I would hike down to the road, then to the nearest town, find a place to purchase the cement, hire a team of mules, load the cement, and carry it up the river valley to the base of the mountain on which Goje rested. The mountain itself, ascending 3,000 feet from the river, was too steep for the mules, so Ashramji would recruit a team of about seventy volunteers from the community and meet me at the bottom of the mountain. We could then, he proposed, carry the bags up on our own. I told him that each bag weighed about a hundred pounds, and we should split the bags in two. I said even that would be a lot—fifty pounds per person—and we may need more people.

Ashramji smiled. "No problem," he said. "When do you want us to meet you?"

"How about sunrise four days from now?" I said.

Ashramji agreed, but I had serious doubts. Even if I made it back in four days, I wasn't sure that he would actually be there.

The Gurung have a different concept of time; they don't wear watches or have clocks and tend to live in the moment. But off I went with a local translator. We descended the mountain, located a vendor, and bought the cement that we needed. I found a guy who had a couple dozen mules for hire, and we began the trip back up the mountain, each animal carrying at least one bag on its side. Our little entourage must have been quite a sight; to get back to the base of the mountain we had to cross three rivers, and if any bag had fallen, it would have been ruined. But the donkeys were sturdy, even in the currents. They made their way along narrow passes and hairpin turns, and we reached the base of the mountain just after sunset on the third day. I was too tired to worry about whether Ashramji would be there in the morning.

Before the sun came up, Ashramji found me asleep and woke me. I was astonished to see him. Then I saw the volunteers who were quietly standing by. He had brought only thirty-five villagers, half of whom were women. A few were wearing flip-flops; the rest were barefoot. My heart sank. With so few people, each would have to carry a bag weighing a hundred pounds up the mountain. Some of the women themselves didn't even weigh a hundred pounds! I shared my misgivings with Ashramji, saying it would now take several trips, and we would lose precious time. He just chuckled.

The villagers leaned over, loaded a sack each on their back, and, using some rope, strapped the load to their forehead. I weighed 180 pounds and was a fairly strong hiker. I strapped on a bag, walked about six steps, stumbled, and fell over. I had no idea how we were going to survive a 3,000-foot ascent, but the sun was starting to rise, so we began walking.

After about a half hour on the trail, we came to a dilapidated rope bridge with loose wooden planks that spanned a raging river. We could have taken a three-hour detour to avoid the bridge, which made sense to me, but Ashramji insisted we were going to cross it. With the bags of cement on their backs, the villagers walked across the bridge as it swayed in the wind thirty-five feet above the rocks and water. I trusted Ashramji, but that bridge made me plenty nervous. I looked down to choose each of my steps carefully. Where the planks were missing, I could see the thrashing water, and I could hear the thundering rapids even over the stiff wind blowing me sideways.

One after another, everyone crossed safely. The next time I came down the mountain to make the crossing, the bridge had collapsed.

On we climbed. Not only was it steep, but we had to negotiate some difficult passes and sharp turns in the trail; one misstep, and you would fall 2,000 feet. It was a warm day, and after about four hours the villagers, hungry, sweating, and showing some strain, took a brief rest. But they were determined to continue, knowing what each sack of that cement meant to their village. They started walking again, but instead of slowing down, they started climbing faster. Then they began singing. I noticed that the village leaders were carrying the heaviest loads. During the climb's toughest points, they started singing louder and louder still. They snacked on cold rice and lentils from their pouches, and, when they passed through a village, they asked for tea. We hiked and climbed for twelve grueling hours, and in all my life I have never seen such endurance and strength. When we reached Goje it was almost dark, but the team still had the energy to sing. A crowd of villagers lined the trail and began to cheer, not because of their neighbors' amazing feat—the Gurung perform remarkable physical activities all the time—but because they now had cement and could start building the foundation of their school.

What the villagers brought that day were only the first thirty-five bags of cement; they would have to carry more than two hundred bags to complete the school.

The real heroes were the Gurung women who hauled the bags up the mountain. In Malawi I had seen how dedicated the Misomali women were to education, when they carried the bricks on their head to the work site, but Goje showed me the women's *strength*. My job was to help unleash that strength—in Goje and beyond—to build these schools.

By 2009 we had built 347 schools and were working in Haiti, Nepal, Nicaragua, Malawi, Mali, and Senegal. We no longer relied on Habitat for Humanity or other nonprofits to choose our villages. In fact, after the first three schools, we have selected every village where we've built, which we realized was the most important part of the process. I had seen too many cases where aid created an attitude of entitlement while diluting the community's spirit, so we sought out villages that had received minimal foreign aid. We hired country directors wherever we operated. College-educated and highly professional, they would receive requests from communities and, through visits, surveys, and interviews that could span months, would determine which communities were willing to support a school. We wanted to be in the villages that wanted us to be there and were willing to make education a priority.

Now, before breaking ground on any school, we met with government officials at the local and regional level, the education ministry, and other nonprofits. BuildOn's job is to help create a permanent structure; the government or the NGOs, as well as the village, needed to sustain it with teachers, books, and other learning materials. Beyond logistics, these other parties have to be willing to contribute because their buy-in set the right tone: *We're all making sacrifices; we're all in this together*.

Above all, we wanted the villagers to understand that this was their school, not ours. Across the developing world, mistrust of the white man runs deep. When I work on a project, I'm usually asked to speak at the opening ceremony. After introducing myself in the native language, I switch to English, mindful of the importance of my first sentence. I never say, "We are here to build you a school" or "We are here to create new opportunities for you." I start out by explaining, "We are here to learn from you."

Once a school is built, we find ways to deepen our involvement in the community. That was how I met Komba Dumbia on a hot evening in the village of Masablah in the heart of Mali, in a schoolhouse with oil lanterns flickering. It was 2009, and I was with students from the South Bronx to build a school in another village, but we were in Masablah to see one of our finished schools. Komba was sitting in the front row, dressed in colorful African garb, a silver-colored bracelet on her wrist. She had very dark skin and carried herself with regal dignity. It was 10:30 at night, a time when most villagers were asleep, and the temperature was still over 100 degrees.

But every seat was occupied, all by women; some sat on the ground or stood outside the building, watching intently through an open window. Many women were breastfeeding. We had originally built the school for children in the primary grades, but it was now being used for an adult literacy class.

Our mission had expanded. At some point, we realized that educating the kids alone could upset the generational balance of a community. How would parents react if their kids were literate but they were not? Equally important, how could they help their children with their homework if they themselves couldn't read or write? Our adult literacy classes addressed those issues while also strengthening our ties to the community. We train locally literate people (in some cases, the existing teachers) to teach the adult classes. Each community chooses its own curriculum, letting the adults determine what they want to study as they learn to read, write, and count. Some adults choose to learn more about prenatal care; others want to learn about irrigation or improved agricultural techniques; others, about how to stop the spread of AIDS and malaria. Almost all want to learn about micro-enterprise and becoming more economically self-sufficient. The point is, *they* decide.

Our staff's involvement in training the teachers requires them to stay in the village and monitor the school during the day. We also create explicit incentives for the village to adhere to its commitments. If after three years the school is educating an equal number of girls and boys, we will build a second school for grades four through six.

Mali was a classic example of our new approach. Gender discrimination there is particularly bad, and we found that in some villages, parents would send their kids to school for a couple years but then pull the girls out. The promise of a second school, however, motivated them to let all their children stay. It also allowed us to build more schools and gave more children from each community the chance to go further with their education.

Masablah was proof of how popular the adult classes were, and I was fascinated by Komba, because she was so intent on the task at hand: she was learning how to write—specifically, how to hold a pencil for the first time.

During a break, I approached her and, through a translator, introduced myself. At fifty-five, Komba was one of the older women in the room, proud and serious. She was missing several front teeth, which was oddly endearing when she flashed her brilliant smile. She told me that she had two granddaughters who attended the school during the day.

"You must be very proud of them," I said.

She said she was.

"And you must be proud of yourself," I said, "learning to read and write."

"I am," she said, "but I'm more ashamed than proud."

"Ashamed? Why?"

"Because I've lived my whole life in the darkness of illiteracy."

I thought I knew what it meant to be shackled by illiteracy—reduced earnings and abject poverty, less access to health care—but I had never associated illiteracy with shame. I was surprised, but I shouldn't have been. Illiteracy in developing countries remains one of the great scourges of our time. According to UNESCO, in 2009 some 793 million adults, two-thirds of them women, lacked basic reading and writing skills. Adult literacy rates were below 50 percent in eleven developing countries, including Chad, Ethiopia, Haiti, and Senegal. Mali's adult illiteracy rate was an astounding 93 percent. Lack of education has always hindered economic development, but it's even more crippling in a world that is fast becoming wired for the information age. That world puts an even greater premium on reading, writing, and numeracy, which should no longer be seen as just an advantage for the elites. These skills are necessary for all.

The United Nations has rightly declared that education is a human right. If we truly believe that, then the human rights of well over 1 billion people, if you include children, are being violated every day.

My conversation with Komba stayed with me, and I went back

to see her the following year. I knew that she had been denied education as a young girl, but that was the least of it. She had been mistreated far more severely, in a way that typifies gender abuse across Africa and in other developing countries.

Mali itself, in western Africa, is among the poorest countries in the world, with half the population living below the international poverty line of $1.25 a day. For my next trip to see Komba, I was with our country director, Alhousseyni, and one of our project coordinators, Aline, who was also our translator. I thought it important that another woman be present. Komba knew we were coming, and she welcomed us to her hut. She was wearing her finest clothes: a blue-and-yellow head wrap and a long, bright green-and-yellow gown; she also had on her bracelet, a necklace, and a ring. We sat beneath a mango tree, and as she began speaking, what struck me was how much more confident she seemed compared to the previous year. Then, she was fully engaged and always poised, but now she was uninhibited, even buoyant, answering highly personal questions with great candor.

Komba grew up in the village of Lasso and was very close to her father, Tenima, who was a Koranic priest as well as the chief of the village, a position he inherited from his own father. Tenima liked to buy nice clothes for Komba, a luxury in Mali, and he would bring her close and talk to her and make sure she knew how much he loved her. But when Komba was six, she awoke one morning not to the usual sound of the pounding mallet but to her mother crying. Tenima had died during the night. Because he was the chief, someone played a special drum with a certain beat announcing his death, and everyone came to their home and then fanned out to tell other villages. Tenima's body, dressed in white, was laid out for mourners to view. He was buried that morning.

Women were not allowed in the cemetery, Komba said, because the village elders believed that women were weak and would cry, which might anger Allah. There was, however, a "special cry" for women when someone died, a silent cry, and Komba said that was how her mother wept. "We could see the tears but not hear the sounds."

When Komba talked about her childhood, she assumed a different posture. She looked down and kept her voice low, and the sadness seemed to return. It took a long time, she told us, to recover from her father's death. "I felt an empty space in my heart. I didn't have the things that other girls had because I didn't have a father. I used to cry a lot."

Komba was one of four children, and after her father's death the family fell into crippling poverty, even by Mali standards. Their mother had to work in the fields, and the young children had to increase their chores at home. Komba learned how to cook, but she was too little, and she dropped a heavy pot on her leg, which caused a bad burn and left a scar. The job she hated the most, however, was pulling water up from the well.

There was no school in the village, but when Tenima was alive, he sent his oldest son, Nana, to a school several miles away. The family of Komba's mother lived in that village, so Nana stayed with them. He finished at least grade six and became a police officer, a prestigious job. Tenima believed in formal education, and Komba told us that he would have sent all of his children to school had he lived. But once he died, the other children had to help out at home, and none were educated.

Komba then talked about another part of her childhood, one that brought an even darker shadow of sadness to her face. When she was young, she told us, her uncle forced her to be circumcised. Carried out on girls between infancy and age fifteen, the procedure, known as female genital mutilation (FGM), typically involves the total or partial removal of the clitoris. The practice has absolutely no health benefits and is a brutal form of gender discrimination.

In big cities in Mali and other African countries, trained physicians might do the procedure under somewhat safe conditions, but health risks loom even there—and the risks are far greater in the villages. In places like Masablah, the women who do the cutting have no medical training, use unsanitary knives (at best), and operate on a dirt floor in a hut or under a tree. There is no anesthesia or pain medication. The pain is excruciating and lasts for days if not weeks. The girl is usually not fully healed for months.

Still, FGM is widely practiced; according to the World Health Organization, about 140 million girls and women worldwide currently live with the consequences of FGM. Although it is also performed in some countries in Asia and the Middle East, in Africa an estimated 92 million girls, age ten and older, have undergone the procedure.

FGM endures for cultural, social, and religious reasons. Because it reduces the woman's enjoyment of sex, men believe circumcised women will more likely be faithful to their husband. In some societies, FGM is considered a cultural tradition or is linked to ideals of femininity or beauty. There is also tremendous ignorance and superstition surrounding the practice. Some believe that if the clitoris is not removed, it will obstruct childbirth. I have often heard, "No man will marry an uncircumcised woman" or "If a woman does not have the circumcision, she will be unclean physically and spiritually."

I had always assumed that men encouraged FGM out of ignorance, so I was both surprised and mortified when I spoke to educated men in Africa who knew the procedure carried no health benefits, increased the risk of birth defects, and destroyed sexual pleasure, yet they still insisted that their daughters suffer the practice. Why? Because they would then be more desirable for marriage. That attitude was a cold reminder that for all my faith in education, education alone cannot eliminate terribly damaging but deeply ingrained traditions.

Komba was seven years old when she was circumcised. As she described for me through our translator over two days of interviews, when she was fifteen, her mother told her that she was to be married to a man whom she had never met. Her uncle had arranged the marriage to a fortune-teller who was also a medicine man. Komba told us that it was a blessing to obey your parents, so that's what she did.

The two families exchanged Kola nuts, another marriage tradition, but there was no wedding celebration.

"My husband was a tall man, strong enough, and light-skinned," Komba said. "The first time we met, I was very frightened. I didn't know whether he'd be a good husband or not. It was not easy for me to talk to him."

Shortly after marrying, Komba and her husband moved to the Ivory Coast, which abuts Mali on its southern border, and they stayed there for five years. Though separated from her family, Komba enjoyed meeting the different tribes in that country. When they returned to Mali, they settled in Masablah, near the city of Bougouni, in the southern part of the country. There Komba experienced both her greatest joys and most profound losses. She gave birth to five children, but only two—a daughter, Marium, and a son, Moussa—survived. Two other boys died shortly after they were born; they did not yet have names. Komba said the village had no medically trained midwife, "just some old ladies." Another son died at age three from malaria. His name was Bourama.

Komba told us that although she had lost her last child more than twenty years ago, the pain was still there, and when she thought of any of her deceased children, or when she saw someone who would be the same age as one of them, she couldn't help but cry.

After her last child was born, Komba said she was having pains in her stomach and was told they had to do with giving birth. She had an operation but was never told what was done. After the surgery, she didn't have any more children.

When Komba was in her thirties, her home life took another dramatic turn: her husband introduced her to his second wife. Polygamy is legal in Mali and frequently practiced, but when a man wishes to take a second wife, he is supposed to receive permission from the first wife. Komba's husband had never asked her for permission. The second wife, Chatou, was fifteen years younger than Komba, but unlike Komba, she had a large wedding ceremony with her—their—husband. The bitterness was still evident in Komba's voice as she told us this.

Then the husband married a third wife, Safiatou, who was ten years younger than Komba. She too had a wedding ceremony. Komba described this development in a flat voice, as if she was resigned by then to her diminished role. Both Chatou and Safiatou also had children, and for a number of years, this extended family stayed in the same village.

Komba said her husband preferred the other two wives over her. "I felt less and less love," she said. "When he would come home, I'd ask if he's okay, and he'd get angry. We argued all the time. I always tried to be on good terms and avoid disputes, but it didn't work."

The husband traveled frequently to other villages, and on one occasion, when he returned, he said that Chatou had accused Komba of sleeping with another man, and their husband beat Komba with a whip. Komba absorbed the beating because she had no choice. If she left him, she would end up homeless with two children, and they would have to live like stray dogs.

It took a clever ploy by Komba to stop her beatings. After another, more severe whipping, she convinced her husband that she was in terrible shape and begged to see a doctor. Her husband took her. The doctor knew Komba, who privately explained to him what had happened. Incensed, the doctor agreed to help. He spoke to the husband and threatened to turn him in if he ever beat Komba again. He could end up in jail, and the threat worked perfectly. The husband stopped beating Komba as well as Chatou.

Komba had outsmarted him. She knew that she herself couldn't approach the police—she had no standing—but a male authority figure could.

Komba is still married, but her husband is now usually absent from Masablah, spending most of his time with his third wife in another town. Komba and Chatou remain here, and Komba speaks of her husband as if he doesn't exist.

"I am against polygamy," she said. "It's very difficult for a husband to be fair to three wives."

★　★　★

When buildOn came to Masablah, the village selected Komba to be on the leadership committee, and she told us it was a milestone in her life. She understood the committee's importance to the future of the community. "The people trusted and respected me," she said.

Komba signed the covenant with her thumbprint—not with sadness, she told us, but with the hope that her granddaughters would soon be able to read and write their own names. She signed it right in front of the elders, the very men who had denied her an education. It was a solemn but dramatic moment. Watching the women stand up and sign the covenant, the men recognized that they would no longer have absolute control of the village. It won't happen overnight, but the promise of gender equality could eradicate patriarchal traditions stretching back thousands of years. Komba's thumbprint was the act of a nonviolent revolutionary.

Komba told us that she asserted her new authority as soon as construction of the school began. "I was the first woman on the work site," she said. "It was a good example to all, and I made everyone get there on time. . . . When I saw people hand out the tools and we began to dig, my dream was becoming a reality."

She did not shirk her duties even when tensions flared. "If there was ever a misunderstanding between two people, I would step in and solve the problem," she said. "I also participated in decision making on punishing people for coming late or fighting."

The school was completed in ten weeks, which is typical for us. The building now holds 166 students, seventy-three of whom are girls, and six teachers. Two of those students are Komba's granddaughters.

And for Komba herself, she has experienced a miracle. "I never thought I would be able to hold a pencil, write a letter, or read anything," she told me. "The first time the instructors gave me a pencil, I put it on the table and told them, 'I cannot do it.' They laughed and said, 'You can do it.' So I took the pencil again and tried to write, and they helped me. I went home and wrote the same letters over and over. Every night for hours. Read and write! Read and write!"

Mastering those skills, she said, "was my proudest moment. I have been reborn. . . . I can now teach people and unite them. I am now the president of all the women in the village. This is a new position. I would not have been able to do this before."

Improved health care has been among the biggest changes in Masablah. "We used to not be interested in child vaccinations," she said. "Today, all children in the village have been vaccinated. We are also engaged in prenatal care for the first time. In the past, we would not take a sick child to the clinic early enough. Now it's the first thing we do." Komba said she now understands that malaria comes from mosquitoes, which she did not know when her son died from it.

The village has also realized direct economic gains. A group of women, led by Komba, borrowed the equivalent of about $2,000 from a Dutch NGO, and they used the money to purchase a machine that pounds shea nuts and millet. When crushed and processed, the nuts produce a nut oil that can be used in cooking or for skin and hair products. The millet is ground into flour. Consider the implications: the women had to negotiate the terms of the loan and had to sell their products in the market. "We have to calculate costs, savings, and gains," Komba said. "We are more productive, and we can put our destiny into our own hands."

She knows how different her life would have been had she been educated at a young age. "I would not have married my husband," she said. "I would not have stayed and gotten married in the village. I would choose my own husband. I would have liked to have been a doctor."

Then Komba told us something about her daughter that really caught me off-guard. "If she had gone to school," she said, "I would not have let Marium get married the way she did."

"How did she get married?" I asked.

"She was her husband's second wife."

At first, I couldn't believe that the very woman who herself had suffered in a polygamous relationship, who loathed the practice, would allow her daughter to be put in that position. But then it made sense: a woman without education, in this village, in this country, has no standing.

Now Komba has a new cause: she wants to end female genital mutilation in Masablah, where for hundreds of years it was mandatory. Komba herself would still abide by it had she not learned of its dangers in her classes; now she insists that her family will no longer be victimized. "I won't let my granddaughters get circumcised," she said. "Even if the father insists, it is not he who will do it. I will make sure it is not done."

I asked Komba what would happen if the father did not agree. She said it wouldn't matter. "Men don't do the procedure," she told us, "so we'll just tell him it was done, and he'll never know." And she laughed.

Komba has made her case to the women of the village, and her campaign to end FGM has made tremendous progress. The practice has been nearly eliminated in Masablah, and Komba is just getting started, as she is taking her message to all who will listen.

Self-assured and cheerful, Komba spoke to us that day as a liberated woman. It was inspiring. When I asked her how the school would affect the future of Masablah, she said this: "If you educate a boy, you educate one person. If you educate a girl, you educate an entire community."

The women raise the children. Educate them, and you educate the next generation.

I spent two days with Komba, listening to stories about her life and her village, and before we left, I reminded her of her comment from the year before, when she said that she had lived in "the darkness of illiteracy."

"Yes," she said, "but now I am living in the light, and my granddaughters are living in the light!" She then picked up a slate board and wrote some words with a piece of chalk in her native Bambara language. "Share this," she said, "with anyone who will listen."

The message was only a few words:

Awnice yeelen kola. "Thank you for bringing the light!"

CHAPTER 10

Jack's First Day

The Great Recession that began at the end of 2008, after the global financial collapse, took a toll on nonprofits. Over the next two years, many had to scale back significantly while others shut down entirely. BuildOn was affected, but thanks to the many people who supported our cause, we continued to expand. In 2009 and 2010, we built ninety-two more schools, increasing our total to 393. Meanwhile, we changed strategies for our after-school programs in the States. Seeking to make a greater impact, we developed more intensive service programs and increased the number of kids we reached by 30 percent. But we did this in a narrower group of economically distressed schools, lowering our overall number from 130 in 2008 to 110 in 2010.

The year 2010 was a milestone for buildOn, as we had survived the economic storm without any cutbacks or program reductions, and we were beginning to return to expected growth rates. It was also to be a milestone for our family.

Jenny and I had two sons by then; Quinn was born in 2007. Jack was entering first grade at Stark Elementary School, and we were excited about the next phase in his young life. He was an early reader, confident, and eager to learn, and we were sure he would thrive in school. Before I left for work on his first day of school, Jack stood at the front door, his hair bleached from the hot sun and his body still carrying that summertime glow. He had a big dimpled smile on his face, and as I aimed my camera, Quinn gave him a hug.

That afternoon I was rushing to catch a train for my next meeting, bound for Manhattan, when I flipped on my BlackBerry and saw a message. The voice mail was from the nurse at Jack's school. There was a problem, but no details were given. I immediately called Jenny, who was already racing to the school. Jack had collapsed in the hall, and the nurse was about to call an ambulance. But Jenny didn't know anything else.

"Meet me at the hospital," she said.

I tend not to be a worrier, so my first reaction was that the school had probably overreacted. Jack had never had any medical issues and was the picture of health, an active, inquisitive kid who loved to draw and paint, a fearless ocean swimmer with an inventive streak that amazed us. When he was three, we found some scrap wood at the school across the street and hauled it to our house. He asked me to take him to the hardware store, where he picked out seemingly random items: a hook, some wheels, nails. We also went to the paint store. Though I had no idea what he was doing, when we got home, he began building an enormous wooden structure (six feet wide and seven feet long), hammering six-inch nails, making a propeller out of paint stirrers and circuits out of fuses, attaching wings and wheels, constructing a shovel for its front, and adding colorful pushpins. He even built a seat. He would take it apart, reassemble it, and add new parts, imagining something that no one else could see—and this continued for a full year. The remarkable contraption was a combination of his two favorite machines, a helicopter and a bulldozer, so he called it his "heli-dozer." He painted it green and white, in proud tribute to my alma mater, Michigan State. That sturdy heli-dozer survived in our backyard for three years.

Now something was wrong with Jack? Impossible. The boy seemed bulletproof. We took his training wheels off his bike just after he turned four, and he rode with a joyous verve, doing figure eights, careening around corners, riding even during our cold winters, wearing his hat and gloves. It was as if the bike opened a whole new world for him, one of speed, excitement, and freedom.

I arrived at the Stamford Hospital and saw Jenny pull up with Jack in the back seat. Her parents were in the car as well. Apparently the school never called the ambulance, so they had taken Jack on their own. He was alert, but his body was limp. I carried him into the Emergency Room, where we filled out papers and answered endless questions. We were eventually sent to an observation area to wait for a neurologist.

Jack's teacher had told Jenny what had happened, and Jenny had asked her to write everything out. According to her notes, the day had gone smoothly until lunch. Then, on Jack's return from the cafeteria, he fell behind. When a student said, "Jack's not coming in," the teacher walked into the hall and saw him drifting, his blue eyes glazed over. She called for him but couldn't get his attention. She reached out her hand. He took it but then lowered himself, spun to the ground, and fell in a heap. His eyes popped open and rolled back. His body shook with tremors. He was having a massive tonic-clonic seizure, though no one knew it at the time, and he was still seizing when the nurse arrived. He remained unresponsive as his arms and legs continued to tremble. Jack finally came out of it on his own, but the harrowing event left everyone shaken. He stayed in the nurse's office, disoriented and crying, until Jenny picked him up.

He had stabilized by the time he reached the hospital, and he was able to talk to us as we waited for the neurologist. At dinnertime, I brought in some food from the cafeteria, and he devoured his hamburger. We had no idea why he had had a seizure—no one in the hospital was even using that word—but we thought his revived appetite was a good sign. Jenny's parents left the hospital to look after Quinn. As Jack lay with his back to us, we passed the time with the television on. We were all pretty calm. Then I looked up and saw Jack's head twitching.

"Jenny," I said.

We looked again, and Jack was convulsing. His body stiffened, his mouth began to froth, his lips turned blue, and his eyes popped wide open. He stopped breathing. He was having another seizure, and we shouted for help.

Five or six minutes passed before the seizure eased. But when you're holding your son helplessly as he convulses, every second seems like an eternity. Jack was given a shot of Ativan, which changes the electrolyte channels in brain cells to depress brain activity. A powerful drug, it put Jack to sleep, and he was soon admitted. Jenny slept next to him in his bed, though she was awake for most of the night, fearing another seizure. I jumped into a vacant pediatric bed in a room across the hall, which was a little awkward in the morning when a nurse opened the door and asked, "What are you doing here?"

That day, amid frustratingly vague statements from the neurologist, Jack was to receive an MRI, which meant he'd have to lie still in a scary, dark, clamorous tube for twenty minutes. This proved impossible for Jack, who was too frightened and agitated to comply. So Jenny squeezed in the tube with him. With Jack on his back, she lay right on top of him, her hands clasping the sides of his head, talking to him, trying to keep his head still and his emotions in check.

After walking through a metal detector, I entered the MRI room, and even with my earplugs, the noise—the incessant pounding of the magnets, like multiple jackhammers at close range—was earsplitting. The isolated technicians, viewing Jack's brain waves on their monitors, seemed to be in another world. I felt horrible for Jack as well as Jenny, swallowed in that metal tomb. Then I saw Jenny's legs kicking through the end. I ran over and looked in. She was screaming, pounding her fists, trying to escape. I ripped out my earplugs to try to hear her, and then I saw Jack. His body was shaking as if an electric current was flowing through it.

I helped pull Jenny out, then I turned to the technicians and began waving my arms. "Turn this thing off! He's seizing! He's seizing!"

They immediately turned off the machine. Jenny would have nightmares about it for months. The technicians also pressed an emergency button—erroneously—that signaled a patient was coding. Soon about fifteen to twenty medics descended upon us to revive Jack, but they couldn't do anything to stop a seizure, and the misunderstanding just added to the tension.

Jack was given another shot of Ativan, which we hated. Our family tends to avoid using pharmaceuticals unless absolutely necessary. We rarely take aspirin and don't even like additives in our food, preferring organic milk and bread without preservatives. Now Jack was being shot up with a potent drug that was leaving him in a stupor. And we had no diagnosis.

I spoke to the neurologist, who acknowledged the difficulty of Jack's case. "It's beyond us," he finally conceded. He advised that we take Jack to the Intensive Care Unit at Yale University, about forty miles away.

Jack had never been afraid of ambulances, but by the time he was ready to leave, the drug had worn off, and he was terrified. Moreover, he was determined to fight us with all the power he could summon. I helped put him in the ambulance, and he thrashed out, kicked, bit, and screamed at the attendants, who had to strap him down. As Jenny later said, this fifty-pound boy, fueled by adrenaline and fear, had the strength of ten men. I stood there as the back doors swung shut, hearing Jack scream, "Help me! Help me!"

The full significance of the crisis hit me. Was my son going to die?

Jenny rode in the ambulance but had to sit in the front seat. She could hear Jack yelling and fighting. I drove our car to Yale but was far behind the ambulance. It was the Friday before Labor Day weekend, with terrible traffic on I-95, and when I reached the hospital, I saw Jack hooked up to EEG wires, oxygen monitors, IVs, and other machines. That was unnerving enough, but he also had his arms and wrists strapped to the bed. Apparently he had scratched one of the doctors and kept ripping the wires out of his head. The attendants told me they feared he could hurt someone or himself, but I was still outraged that he was strapped down like a prisoner. I told them they had to take the straps off, which they did, and I went to his bed and embraced him. As I held him, his fear finally subsided.

In preschool Jack scored two years above his age level on the assessment tests, but now he didn't know his last name, couldn't remember his birthday, couldn't walk. He couldn't brush his teeth and couldn't feed himself. He couldn't watch cartoons on TV without getting upset. We kept asking the neurologists if our son would be okay. Would he end up in a coma? Would he be able to talk clearly again? They couldn't even tell us if he'd ever come home. They had no answers.

The medical tests continued, unbelievable in number, and some were painful and even spooky. Already hooked to an IV, Jack was given an anesthetic and taken through the dark bowels of the hospital, but it freaked him out, and he fought the medics. Finally sedated, Jack required a spinal tap, in which a long thin needle is inserted into the spinal canal and fluid is drawn. Jack fought the second spinal tap as well. The doctors were constantly drawing blood and sending it to the CDC. They gave him CT scans and another MRI; they had him evaluated by psychiatrists; they had him quarantined and made all visitors, including Jenny and me, wear face masks in case he was contagious.

Jenny and I slept on cots and stayed with Jack full time. The only place to get any fresh air was on a roof-top patio, and one day when I was there, two pastors approached me. They were aware of Jack's fragile state and asked me how I was doing. I told them as well as possible. They asked me what my faith was. I told them Roman Catholic. They asked if I felt helpless or alone. Was I asking questions like *Why Jack* or *How could God let this happen?* I smiled and said I knew what their real questions were: Did I still believe in God, or was I angry at Him? Had my faith in God held up, or had it been shattered?

They knew I could be at a crossroads, and though this was the most painful test I had ever faced, I didn't hesitate with my answer. Though my faith is personal and I don't wear it on my sleeve, I know it is a gift from God, and it sustained me during this moment of truth. I told them not to worry. My faith had not been shaken.

They were relieved, as I'm sure they feared they had "lost" one. They were nice guys. We talked a little while longer, they gave me their cards, and we said a prayer for Jack.

After two weeks Jack was moved to a special ward full of beds that were adjacent to video cameras, which filmed him every minute of the day; a nurse watched the video monitor day and night to mark any sign of a seizure. He also had about twenty-five wires hooked up to his head to capture and record all neurological spiking. He could rarely get out of bed, and when he did, he had to drag with him an IV as well as the EEG circuit; both were mounted on a pole on wheels. His grim confinement was made even worse by the cramped, dingy hellhole of a room in which he now had to stay.

After nearly three weeks the doctors finally met with us to give us a diagnosis. Their tone and body language signaled bad news: meningo-encephalitis, an insect-borne viral condition that resembles both meningitis and encephalitis, an infection of the brain and the spinal fluid. It must have been from a mosquito bite that summer. A completely random event. A fluke. He was lucky to be alive. We then understood that when Jack was screaming "Help me!" and ripping the EEG wires out of his head and battling *everyone*, he was fighting off a deadly virus; he was fighting for his life. It was his tenacity, his will to live, that saved him. That, and the grace of God.

But though we had a diagnosis, we had no prognosis. Jack, we were told, might recover some day, but the doctors couldn't tell us to what extent he would regain cognitive brain function. Would he be able to relearn his name and walk and talk again? Would he be able to read or swim or draw or play with his little brother or hug his parents or do all the things that he loved to do?

Those were brutal questions, but I tried to keep perspective. Only a few months before Jack had collapsed, I had spent time in refugee camps in Haiti after the devastating earthquake had crushed so much of that country. I met children without parents, parents without children; I saw cities without food, water, or shelter; villages without medicine, a land broken in every possible way. I have also witnessed extraordinary courage in my life—from Rayia Gaddy to Komba Dumbia to the countless others I have met in our program. Their strength was my strength, and because of them, I know what the body can endure and what the spirit can overcome.

If Jack had been Haitian, even without the earthquake, he'd be dead. Instead, he was alive and receiving state-of-the-art care.

Those thoughts brought moments of relief. But they passed all too quickly. In other moments, sitting in this airless chamber, amid the surveillance cameras and alien wires and oxygen monitors—everything our insurance, education, and money could provide—I couldn't help but wonder if Jack would ever ride his bike again.

CHAPTER 11

The Path to Redemption

Jack's condition stabilized enough for him to come home in October. Jenny, who had quit teaching after Jack was born, became the point person, giving him his meds, working with the doctors, and reintegrating Jack into his life. And I went back to work. I had to cut my hours some, did fewer service projects, and reduced my travel when possible, but now that Jack was home, I could again travel with students on their trips abroad to build schools. By now we were running about eighteen treks a year, and they were my favorite part of the job.

We know that the motives to make such a journey can vary, but for the most part the students are looking for an opportunity to serve, for an adventure, for something that's dramatic and meaningful. Some students are also looking for someone to talk to. One student I'll never forget, whom I'll call Johnny, sure was.*

Johnny was from the South Side of Chicago and was part of a group of students who went on a trip to Nicaragua in 2010. I was on the trip as well (it was before Jack's diagnosis), and I ended up sitting with Johnny on the long plane ride from the States. I had found an exit row by myself, and he asked if he could sit with me. Instead

* Some names and identifying details of those portrayed in this chapter have been changed.

of taking the window seat and giving us a little space, he chose the middle seat, right next to me. He was about five feet eleven and had a sturdy, athletic build.

Sometimes friends or colleagues ask me how I connect with young people, and I tell them I have a radical approach: I talk with them. If you want to forge a real connection with a child or teenager, you can't ask him questions and then be indifferent to his answers. Kids will detect the dishonesty and respond accordingly. If you're willing to genuinely listen, follow up with good questions, gently probe, and show that you care, kids will open up. They realize you respect and believe in them. They *want* to tell their story.

My initial conversation with Johnny over a six-hour plane ride unfolded in that fashion. He grew up in trailer parks in the Chicago area. He met his father only once and was raised by his mother and stepfather. Neither parent had steady work, so the family, including Johnny's half-sister, was evicted from single-wide trailer homes and apartments nine times in twelve years. Eventually Johnny didn't even bother unpacking his boxes. The family relied on soup kitchens for food and routinely had its water or electricity shut off. Instead of a bath or shower, Johnny would bring back jugs of water from neighbors, put the water in bowls, heat them in the microwave (when the electricity worked), then wash with a sponge and soap. Even when the water was flowing, they had to boil it before drinking. (That's what the sign in the trailer park advised.)

But, as Johnny told me, poverty wasn't his biggest problem; his stepfather was. Richard sold drugs out of their home, was put in jail on several occasions, and was physically abusive toward him and his mother. During one domestic fight, the police arrested Johnny's mom when Richard claimed she was the aggressor.

Gangs, drugs, and violence were all part of his neighborhood and his schools. Basketball was his most promising outlet; he was a standout point guard pushed by his stepfather so he might someday get a college scholarship. But as Johnny acknowledged to me, he lacked discipline and self-control. In school he got into fights that led to suspensions two or three times a year.

As a sophomore in high school, he said that he stayed clear of the school's pervasive drug culture, where marijuana was routinely bought and sold on campus, but he struggled to fit in. The gangs were well organized, and with no support from home, he thought that a gang could give him purpose as well as protection. A cousin had already joined one for just those reasons. Johnny's strength and fighting skills made him an attractive recruit, and gang members were urging him to seek out a new family. It would be hard to say no.

He heard about buildOn when the school's public address system announced a meeting. The school required each student to do forty hours of volunteer work to graduate. Not everyone did their hours, and tracking the students was difficult, but Johnny thought he should fulfill the requirement and decided to attend the meeting. About a dozen other kids showed up, and a young program coordinator talked about buildOn's goal to make a positive impact in the community, about its weekly meetings that buildOn members were encouraged to attend (they were fun, social, and productive), and about its approach of openness and inclusion.

Something about the presentation, and the program coordinator, struck a chord with Johnny. Soon he was doing his first service at a food bank. When kids at school asked him why he joined buildOn, he would say, "To do service," prompting blank stares or quizzical looks. But at the meetings themselves, the students expressed interest in him for reasons other than sports or fighting. "You have a common interest," Johnny told me. "You're helping people smile, and you're working together. You're part of something bigger and have a common purpose. I never had that in my own family."

At the community center, Johnny was asked to tutor a girl whose father was in jail. Tanya was in second grade, about the same age as Johnny's stepsister. She was having trouble with math, so he went to the center twice a week and brought Pepperidge Farm Goldfish to demonstrate basic addition and subtraction. He spoke to her about her classes, her home, and her father. A shy, dark-skinned girl with pigtails, Tanya gradually opened up, and by the time the year was over, she had learned her multiplication tables and had connected with a new friend. "She thanked me for being there," Johnny recalled. "I had never had that experience before."

Other volunteer opportunities came his way: at the Veterans Center, churches, soup kitchens, marches. He did a hundred hours of community service in his sophomore year alone, and he left his old friends and only associated with his new ones at buildOn.

That year he heard that students could apply for the trek to Nicaragua. Johnny had rarely traveled out of state, didn't have a passport, and thought he'd never be selected. During the interview, he was asked why he wanted to go. He pondered the question and then said, "I think it will change my life." He was also asked if he'd mind digging ditches in blistering heat or hauling concrete. "I'd do those in my sleep," he said.

"Can you live without electricity?"

"I already have."

When the program coordinator called and said, "You made it," Johnny dropped the phone in disbelief. He was heading to Nicaragua.

Our flight to Managua was the easiest leg of the trip. From the airport we boarded a bus and drove ninety miles north to Esteli. We got some sleep in a ramshackle motel, took a walking tour of the town (murals celebrated its role in the Sandinista Revolution), then took a bus to yet another town, where we were met by the mayor of the district. He had petitioned buildOn for a school; as we now did with all our schools, we worked closely with the local authorities on planning and logistics, including travel. We still had to drive three more hours along dirt roads, and the mayor provided us with several SUVs and pickup trucks.

I borrowed our country director's Yamaha dirt bike because they had no room for me in the vehicles. The mayor, in his straw hat, became our new escort. That an American nonprofit group had mustered a volunteer workforce to build an elementary school here, while also dangling the promise of a long-term partnership to build even more schools in the district, had put his forgotten community on the map.

For the final stretch, we rode through the mountainous jungle, where barefoot children walked for hours to help pick coffee beans. Our destination, near the Honduras border, had a fitting name, La Soledad, which means "isolation" or "loneliness."

It was a balmy afternoon, and the eighteen-hour trip alone had tested the kids, but they were already survivors in their own right. In addition to Johnny, there was Sh'quena, whose mother had been car-jacked at gunpoint a few days earlier, and Alisa, a charismatic singer who had recently been evicted from her home.

Dressed in white buildOn T-shirts, our group walked into the village and were met by curious stares from the Nicaraguans. Most of the four hundred or so people who lived there turned out to greet us. They knew something extraordinary was about to unfold, but for an awkward moment, neither side knew where to begin. The language barrier was an obvious hurdle. Most of the Americans didn't speak Spanish very well, and most of the Nicaraguans had limited experience with English.

Suddenly a small band of musicians with battered guitars and over-worked accordions struck up a festive song to welcome us, and Alisa decided there was only one way to break the ice: she began to dance, swinging her hips and waving her slender arms with abandon. Jacqueline quickly joined her, and, laughing with relief, some of the villagers jumped in as well. The party was under way. The adults danced while the children circled and watched in amazement. When Alisa sang, accompanied by guitarists from La Soledad, the cultural divide closed.

The village had agreed to shelter and feed us, and as the first evening fell, we began pairing the kids with their host families. Alisa and another girl settled in as the guests of an extended family whose sixteen members, including a pregnant woman and a deaf-mute girl, were already crowded into a few small rooms. Johnny and two other boys headed off for the long hike up and down three hills to a hut where their host family lived. I aimed my flashlight up a steep mountain path with Leonardo, who offered me a place to sleep in his small house, built with local timber, a dirt floor, and a flimsy roof. But I preferred his dirt porch, where I unrolled my sleeping bag and closed my eyes beneath the stars.

For me, this trip to Nicaragua had several purposes. In addition to building in La Soledad, I was going to visit a school in El Rodeo that we had built the year earlier, the one that Rayia had helped with shortly after her brother was killed. I woke up at 4:30 one morning in La Soledad, and with one of our Nicaraguan project coordinators, rode a motorcycle for two and a half hours to the town of San Rafael del Norte, where I met our country director. We then drove for four hours in a four-wheel-drive vehicle through low-lying farmland and then back up into the mountains and jungles. When the road ended, we were in El Rodeo.

The villagers had been told that we would be paying a visit, and the entire community of more than a hundred people met us. All were wearing their best clothes; some had walked more than an hour to be there. I'm sure they assumed we had come to look at the new school, which would be a proud moment for the community. The structure was set into the side of a mountain. With pickaxes and sledgehammers, the workers had removed many tons of rock to create a level space for the foundation. The result was a school with a breathtaking mountain view.

I told the village leaders that I wasn't there just to see that building. I explained that one of our students had worked on it last year not long after losing her brother. I told them that I had spoken to Rayia shortly before I made this trip, and she had a message for the village: "No matter how far apart we are, I love you and I miss you."

One of the women immediately had a message for Rayia: "We love you very much. Please don't feel lonely about the loss of your brother. Because when we lose someone physically, they still live in our hearts."

A minister offered a prayer, and many parents joined in with their own. I walked over to the school and pulled out of my duffel bag a plaque that I had had made in Managua. The plaque dedicated the school to the spirit of Vandell with the words *Oh Yes You Can Rayia!* I told the villagers that those were the words that Vandell had told Rayia in a moment of despair, when she questioned whether she had the strength to make the trip to Nicaragua. "Those were the words that inspired Rayia to overcome her fears, and I hope they will be the words that inspire generations of students in El Rodeo." The community erupted in applause.

I had concrete anchor bolts to attach the plaque in the school. I put it on a blue wall near the doorway, at the students' eye level. The headmaster then dedicated the school, saying that the spirit of Vandell would live on for as long as this building stood near the top of this mountain. I took out my camera, and as a group of children gathered around the plaque, smiling and laughing, I took the picture.

Back in La Soledad, it was time to break new ground. On our first day at the work site, I looked down in the field where the new school would be built. The twenty or so villagers, all men, who had volunteered for the first construction shift looked skeptical when they caught sight of the American contribution to this labor pool. I could understand their concern. The Nicaraguans, after all, were *campesinos* honed by a lifetime of hard physical labor, accustomed to carrying heavy bags of coffee beans on their back for hours at a time or clearing thick woods by hand with their machetes. I had a couple of gangly teenage boys on my team, and the rest were girls who, until that morning, had no idea how to mix concrete or tie rebar to reinforce the pillars and beams. They would be expected to shovel gravel and haul cinder blocks just like everyone else. There was a good chance that the Nicaraguan men would want to help the girls rather than accept them as equal partners.

As preparation for the trip, buildOn sponsors three or four workshops for the students, which cover everything from learning basic foreign-language skills to eating unfamiliar foods to sleeping without a bed. The students do a service project that's strenuous, such as working in a community garden, which forces them to shovel and dig. We try to teach them to work hard and be good ambassadors. The kids also learn a great deal about cultural differences. In this instance, despite their studded jeans and color-coordinated sweatbands, the girls knew they were to politely resist any chivalric efforts to separate them from their pickaxes. As if on cue, Alisa and Jacqueline greeted their new coworkers with a cheery "Buenos Dias!," then flashed their "Bring it on" smiles and joined the crew digging the foundation. Smiling to myself, I joined them.

In truth, the students have little idea what it takes to build a school. Many of the kids are muscular, strong, and tough, but they've never actually done manual labor under a hot sun. With sweat pouring off them, mud streaked across their face, and cement mix splashed on their boots, they often tell me that they've never worked so hard in their lives.

In La Soledad, I staked out an eight-by-five-foot rectangle near the foundation where we would dig a pit latrine for the children. It needed to be twelve feet deep, which was deep indeed considering that our only tools were pickaxes and shovels. Even mixing hundreds of pounds of wet concrete seemed easy compared to this job. I always ask for volunteers to dig the latrine but rarely get them. But this time Johnny immediately stepped up, while the other students paired off with the Nicaraguans elsewhere on the work site. I've had some of my most meaningful discussions while digging pit latrines. The hard work frees the spirit, I guess. Not long after we began swinging the axes, Johnny fell into an easy conversation.

He confided how bad things were at home, noting that his family was on the verge of eviction again, and he didn't know how that might affect what high school he would attend or what basketball team he would play for. The uncertainty complicated his dream of getting a college scholarship. He acknowledged that his coach and teachers created a safety net that he didn't have at home. A couple of weeks before he left for La Soledad, his mother and stepfather had had another fight, during which Richard, reeling from alcohol, slammed Johnny's mother up against a mirror hanging on the wall. It cracked against her head, and then he smashed a bottle on her face, opening a gash near her eye. Johnny picked up a baseball bat and warned him, "Back off."

It was the first time he'd stood up to his stepfather, and he tried not to show his fear. Richard, who stood a half foot taller and weighed at least a hundred pounds more, looked at him hard. "I'll fucking kill you," he swore before walking out. Johnny didn't doubt him. When Richard returned home two days later, a tense silence hung between them. Johnny was grateful when it was time to leave for Nicaragua.

We had been there for about a week when a different dimension of Johnny emerged during one of our lunches. After we polished off some rice and beans, he mentioned that he had written a poem. I knew he was introspective but hadn't realized he tried to channel his thoughts and feelings into poetry. "I'd like to read it," I said. Johnny pulled out his ragged journal with a worn purple cover and turned to a page titled "Two Worlds," in which he wrote about the village and his home back in the States. I thought the rest of the team would be interested as well, so I suggested he read the poem to everyone after lunch. Johnny told me that he didn't think he could do it. Then another possibility occurred. "Would you read it for me?" he asked.

"Are you sure?"

He nervously looked down at the poem and then back up at me. "Definitely," he said.

"Sure," I told him. "It would be an honor."

Once I settled everyone down and explained what was going on, Johnny gave me the journal, his hand slightly shaking. He was embarrassed and nearly overwhelmed, but I admired his courage. I began reading "Two Worlds":

Everything seems normal to me,
It's almost the same.
Everything I see,
gives me pain.

Everyone works so hard,
To make ends meet.
Time is always of the essence.
It's rare to get a treat. . . .

Now I see what it means
to live in real poverty.
No electricity means no light.
Never putting up a fight.
I can see outside
and use wood to cook.
Here I haven't
seen a book.

Washing clothes by hand,
or pumping drinking water.
Seeing all this,
makes me wonder.

I know this because
I have poverty at home.
I know it isn't right.
Scared to be robbed
or to get stabbed.
Moving from house to house,
Worrying about being kidnapped,
Water cut off,
and freezing in the cold

> *But things here can*
> *Always get better.*

The students were silent as I read, which wasn't typical of this group, and when I finished they broke out in applause and thanked Johnny for being so honest. In an instant, his anxiety vanished, replaced by pride and confidence. His candor had a remarkable effect on the whole group; it opened up a broader discussion about the culture of poverty, here and back home, about water and electricity and being cold, and the difference between needs and wants: What do you *need* to be comfortable, as opposed to what you *want*? I was surprised by what I heard. Several of the kids identified heat as a want, not a need. "You live in Chicago," I said to one of the students. "The temperature in the winter can get below zero. How can heat be a *want*? You don't *need* heat to keep warm?"

A student talked about her heat being turned off in the winter. She said her family made do: three of them would sleep in one bed to stay warm. It worked, so for her, heat really was more of a want than a need. Another girl said that also happened to her family. So I asked, "Who here has had their heat turned off?" Out of fifteen kids, eleven raised their hand. The acknowledgment bonded them closer together, while reminding me that an entire swath of children live in a world with which most Americans have no connection.

I made several trips to visit Johnny in the hut where he was staying, and we continued our conversations during walks along the ridge top. He told me that Richard thought his fighting prowess could be put to "good use."

When Johnny was thirteen, Richard told him that he, Johnny, needed to bring in some money or they'd be evicted again. He drove Johnny to a large house set far back from the street. They entered a side door, went downstairs, and in a darkened room with black walls saw about a hundred men gathered on the concrete floor. Two fighters came out in bare feet, stood in the center of the group, and began pummeling each other. The brawl, a combination of boxing and wrestling, continued until one combatant surrendered. There were no breaks and no real rules. Each fighter had a sponsor, who would put up $100 or more. Some in the crowd placed bets as well. Others just watched for amusement. The spectators kept their voices low to avoid drawing the attention of anyone outside the house. The winner would walk away with a couple hundred dollars in prize money, the house got a cut, and two more fighters would take the floor.

Johnny said he had no idea such places existed, and he thought it barbaric. So he was not pleased when Richard told him he'd be fighting next. He didn't want to, but he felt he had no choice. He took off his shoes and waited nervously while Richard put down his $100. He was finally called into the ring and saw his opponent, a kid not much older than he, about the same size, with a vacant look in his eyes. Johnny told me, "You could tell he had done this before. He looked dead. He had no soul."

The fight began, and it appeared to Johnny as if everything was moving in slow motion. The kid got in a few punches, but Johnny was too strong and fast, and after a couple minutes he knocked the boy down with a punch. "Don't get up," Johnny said.

But the kid got to his feet and resumed the fight, and Johnny again put him on the floor. Finally, after getting knocked down a third time, he took Johnny's advice and stayed down. The fight lasted about four minutes, but it seemed to Johnny to drag on for hours.

"I knew you could do it," Richard told Johnny. He kept the prize money for himself and took Johnny to McDonald's.

At Richard's insistence, Johnny continued fighting, gained a reputation as someone not afraid of older fighters, and earned his stepfather as much as $500 for a single match. He fought four more times, winning three, but then he told his stepfather that was it: if Richard continued to arrange fights, he would lose on purpose. His career as a basement brawler was over, and Richard lost his easy payday.

Johnny also brought me up to date on more immediate concerns. He told me he worked at a movie theater to help pay the bills, but he assumed Richard used the money for alcohol, and he feared he would be back to getting goods at the food bank or begging showers from a neighbor after the water was shut off.

The family that Johnny was staying with appeared to own the poorest house in the village. It was made of rough timber, with many gaps between the planks, a dirt floor, and a porous plastic tarp that stretched across one end of the structure to partially cover some of the holes. A strong rainstorm would knock it over. As I learned during my visits with the family, Buenaventura, the dad, had brought his wife, Maria, and four children to La Soledad only three years earlier, after hearing that the land was cheap. But it wasn't cheap enough. After the first meager harvest, Buenaventura realized that they needed more land to survive. His children were hungry, their reserves were dwindling, and he was desperate. So Maria and their four boys—a thirteen-year-old, a nine-year-old, and six-year-old twins—pitched in to farm what little land they had while Buenaventura and his brothers worked as day laborers, which allowed them to buy some rice and beans. They made it through and now had enough land not only to feed their children but also to plant coffee as a cash crop.

Buenaventura immediately took Johnny under his wing. Johnny could relate to the tough times and was inspired by how the family came together to meet its daily challenges. Buenaventura was everything his own stepfather was not. He would take long walks with Johnny and explain which berries were good to eat and which were bad, and when Johnny ate one that wasn't yet ripe and cringed from the bitterness, the patriarch laughed with gusto.

Johnny spoke little Spanish, but he used a cheat sheet and found ways to communicate. He and the oldest son, Enrique, worked side by side on the work site, then Enrique would help his father in the field. "He was the hardest worker I've ever seen," Johnny later told me. When they reconnected in the evening, they greeted each other with an elaborate fist-bump handshake. Johnny played catch with the younger brothers in the dirt yard, gave them rides on his shoulders, taught them the card game Uno, or kicked a soccer ball made of bunched-up rags tied together with some salvaged string.

Johnny had brought a book and was struck by how interested the twins were in it. "They would try to say the words in English, and they'd say them wrong and just laugh," he told me. "It just brought us a little bit closer."

The two other buildOn students who stayed in the house usually spent their free time with the other Americans, but Johnny stayed with the family and found ways to help out. Making the tortillas, for example, required Maria to grind corn each day with a mallet. After a few days, Johnny asked if he could do it, so grinding the corn became his new job. "It was hard, but I tried to make it festive," he said. The family would feed the three students first, then eat when they were finished. But after several days, Johnny motioned to the kids, "Hey, come eat with us." And they did.

Beyond his host family, Johnny easily made friends throughout the village, including with the pretty teenage girls in La Soledad. While he was shoveling out a pit, they would shoot quick glances at him and then dissolve in fits of Spanish whispers and giggles. The prettiest one, Juana Maria, sometimes peeled off from the group to stand near Johnny and watch him quietly. At first, her physical closeness surprised the American kids, who have a different sense of personal space than the Nicaraguans. If they spotted any of the Americans sitting alone outside, just taking a breather, a handful of villagers, usually the women and girls, would come up and stand silently or, if invited, sit down. The American, only after attempting to fill the silence with English or halting Spanish, would soon realize that the Nicaraguans were not expecting to be entertained or even acknowledged beyond a nod and a smile. The villagers had an almost Zen-like ability to fill space with a gentle, warm energy. For the American teens, so accustomed to the constant stimulation of raucous hallways, noisy streets, blaring headsets, and droning TVs, the concept of companionable silence was new and enlightening.

★　★　★

As the end of our two weeks in La Soledad drew near, the walls of the new school were growing higher by the day. After we left, the villagers would continue along with our construction supervisor and a team of skilled labor, and the school would be complete in another eight weeks. The afternoon before we were due to leave, the sound of guitars and singing drew everyone to the field across from the school for a farewell celebration. A villager named Marvin charmed most of the American girls into dancing with him, and Juana Maria turned up at Johnny's side, dressed in her best Sunday blouse and denim miniskirt. Johnny blushed until Alisa and Jacqueline coaxed him into the grassy circle to dance with his beaming admirer.

Privately Johnny's good-byes were less jubilant. I had been at his house the day before with a translator, Cairo, while Johnny was hanging out, laughing and playing catch with the brothers. He was teaching the twins how to throw a baseball when he suddenly became very somber and had to sit down to collect his thoughts. The family sensed something was amiss and quietly gathered around. After a long pause Johnny looked up at Buenaventura and broke the silence. "This has been the best two weeks of my life," he said softly. He looked around and confronted the inevitable. In two days he would leave La Soledad and would never see them again. "I don't know how I will be able to say good-bye," he confided.

Maria began to cry, and tears began to roll down Buenaventura's brown cheeks as well. It is rare for Latin American men to show that kind of emotion, but Buenaventura, still weeping, wrapped Johnny in a tight embrace.

Then he stood a little apart from Johnny, put his hands on his shoulders, and looked him in the eye. "You are my son now," he told him in Spanish. "You will always be part of my family." Johnny had never heard such unconditional love spoken aloud. So many people had taken so much from him, but no one could ever take that away.

★　★　★

I return from every trek both exhausted and exhilarated; the experience, regardless of country or village, is always filled with so much emotion. But that trip to Nicaragua was unusual for some of the connections that I made and for its moments of intense drama, both in La Soledad and in El Rodeo. I couldn't just walk away from it all.

That summer Jenny and I invited Johnny to live with us for a few months; his family had been evicted again, and his living situation had gotten even more toxic. We thought he needed some distance from home, and he quickly became a part of our family. As he spent time with our two boys, he became like an older brother to them. I saw his gentleness when he read to them at night and taught them to play basketball.

Johnny asked me questions about my faith as he struggled to find his own religious bearings. On one occasion, he talked about his biological father, whom he'd met only once and who provided no financial support. He described the anger he felt toward him, and bitterness, yet part of him wondered if he should try to reach out. He was troubled by the lack of a relationship, and he had some sense that the Gospels could give him guidance.

I agreed. I couldn't tell Johnny what to do, but if he considered himself a Christian, he could think about what Christ would do. And he knew the answer to that. Christ teaches that forgiveness is the ultimate expression of unconditional love, forgiveness as an act of grace. His father had abandoned him, and through God's love Johnny could overcome the anger and bitterness he felt. As Tolstoy wrote, "It is possible to love someone dear to you with human love, but an enemy can only be loved with divine love. . . . Human love may turn to hatred, but divine love cannot change. Nothing, not even death, can destroy it. It is the very essence of the soul."

I was always moved by this passage in *War and Peace*. In Detroit, I had seen how Arnaz had called on the power of divine love to forgive the man who had murdered his own son. Johnny called on that same force to forgive his father.

Johnny asked me what church he should join. Drawing from the teachings of Gandhi and the Dalai Lama, I tried to explain that all religious traditions have value and lead on a path to peace with God. When many were converting to Hinduism because of him, Gandhi encouraged them instead to become more invested in their own faith. He suggested that if you are a Muslim, be a better Muslim; if you're a Christian, be a better Christian; if you're a Jew or a Buddhist, be a better Jew or Buddhist. I couldn't tell Johnny what path was right for him; I could tell him what worked for me, but he would need to find his own peace. He thought a lot about his faith and did his own research. In later visits, he brought a Bible with him and read it at night, jotting notes in the margin.

On that first summer visit, Johnny brought a journal with him, not of poetry but a diary, and one night he asked me to read a long section. I knew that he had had a violent childhood, that he had fought others and had been beaten himself, but I was stunned as I read about far more horrific experiences. Johnny and I were the only ones home, and he paced nervously through other rooms as I made my way through the pages. I read, "No one knows what I have done but I will write everything in this journal." He described how he sold heroin with a relative when he was thirteen.

> *I have shot a man before. He was in his early 20's. I feel horrible. Every night I see him in my sleep. It was an accident. . . . I was dealing and the guy was a customer. I was alone and he pulled out a knife. He then stabbed me in my thigh twice so I grabbed his gun in his pocket, closed my eyes shut and pulled the trigger.*

Was this true? Could he have survived all this? I looked at Johnny, and he showed me the knife wounds on his thigh. It was important for him to tell me about these events. He had never told anyone, and I knew I needed to be there for him. I told him that I loved him as a son, and we prayed together, asking for grace and forgiveness.

Over the next several weeks Johnny and I spent a great deal of time talking about the shooting, or "the incident," as he called it. He told me that he felt "very insecure" afterward because he thought people were talking about him. "I felt really guilty and scared," he said. I knew he had a hard time sleeping. I would go downstairs to meditate at 5:30 in the morning, and he was often awake and had been for hours. Three years had passed since the incident, but the nightmares had not gone away.

Johnny's freshman year in high school was pivotal. By then he had stopped selling drugs, and his relationship with his mother had improved; he came to realize how much she really did love him. Helping his mother, he said, made him want to do more for others. That's when he joined buildOn, which gave him that chance.

"It made me happy to see others happy," he said. "Just helping them. But I'd never thought I'd like helping people. I always thought to help someone you had to be better than them. But now I know that isn't true. Because someone needs help doesn't mean you're better than them. They just need a little help. And doing that gives me joy. It takes my mind off all the bad things in my life. It's a way to escape what I've been through."

The night I read about the shooting, I lay awake thinking about the gravity of it all. Not all my thoughts were encouraging. I considered how this young man, who was capable of selling heroin and committing a very violent act, even though in self-defense, was living under the same roof as my wife and two young boys. I had immediately told Jenny about what I learned, and, like me, she tried to absorb it. It soon became clear that this was a test of my own faith and a test of Jenny's as well. To what extent could we trust Johnny? Did we truly believe in redemption?

Thanks to God, we never wavered. We now knew Johnny well, and we knew what drove him to serve: his desire to prove to himself that he was a good human being. Though we prayed together and asked God for forgiveness, that alone wasn't sufficient. Serving others was his path to redemption. Compassion allowed him to transcend adversity and to overcome his past. I had always believed that this path is available to everyone. We just have to be open to it.

Johnny was, and it made all the difference. He stayed with us the following summer as well, and he has truly become part of our family.

Every year I make presentations to buildOn stakeholders across the country. I'm grateful to speak to audiences of five hundred to more than a thousand, and we have raised more than $2.3 million in a single evening. Along the way, I've shared the stage with such buildOn supporters as the television journalist Ann Curry and Barack Obama. When Senator Obama spoke at one of our Chicago events in 2007, he said of our students, "What they are learning is the ability to . . . stand in somebody else's shoes." (President Obama is now an honorary board member.)

But the most powerful speeches I've heard come from the students themselves. They deliver the keynote addresses at all buildOn events, knowing that when they step up to the microphone, they represent thousands of students from across the country. It's one of the biggest moments in their lives.

At one event, I asked Johnny to speak, and few will forget his first line: "I have done over 230 hours of service through buildOn, and I can tell you that if it wasn't for buildOn, I would be dead or in jail."

At another event, I invited Rayia. I gave the audience some background on her story, including how her trip to Nicaragua helped her overcome her grief. I then announced the dedication of the school in honor of Vandell. Rayia was overcome by emotion. I presented her with the framed photograph of the school she had helped build, the picture I took of the children surrounding the plaque. "Now generations of children will know the name of Vandell," I told her, "because of what he shared with you and what you did to help build that school."

She received a standing ovation, and she wept as she stepped up to the podium to accept the picture.

"To start off," she said, "I must ask you all to close your eyes. Think about your teenage years. Relive the moments you felt happy, loved, and you laughed. Now think about the moments you felt alone, sad, scared, unwanted, and felt like you had no purpose. You wanted—no, you needed someone to reach a hand out to you. You can open your eyes now. BuildOn gives me and hundreds of other students the hand we need and the purpose we want."

By the time Rayia graduated from high school, she had done more than seven hundred hours of community service, an extraordinary total, and she had won a full scholarship to Bowling Green University—for service! Johnny is now attending a trade school to be a licensed tradesman.

Both Rayia and Johnny are reminders that kids who live through violent or tragic circumstances can overcome those conditions, redeem whatever mistakes they have made, and find meaning in compassion toward others. Both of them realized this at home and in Nicaragua. If you help one community, one village, or one child, the effects can last for weeks, years, or even a lifetime, like a ripple on a still ocean that extends into the horizon. That's how you change the world.

CHAPTER 12

Staying Together

In July 2010, two months before Jack's illness began, we had some painting done on our house. The house itself was over a hundred years old, so we hired someone who was licensed in lead-paint remediation. We left town to visit my mom in Michigan but gave specific instructions to the contractor that he should follow the protocol to ensure that poisonous dust was not released into the air. Among other things, that meant if he used any power sanding tools, he needed a special suction device to capture the dangerous particles, and he was to quarantine the house section by section to ensure that any loose particles were confined.

But when we returned, Jenny immediately noticed a thin layer of white dust on *everything*. "We can't stay here," she said. I wasn't as certain, but she convinced me that we had to leave and get the house tested. Before the results came in, I left for Mali to help build a school with a group of kids from Detroit. We didn't have cell phone coverage in Mali but could use a satellite phone, which meant I had to stand in an open field to call Jenny. So there I was, baking on a hot, barren field in the middle of West Africa, listening to my wife on a static-filled line telling me that our house was pretty much a toxic dump.

Our painters, it turned out, had used a high-powered sander on the window sills, and with the temperatures in the high 90s that week, they cranked open all the windows, left the attic fan on, and set up some floor fans as well. The result: a wind tunnel that blew noxious dust into every corner of the house.

Jenny and the boys stayed with her parents for several weeks, and I joined them when I returned from Mali. Johnny was with us as well, and he became part of our search for a quasi-permanent dwelling. Some friends were traveling overseas, so we moved into their house for a week. We drove up to Rhode Island for vacation. When we returned, we headed over to the house of my friend and colleague, Marc Friedman. I had shown up on Marc's door when I quit GE and needed to lower my rent; now I was crashing at his place with my whole family. As generous as ever, Marc even gave us his master bedroom, where Jenny, the boys, and I slept. We were living with Marc when Jack collapsed at school.

All the while, we had to decontaminate our own house, which began with a giant purge. We threw out beds, rugs, air-conditioners, the television, slipcovers, futons, a stereo, and speakers; we ultimately filled three Dumpsters. All our clothes were either washed several times or tossed out. We hired the best lead-abatement expert we could find, and the total cleanup cost, including replacing our damaged goods, was nearly $30,000. The painter refused to cover the costs, and our insurance covered none of it.

It was a crazy, stressful time. The challenges for Jack were obvious, but these were also difficult days for Quinn, removed from his home and then separated for three weeks from his brother and parents. That's a significant burden for a three-year-old. One time Quinn visited Jack in the hospital after Jack had had a bad seizure, and Jack's verbal skills had dropped to Quinn's level or maybe even lower. Instead of an older and a younger brother, they seemed to be par. But what hadn't changed was their affection for each other. Quinn crawled into bed with Jack to snuggle, to play together, and to watch a movie. It was beautiful and sad.

When Jack was released from the hospital in the third week of September, we weren't yet in our own home, but at least we were reunited as a family. We finally moved back into our house after three and a half months. Including the hospital, we had slept in six different places—seven for me, counting Mali. Our house had never been cleaner, though, and our own beds felt good.

Jack's medical condition did not improve. Even with the medications, he continued to have seizures, and one of his meds had particularly harsh side effects. Though the doctors had tried to prepare us, the effects were still tough to witness; the drugs made Jack belligerent. We met with a neurologist in Stamford, who tried adjusting the dosages, but it was as if he was aiming at a constantly moving target. The adjustments never worked. After one prolonged seizure, we ended up back in Stamford Hospital's Emergency Room, where we had started a month earlier, only this time it seemed worse. Jenny and I once again had to fill out all the paperwork and answer all the questions. By now Jack understandably hated the ER, and it was all we could do to keep him from taking the place apart. We couldn't get out of there soon enough.

Some of our greatest fears centered on the nighttime. If Jack had a seizure that went unnoticed, we were told, he could either suffocate or suffer severe brain damage. When he was at Yale, a nurse watched him the entire night on a monitor, or an attendant sat at his side and stayed awake through the night. When he was at home, Jack slept on an air mattress next to our bed, and Jenny would stay awake for all or most of the night to keep an eye on him. I had trouble sleeping in those days, so I would often sit by his side in the wee hours of the morning, watching and praying.

Jack was not able to return to first grade that fall, but he never lost his daring attitude. When he was initially hospitalized, the doctors told us very little about what to expect. I worried that he would never return to the fun, fearless boy he had been before; if he couldn't hold a pencil or use a spoon, how could he ride his bike? But a day or two after he was released, he insisted on taking his bike out. We were at Marc's, so I went back to our house, decontaminated the bike, and brought it over. A blue-and-silver mountain bike with six gears, a front shock, and hand brakes, it was an impressive piece of equipment for a six-year-old. As soon as Jack saw it, his face lit up, and he jumped on it. I put on his helmet, and off he pedaled. He was a little wobbly at first, and Jenny was petrified, but he rode up and down the street, the smile never leaving his face, a moment of triumph.

"I guess I can still remember how to ride my bike," he said when he got off.

Our concerns about overnight seizures were valid, but we needed a more practical way to keep vigil. So we mounted night-vision cameras on his bed, and when he went to sleep at 7 or 7:30 in the evening, we could watch him on a portable monitor. We then moved the monitor next to our bed so we could watch him through the night. In addition to those cameras, we kept a hand-held, high-definition Panasonic camera nearby so we could capture a seizure on film. We were advised to do this so the doctors might learn what part of the brain was causing the seizure. Sure enough, we caught one on film, a terrible tonic-clonic episode. It was the longest I had ever witnessed, ten or eleven minutes. Our neurologist had told us to wait that long before giving the emergency medicine. Jack's eyes rolled one way, then the other. His body stiffened. Then he trembled. His lips turned blue because he had temporarily stopped breathing. It was excruciating to watch for even a second.

We called our neurologist that night. He didn't need to see the video to realize that Jack's case was beyond him and to suggest that we seek out more advanced care in New York. It was late January 2011, five months since his first seizure, and we were no closer to controlling them. We met with two highly respected neurologists at Columbia University and New York University. Both gave us the same advice: Jack needed to be readmitted immediately. His current medications, including Keppra and Trileptal, were no longer stopping the seizures; we essentially needed to strip away his existing meds, start from scratch, and find a more effective mix of drugs.

We chose to work with Drs. Orrin Devinsky and Judith Bluvstein at New York University. Dr. Devinsky had written the definitive book on epilepsy, and Dr. Bluvstein was a pediatric neurologist who eventually took over Jack's care. They admitted Jack to the pediatric ward at the New York University Langone Medical Center. There were patients from France, Scotland, and South America; it was a good sign, I figured, that others had traveled so far to be there. The doctors told us they expected Jack to be out of the hospital in two or three days.

They began to draw down his meds, and there was a brief period, when his old drugs had left his body but the new ones had not yet taken effect, in which my son reappeared. He was lucid, bright, curious, the old Jack. We had a wonderful conversation—about the monitors, the medical equipment, the gizmos in the ER room—and my hopes soared that we would get back on the right track.

But it didn't happen. Jack tried low doses of other meds and was ultimately put on Lamictal, but it had to be introduced slowly because a lethal rash could develop. The seizures returned, as did the side effects. Jack was once again enveloped in the pharmacological clutches of modern medicine. As we've discovered, the brain is too sophisticated and complex for modern medicine to control, and the effort itself often feels like a roll of the dice.

I had seen a great deal of undeserved suffering, both in this country and abroad, and those experiences had been a personal wake-up, leading me to my life's work. But watching Jack now was a reminder that my family and I were not immune from unbearable agonies. Suffering is part of the human condition, and when you realize that modern science cannot eliminate that suffering, you can rely only on that which is always present: God. Only through faith and prayer would we get through. So I prayed.

Two days passed at the hospital, and then three, then four, and the seizures continued. Jack wasn't going anywhere. Neither were Jenny and I. We lived in Jack's room, Jenny sleeping on a reclining chair and I on a mat on the floor. I brought my work in, running a board meeting by phone. The only time I left was to go for a run or to bring in food.

A week passed, and now a new problem emerged. In three days I was supposed to leave for Nepal with a team of students from the South Bronx, and once there we were to break ground on our four-hundredth school. A camera man would be meeting us to shoot footage for a story that would air on CBS News. I was torn about whether I should go or stay. I hadn't traveled anywhere since Jack had collapsed in September, and I hated not to be out in the field. But the thought of being away from Jack was worse. Nothing is worse than watching your own child languish. How could I leave?

I spoke to the doctors, Jenny, and Marc, and they all told me the same thing: Go to Nepal. I couldn't do much for Jack in the hospital, and as Dr. Bluvstein finally put it, "You have to keep living your lives, and besides, someone has to pay for the insurance and the hospital bills."

So I decided to go. Two days before leaving, I tried to explain to Jack what would happen. He didn't seem to understand, or perhaps he didn't want to believe that I would have to leave the hospital. On the day I was to leave, I rolled up my sleeping mat and stuffed it in my duffel bag. Then Jack started crying. I hugged him and said good-bye, and I tried to be strong. Jenny told me that he cried for an hour after I left. It broke my heart.

I had plenty of time to reflect on Jack's condition on my trip to Nepal, one of the most isolated countries in the world. A buildOn team of about twenty flew from New York to London and then to New Delhi. After a long layover, we took our next flight to Kathmandu, Nepal's largest city, then had to fly on a local carrier called Buddha Air to a dirt airstrip near the Indian border, where we jumped in a bush bus for a two-hour drive to the village of Pakariya.

Nepal had always been special to me. It was while hiking there after college that I saw the villagers celebrating their new school, which first got me thinking about how I could make a contribution. It was in Nepal that we built our first school with a covenant, signed by the villagers, describing their contributions to the project, and the covenant became the cornerstone of our entire effort abroad. Over the years I've also been inspired by the Tharus, an ethnic group found mostly on the western plains of Nepal. For generations, the Tharus have either been discriminated against like untouchables or held as slaves in a forced-labor system called *Kamaiya*. What made it worse was that the Tharus were forced to work on land that had been systematically stolen from them. After years of protest, the system itself was officially outlawed in 2000, but the Tharus have remained among the poorest people in the world.

On this trip, at the covenant signing, I noticed a woman in a pale blue dress who had bright red *tika* powder smeared on her forehead. One of the leaders in the village, she had greeted us warmly when we arrived, but now she was the only one at the signing who wasn't smiling. With a grim intensity, she signed the document with her thumbprint.

Her name was Ram Dulari Chaudhary, and I later circled back to her and asked why she appeared so sad. "I've only been asked to sign my name one other time in my life," she said. "And I couldn't do it. All I could do was weep."

Ram told me that when she was a little girl in the 1970s, her father could not repay a debt of 1,800 rupees (about $25). So the *zamindars*, powerful landlords, confiscated their thirty-five acres of land as well as their buffalo and cattle. The family was forced to live in a one-room hut, and Ram began working in the fields from 4 a.m. to 8 p.m., seven days a week. She explained that the *zamindars* had high positions in the government, and the enslaved Tharus would be beaten or starved if they refused to work. They were also refused education, which the *zamindars* viewed as a threat. One Tharu, however, was literate, and he wanted to teach others in the village, but to no avail. As Ram said, "The *zamindars* would not let us see the inside of a school."

But at night, when the *zamindars* were asleep, the Tharus would secretly gather around candles to teach themselves how to read and write. Progress came slowly, but through that effort they became literate, united as a people, and realized how badly their most basic rights had been violated. That led them to petition the Nepalese Parliament for their land rights and their human rights. Over several years, beginning in the 1990s, those rights and their land were restored, until 2000, when the government declared that all the Tharus were freed from the *Kamaiya* system.

Now I understood why signing our covenant was so monumental for Ram. They had won their freedom without firing a single bullet. They were liberated by education. And we would have the honor of working with Ram and the Tharus to build their first school. Ram concluded by saying to our students, "Because of the school we're building here together . . . because of you, no one will ever enslave our children the way we were enslaved." Her words were unforgettable.

I felt deeply connected to the villagers, to the American students, and to the project. I am simply wired for this work. We broke ground on the school, began mixing the concrete, building the foundation, and raising the walls. Physically, emotionally, and spiritually, I felt I was in the right place—except I wasn't. I was talking to Jenny every day on the phone at the hospital, and the updates were never encouraging. Jack was in his own kind of shackles, as he couldn't move the left side of his body. Jenny had support from her family and Marc, all of whom came to visit, but I could tell in her voice that the stress was growing. She kept assuring me that I was where I needed to be and that I shouldn't come home early, but I ended most conversations in anguish.

Finally, during a weekend call, Jenny told me that Jack had had a bad seizure in the middle of the night. Our doctors weren't there, and the resident gave him emergency medications, but apparently not the right ones or not enough. The night staff didn't have the experience of our specialists, and the seizure apparently lasted fifty minutes, on and off, which was verified by the EEG readout the following day. Jack remained partially paralyzed, which freaked me out. Jenny said the residents and the doctors were doing the best they could, but I was infuriated. I had to leave Nepal. Immediately.

I didn't know that I could make any difference at the hospital, but it wasn't fair that Jenny should carry the burden by herself, and I had to be with Jack. I was going home.

But how?

I called Marc and told him I had to get a flight out of New Delhi. It turned out that I wouldn't be able to retrace my steps there by flying through Kathmandu; the fog had grounded Buddha Air. That left one daunting possibility: to drive across the Indian border all the way to New Delhi, about four hundred miles as the crow flies. For medical emergencies, we keep a truck and a local driver in the villages where we work. I could use that truck, and our trip leader said she could get a backup vehicle while I was gone.

I was prepared to leave when Marc called me back and said that British Airways had a flight that left New Delhi for London at 3:30 in the morning. There was only one problem: it was full, and there wasn't another London-bound flight with any seats for three days.

I didn't care. I packed my duffel bag, hugged Ram Chaudhary, and said good-bye to our team in Nepal. I usually don't have a hard time with good-byes, but I did then. In that moment, I felt a swirl of emotions: the honor of being able to bring a school to this community, the bonds I formed with the villagers and our own students, but also the fear of what was happening to Jack.

It was about 10:30 a.m., only a half-hour after I had hung up after talking with Jenny, and I piled into our truck. I had to get to another country with a driver who spoke no English to reach a flight that had no seats available. But at least I would be moving toward home.

We drove through the Terai region of Nepal, a mostly flat, fertile, but deforested swath of land in the southern part of the country. We began on dirt roads but soon made it to a paved highway. We were safer on the dirt roads. The highway was the country's main east–west artery, a two-lane ribbon so narrow that only about six inches separated two cars barreling in opposite directions. We often found ourselves hurtling straight toward a giant Tata truck, whose kaleidoscopic colors would be distinctive in any country. These trucks had vibrant streamers whipping off the sides, bright fabrics draped across the front, gaudy license plates, Hindu Gods or the eyes of Buddha painted on the bumper or hood, and musical horns blaring like the brass section in a bad high school marching band. To pick up extra cash, some drivers charged pedestrians for a lift, then made them ride, precariously, on top of the payload. The guys behind the wheel also enjoyed playing the game of chicken: as two vehicles bore down on each other, the drivers accelerated and defiantly honked their horns to see which one would move over first.

We tried to avoid the gamesmanship and focused on surviving.

It took us about four hours to reach the Indian border. The Indian soldiers, however, wouldn't allow us through, either because my driver was Nepalese or because the truck was Nepalese, or both. Those kinds of bureaucratic tangles always happen in that part of the world, and you just have to find other options. We had more than twelve hours before the plane took off. Rather than keep fighting to get across the border in the original truck, I hired an Indian man to drive me the rest of the way. My Nepalese driver insisted that he leave our truck there and that he come with me, which I thought was endearing. But all the haggling cost us a full hour.

While we were in the car, I had no phone contact with the States, so I didn't know if Marc had made any progress on finding me a ticket. With the sun still high, we passed large tracts of farmland made brown by the dry season; the rickshaws, packed high with belongings, teetering down the road; the trucks and the pedestrians and the cows, some of whom would plop down in the middle of the road and take a snooze. We were in India, and you didn't mess with the cows.

With fog rolling in, we finally reached New Delhi just after midnight, and even that late at night, incredibly, we hit a traffic jam. We had been on the road now for almost fourteen hours, but even with the traffic I still had a chance to make it to the airport on time. Until I realized that our driver had no idea where the Indira Gandhi International Airport was. I didn't know either. Neither did the Nepalese driver. Now a bit of panic, mixed with anger and frustration, began to swirl in my gut. New Delhi is a sprawling metropolis, and we started asking people where the airport was, but we had no clear direction. The fog had gotten so thick that we only had about twenty-five feet of visibility. We finally found the airport, but we were in such a haze we couldn't find the entrance road, and we circled that airport two or three times in search of an opening. We could hear the airplanes but couldn't see them. It was like a terrible dream.

The fog finally lifted a bit, and we stumbled upon the entrance road and motored into the airport. It was about 2:15 a.m., and I wanted to make a beeline to the British Airways ticket counter. But as I dashed in, I was stopped short by the airport army officers, all of whom were carrying AK-47s. These officers, all business, said I couldn't enter without a ticket.

Standing there in my flip-flops with my duffel bag over my shoulder, I was becoming increasingly tense and agitated. I now had only an hour before takeoff. I told the officers that my ticket was inside at the British Airways counter. (That was a gamble, because I didn't know if Marc had managed to get me a ticket.)

The officer repeated that I couldn't enter the airport without a ticket.

I repeated that I couldn't give him my ticket because my ticket was in the airport.

And he answered that I couldn't enter without a ticket.

Back and forth we went, and I could barely contain my frustration, my fear, or my exhaustion. But I knew that I couldn't lose my temper because the solider was holding a very large automatic rifle. I persisted, and he finally allowed me to go to an airport lounge with a computer, where I could retrieve the ticket that I desperately hoped was waiting for me. It was now 2:45 a.m., so I was down to forty-five minutes. I could only pray that Marc had come through. I reached the computer and logged on to my email. No ticket! I envisioned myself stuck in this airport for the next three days. The curry alone might kill me. I had only one hope left. I returned to the security guard and begged him to allow me to go the British Airways counter.

By now the soldier probably figured I was too desperate or too pathetic to be acting. He took me to British Airways, and I asked the ticket agent if there was a seat for me.

He looked up and said that everything was in order. The soldier left, and I was ecstatic. Then the agent said, "There is no ticket for you."

"What?"

Unknown to me, Marc had been in touch with one of our board members, Mark Webb, who was an executive at British Airways. Thanks to a day of frantic calls, Webb had sent instructions to his colleagues in New Delhi to try to get me on that flight. But the flight itself was still full. The agent had just been covering for me to get rid of the soldier.

"Can I speak to the manager?" I asked the agent.

"I am the manager," he replied.

He kept tapping the computer keyboard, looking for a miracle, and all I could think about was Jack and how far I had traveled that day. Everything was a blur, the flight was leaving in minutes, and I was trapped in this nearly empty modern edifice to global travel.

Suddenly the manager looked up and said that, yes, there was a ticket for me. Maybe there was a last-second cancellation. Maybe someone got lost in the fog or smashed a fender or hit a cow. It didn't matter. I was leaving.

The manager printed out the boarding pass and instructed an agent to take me through security and then to the gate. It was 3:15 a.m. We zipped through the metal detector and reached the new Terminal 3, which is the pride of India and about the size of Cleveland. It spread over twenty acres, the twenty-fourth largest building in the world and the globe's eighth largest passenger terminal. Now we had to race through it. Everything was closed: the souvenir shops, the food outlets, the immigration counters. My duffel bag was weighing me down, and I had left my tennis shoes in the truck back at the Indian border, which meant that I had to run in my flip-flops. We ran for at least a half mile. I finally got to the gate, handed the agent my boarding pass, and staggered onto the plane—the last one on.

I turned right to find my seat, but a flight attendant stopped me. "No," she said, "you go left, that way." I had never been in first class for any flight in my life, domestic or international, but there I was. It then dawned on me that I didn't exactly look like a first-class passenger. I was sweating; I hadn't bathed in four days, hadn't shaved in a week. My pants and T-shirt were muddy, and my feet were caked with road grime and dirt. It seemed that everyone was looking at me, wondering how I managed to sneak into the luxury coach.

But I was suddenly living like a king. A comfortable chair that turned into a bed. Complimentary soft pajamas. Slippers. An eye mask. Sumptuous meals. White wine. Cold beer. A flat-screen TV. Constant pampering. I was even able to wash my feet. I explained to an attendant that I was in Nepal building a school and the ticket was donated; then I told him how my long haul to the plane had left me in such terrible shape. He just laughed. He said the attendants had been talking about me since the flight took off; they had assumed I was some sort of eccentric Internet millionaire.

I got to London, then flew to New York. It was all possible because of Marc Friedman and Mark Webb, both of whom knew about Jack. How lucky I am to have them.

It was fifteen degrees when I landed at JFK, and I went straight to the hospital, still in my flip-flops. Jack was in his pajamas, and I gave him a big hug and kiss and told him I loved him. He hugged me back tightly and said, "I love you too. But you need a shave!"

Jenny provided more details about the recent medical challenges. Jack had been through a cycle of seizing and vomiting. At the same time, he had begun faking seizures, either to get attention or just as a game so he could watch Jenny and the nurses jump into action. Then one evening his left side began twitching, and he had a strange half-smile. Initially everyone thought he was play-acting again; this didn't look like a normal seizure. But the twitching continued, minutes kept passing, and Jenny realized that this was no act. Her sister, Kelsey, who is a nurse practitioner, was with her, and they tried to convince the nurses that Jack needed help. But the nurses remained uncertain.

Kelsey is a lot like Jenny; she rarely raises her voice. But as Jack continued to twitch, she could no longer restrain herself and finally screamed, "Will you stop talking about it and get the meds!"

A seizure is like a gathering storm: the longer you wait, the more power it generates. By the time Jack received his emergency medication, it was too late. Another drug was used, and then another, but the hurricane had already been unleashed. The attending neurologist was brought in from another emergency, and he talked to Jenny about trying a new drug, what Jenny called "the lesser of two or three evils." By itself or with the help of the drug, the seizure did stop, but the following day the tests confirmed that it had lasted for almost an hour.

Afterward Jack was on such a massive drug load that Jenny and Kelsey took turns watching him overnight, and for the next day or so Jenny never left his side as he struggled to regain control of his speech and the left side of his body.

As she told me about these experiences, I was again reminded of Jenny's remarkable poise and grace under agonizing conditions, all of which, I was certain, had a calming effect on Jack and sustained him through the worst of the trauma. I thought about my stressful journey from Nepal and realized how it paled in comparison to the terrifying ride that Jenny had just been on. "Sunshine" had not walked outside the hospital in twenty days, and she remained unfazed, resilient, and beautiful.

I felt as though I had traveled through a time warp, from the scrubland of Nepal to the neurological mecca of a Manhattan hospital. The doctors kept tinkering with different medications, and we remained in the hospital another two weeks. Jack's stay finally reached thirty-three days, but he hadn't gone for more than a day and a half without a seizure and was no more stable now than when he arrived or, for that matter, when he was first diagnosed. He was safer in the hospital, but he couldn't live the rest of his life inside the pediatric ward of the Langone Medical Center. He needed to get out, play, run, be with other kids, and reclaim his childhood. So we received permission to go home, grateful that our family was together, united in our faith in God but still on the precipice.

CHAPTER 13

Ignition

Just as Jack had to continue with his life and try to get back to school, I had to go back to work. But after my stressful emergency trip home from Nepal, I had to rethink my overseas travel. Before I met Jenny, I spent six months a year traveling to developing countries. After we married, that was gradually reduced to six weeks. When the boys were born, I traveled only four weeks. Now that Jack was stricken, I cut my overseas travels to two weeks a year.

I thought about not traveling at all, but I couldn't stop those trips entirely. Jack was in more than capable hands with Jenny. In addition, my work in the villages meant too much to me and to the organization to give up altogether; I couldn't be the father to Jack that I needed to be if I gave up that part of myself. I was also beginning to draw a connection between Jack's condition and the many hurdles that confront the children in these villages. Both have to face challenges that were not of their doing, and each helped me understand what it takes to overcome the most extreme circumstances.

When I do go abroad, I like visiting our existing schools to see what impact they're having. But there was one village to which I had never returned: Misomali. Devastated by our original experience, I felt lucky that Dave, Erik, and I had gotten out of there alive, and I struggled to bring myself to go back. I remembered the loneliness, the primal nighttime din, the fever, the death. I knew that many of my close friends would be gone. After that initial project, we stopped working in Malawi for nearly ten years, and when we did return, we were up in Kasungu, a twelve- to fourteen-hour drive away. Over the years, members of my staff had sometimes tried to reach Misomali, but they simply couldn't find it. Too remote, too obscure. I really had no idea what became of Thambe FB School or the village. When I left in 1993, I didn't know if the school would survive even five years, fearing that either another flash flood could wipe it out or that neglect from the community, or corruption, would doom it.

Brett McNaught had often heard me talk about Misomali. A broad-shouldered former Peace Corps volunteer, he was the head of our VP of international programs, and in 2011 he set out to find Misomali himself. Though it appears on no map, I tried to guide him in via satellite phone, and, miraculously, he found it. He reported back the good news: the school was still there.

In February 2012 I traveled to Malawi with a group of students from the South Bronx to break ground on our 450th school, with money donated by Madonna. We weren't going to be anywhere close to Misomali, but it had been nineteen years, and Brett's report on the place piqued my interest. I wanted to see for myself what impact the school might have had on the community. I wanted to see my old friends. Steven. The chief. Mr. Joseph. Mr. Gamma. It was time to set aside my troubling memories and return.

Members of buildOn often travel into remote and challenging destinations. Teams have encountered civil wars and firefights in Nepal. We've endured earthquakes, hurricanes, and cholera in Haiti. We've averted violent street protests in Johannesburg, sidestepped coup d'états in Mali, and been laid low by Dengue fever in Nicaragua. We've had to overcome fuel shortages, currency shortages, and cement shortages. Even in good weather, some village roads are impassable. Other villages have no roads, and the locals build them just for the project. Bridges collapse. Corruption persists. As

Nietzsche said, "That which does not kill us makes us stronger." Well, building schools makes us stronger.

Malawi will never be easy to reach. For this trip in 2012, British Airways donated plane tickets, for which we were grateful. The team flew the red-eye from New York to London, where we had an eight-hour layover, and then flew to Johannesburg. After several hours, we took another plane to Lilongwe, the capital of Malawi, boarded an old bus, and drove eighty miles until we arrived in the town of Kasungu to spend the night. The next day we drove three more hours to the village of Kankhumbwa. It was a long haul for the students, some of whom had barely been outside of New York.

As we rambled into the village, droves of children suddenly appeared, chasing the bus, singing, smiling, dancing, all beneath a bright sun against a sweeping panorama of the African fields. The American students stepped down from the bus and waded into the exuberant crowd. Some of the students danced. Others cried. Many watched in amazement. The African children knew we had come to help build a school, but their enthusiasm spoke to an even deeper response to our being there. No one just happens upon this distant village, which didn't have electricity or running water or even the most basic medical supplies, not even a Band-Aid. There was no evidence that the government paid it any heed. But our arrival signaled an important message: *You matter.*

I was scheduled to stay in Kankhumbwa for two weeks, including my side trip to Misomali, but my plans were nearly torpedoed on my very first night. Our Malawian translator, Chris, was a quiet, earnest college student majoring in business; he and I were staying in an empty mud hut provided to us by a host family. Along the walls crawled large cockroaches that, if I'm not mistaken, could also fly—not a good sign. The hut had probably been used for cooking and food storage. It had been pouring rain. Most of my stuff was drenched, and the thatch roof was leaking. I just wanted to find a place dry enough to lay down my mat for the night. I fell asleep quickly.

Chris slept under a mosquito net, but I wasn't using one; I thought I was safe enough taking antimalaria pills. I was asleep only a short time when I felt something nibbling at my left ring finger. Still half-asleep, I tried to thump it with my other hand, but the sudden pain became more intense. I shouted. Opening my eyes, I turned on my head lamp, and there I saw a fat fifteen-inch rat waddling away, in no particular hurry. It had bitten down to the bone.

I thought I might still be dreaming or having a nightmare, so I yelled to Chris. "Can you see that?"

"Yes, I can see it," he said.

The rat had made it over to the wall, scurried clumsily to the top, and looked right at me through beady eyes before it disappeared into the dark. All I could do was curse it and find some toilet paper to stanch the bleeding, though not before my sleep sack became covered in bloodstains.

Chris and I left the hut that night to find rat-free quarters in the village. The host family later confirmed that our hut was known to attract rats because the family did indeed store food there. I appreciated the hospitality, but I think a place that shelters huge rats is pretty much disqualified as a viable lodging option.

The bite itself was a more serious matter than I originally thought. The following day, traveling with some bundled *kwatcha* (cash), I drove several hours to a health clinic at a private school. It serves the country's elite, so it had a full supply of medicine. I was told that I needed a rabies vaccine shot, which would be the first of five such shots that I would need over the next twenty-eight days. But that was only part of the treatment. I also needed H-RIG, Human Rabies Immune Globulin, to be injected right into the wound on the finger. While the vaccine helps you develop antibodies to fight the rabies virus, it takes two weeks to take effect. During those first two weeks, you need the H-RIG for protection. The clinic, however, didn't have any. BuildOn can telephone doctors all over the world through a global medical and evacuation insurance agency, so we called one of the doctors while we were still at the clinic. We put him on the speaker phone, and he confirmed that the H-RIG was needed in case the rat had rabies. Those chances, he said, were "low but not zero." A rat on its own wouldn't carry rabies, but if it had been bitten by a rabid cat or dog, it would then be infected, and a large rat, like the one that got me, could survive such a bite. In other words, it was possible that I could get rabies.

"If I do get it," I asked the doctor, "what are the symptoms?"

"You die," he said.

Silence.

"Okay," I said. "Before I die, are there any symptoms?"

"You become irritable."

He said I had seven days to take the H-RIG, and I assumed we could find it somewhere in the country. I felt fine, but the events evoked memories of my first visit to Malawi. Then, I was able to survive malaria only because I got immediate and decent care at a hospital, beyond the reach of the villagers I was living with. Now I was searching for a potentially lifesaving vaccine that would be unobtainable to the villagers in Kankhumbwa; the only thing their health clinic distributes is condoms.

Three days after I was bitten, Chris and I set out for our long drive south to Misomali. Our seven-day window for the vaccine was still open, so we arranged to stop in Lilongwe at the African Bible College, whose private hospital, I was told, had the H-RIG. But that information proved false; there was no vaccine. Our country director was making calls all over Malawi, but he couldn't find the medicine anywhere. I had four days left to get the shot.

The doctors insisted that I evacuate immediately to Johannesburg or Nairobi, where the vaccine was available. But I had flown more than ten thousand miles to get to Malawi, and I was resolved to go to Misomali and also help build that school in Kankhumbwa. The doctors were never specific about my odds of infection, beyond what the first doctor had said: "low but not zero."

Even without the rat bite, I realize I incur far more risks than people with desk jobs. Members of any single trek, however well organized, might encounter sickness, violence, horrible conditions, or accidents. Jenny tears up every time I leave for the airport to go overseas. But my priorities have always been clear. When I married Jenny, she became as important to me as God. Nothing has changed since, except that I love her even more. When Jack and Quinn were born, they joined Jenny and became more important than all else. I love them more than life itself.

The rat bite brought my dual commitments to family and work into sharp relief. Should I evacuate for the vaccine, or should I continue on to Misomali? Was the decision to stay fair to my family? Am I being fair to them when I leave for two weeks at a time to go on these treks? I try hard to be, but I know there are still risks, and I do worry about the boys. What would happen to them without their father? And I worry about Jenny. If I thought there was any real chance that I had been infected or that not getting the injection might jeopardize my ability to care for my family, I'd have evacuated in a minute. The odds, however, were in my favor, and that's how I see life: as a series of trade-offs between calculated risks and rewards. These trips abroad aren't personal adventures; they're missions to help empower the poorest people in the world.

I was deeply conflicted, but these are the choices I face, and this is who I am. I went on to Misomali.

We had a long drive south, and many of the sights were all too familiar. The average Malawian still earns less than one dollar a day, so while we saw the beauty of the rolling hills, lush from the recent rains, we also passed the shantytowns, with their ragged stands peddling fabrics and souvenirs; the farmers in the road selling chickens tied up like hostages; the bakeries that sell only bread; the children gnawing on raw sugarcane; the conspicuous signs for coffin makers as reminders that death is a booming business; the scrawny dogs and cats, goats and cows, as hungry as their owners; the old women walking along the lonely highway, with baskets on their heads, to a market down the road.

But change was also evident. When I was there in 1993, Malawians lived in virtual isolation. There was no television, even in the cities, and the few newspapers and magazines were controlled by the government. But political reform and improved technology were leaving their mark. Television came to some of the cities in the early 2000s, though it's still a luxury item. Magazines are available, and the Internet can be accessed in some places, though broadband is still rare.

Cell phones, which first appeared around 2005, are probably the biggest advance. Like other developing countries, Malawi has effectively leapfrogged the power grid and gone right to cell towers. To use a phone when I lived in Misomali, I had to walk or ride my mountain bike to a town fifteen miles away. Even then, the phone might not be working, and there would be nothing to do but turn back. But all our staff in Malawi now have cell phones, and I was able to use one to call Jenny from Kankhumbwa every day. While I was driving to Misomali, I could use my smartphone to access the Internet for everything from news updates to Michigan State basketball scores. I could answer emails, send text messages, and tweet. I was connected!

Yet although Malawi is entering the modern age, it is falling further behind other countries. While 90 percent of Malawians still live in rural areas and education remains out of reach for the vast majority, our technology-driven world is creating new opportunities for skilled workers everywhere. To catch up, the answer for Malawi is what it's always been, but even more so: education.

We passed through Blantyre, which appeared to be a bit more developed than before—some newer buildings, more cars, not as dirty—and in the evening we met up with Brett McNaught. He would be accompanying us to Misomali the next day, and he had a place for us to stay that night.

We woke up early the next morning and drove the last ninety minutes high enough in the mountains to cut through the misty clouds. As we approached Misomali, the dirt roads and cornfields looked increasingly familiar. Maybe that triggered the memories. I started thinking about the seven-mile hike I had taken back to the village after nearly dying from malaria, grateful to be alive but alone, and the realization that I could never truly understand what it meant to be a member of the community because I would always have more. I thought about Gatoma. I knew he'd be dead, and I still felt terrible because I hadn't been able to help him. I wondered about his sons. I got choked up and had to fight back the tears.

We parked the truck, and I regained my composure. Brett had gone to Misomali the previous day and told the elders I'd be visiting. When I began walking toward the village center, I once again experienced flashbacks. I recalled all the suffering that seemed to stalk the population. I recalled how Dave had saved me after he himself had almost perished. I wondered where Steven was, my close friend who accompanied me to the top of Mount Mulanje to protect me from the evil spirits. Had he made it? And the chief? And so many others.

Then hundreds of kids, barefoot and in rags, came running up to me and began singing and dancing and reaching out to touch me. I was mourning; they were celebrating. And the tears came back. My legs started shaking and my knees finally buckled. I closed my eyes, bent my head, and fell to one knee, my hand shielding my face. The kids stood next to me, singing right into my ear, touching my shoulder, but the sounds became muffled. I kept my eyes shut and as I sat in the blackness, I saw the faint outline of a cross. I prayed.

Chris later told me that he overheard villagers saying that when I fell to my knee, they thought I had been possessed by a "kind spirit."

We continued walking, with the children blowing whistles and banging drums. Women danced. I tried to wipe away the tears as one of the women, an elder, took my hand and guided me through the crowd. I saw Chief Misomali, just standing there, waiting for me, always patient. Still lean, he wore a tattered dark sports coat, a beleaguered gray dress shirt, and a red-patterned tie. He smiled when he saw me. I walked up and shook his hand, pressed my forehead against his, and we gave each other a hug. We exchanged greetings, and, amid the hoopla, I told him "Thank you, thank you." He smiled, held my hand, and asked me for money to buy a new cell phone.

I didn't know what to make of the question; it was completely out of character for the chief I had known so well. Back then, he never asked me for anything. He was always giving, offering to share his food or space in his compound.

I looked around at the buildings behind the chief. Though we were certainly near the school that I had helped them build all those years ago, I didn't know *which* one was ours. Instead of just the one we built in an empty cornfield, there were five schools! Chief Misomali pointed to ours; with its familiar brown-red bricks, freshly painted blue trim, and white breeze blocks, it looked sharp. But the others were equally beautiful, each similar in size, shape, and color. The European Union and the Malawi government, I was told, had given the village the funding to buy the materials and build four more schools. The original school had not only survived; it had multiplied.

I looked around and realized I was not standing in a cornfield but a courtyard, with gardens, bushes, and walking paths. The villagers had cleared a large swath of land to make it possible, and now they had brought out chairs and tables for a ceremony. The small eucalyptus saplings that we had planted had grown tall, providing shade for the buildings. Misomali had been fragmented physically when I had last been there, with five subvillages, but now it had a gathering spot for the entire community.

I tried to take it all in, but there was so much commotion I almost felt dizzy. Some of the women who remembered me made that unique and friendly call, which sounded like a cry from an Apache warrior in an old western. I did my best to return the greeting.

I found Mr. Joseph, one of the core volunteers, in a blue button-down shirt, a big smile, and a bit of a pot belly—a great sign! I teased him that it was evidence of prosperity. There was Frackson, also part of my core, a dependable and diligent man of few words, now wearing a light-blue cotton T-shirt. I embraced him as well. But what about Steven? I felt like I was swimming in a sea of people, and I kept asking, "Where is Steven?"

Finally, I spotted him. He looked fit, even ageless, in a yellow button-down shirt. We hugged and laughed and recalled the good times on the work site. As the community continued to celebrate, we joked yet again that if he talked too much, then I talked "three much"! Nothing had changed between us.

As we gathered for a formal ceremony, I took note of other signs of progress. The headmaster's house was built out of bricks with concrete mortar; the same was true for three teachers' houses. Some houses had iron sheets for their roofs, a huge upgrade from thatch. At least one roof had a satellite dish, though I doubt it worked. Several electric wires ran overhead. Two new wells had been dug. Adults were riding bikes, which can also be used to carry grain and were considered a business investment.

Dark clouds suddenly rolled in. The skies opened, and sheets of rain soaked Misomali, a classic African thunderstorm. Hundreds of villagers scattered in search of cover. Most of them found it in the classrooms and under the overhangs of the schools. Steven pulled me aside and motioned me into one of the rooms, where we could talk in private. He spoke in a low voice. "This is not the chief you knew," he told me. "That chief is dead."

"What? What do you mean it's not the chief? Who is he?"

"This is the chief's brother. The chief you knew died ten years ago."

I was shocked, heartbroken. I was also angry. The current chief had deceived me and made me believe he was his brother. And he wanted a cell phone!

Steven had more news. Gatoma had passed away, as I had expected; he had been dying when I knew him. But what I hadn't expected was that Gatoma's two sons had died as well, the very boys for whom Gatoma had worked so hard to build the school.

Also dead was Mr. Gamma, who was with us on the site almost every day.

I had had six coworkers, and half were gone. Maybe I shouldn't have been surprised. When I lived there, a nun who ran a medical outpost told me that in this region, the HIV rate was close to 50 percent.

I asked about my old nemesis. "What about Mr. McCrory? What happened to him?"

"He's dead too," Steven said.

I suddenly felt drained. Too much death. And the chief! The chief I knew. He had been such a good friend, and I had just shed tears of joy when I saw him and had hugged him as I would my own father. But it was all a lie. I couldn't get my mind around it. I walked out into the rain to be alone.

The weather finally cleared, and the ceremony continued. There were prayers. There were teacher introductions. There were girls singing and dancing. There were boys performing a raucous skit about how the first school was built. I made some remarks, talked about our efforts years ago. But I felt detached, emotionally exhausted.

Then the headmaster started speaking about the schools and teachers and the children, and he detailed how much progress had actually been made. I looked around and felt my strength slowly return as I made sense of the bigger picture. I realized that it had all been worth it. The work that had been done years ago had paid off in exactly the way that we had all dreamed it might. Although not everyone had lived to see it flourish, the sacrifices had not been in vain. These schools were a living tribute.

When I had left Misomali nineteen years earlier, the village had two teachers and about 150 kids attending classes in a single school. Now it had seventeen teachers and more than a thousand students attending classes in five schools, all the way up to the eighth grade. The headmaster said that improvements in education had many benefits, including greater trading opportunities and micro-enterprises, increased agricultural yields, the distribution of health care information, and increased pride and self-esteem.

I agreed, but in my opinion the most amazing change was this: when I lived there, Misomali's five subvillages all had male chiefs; now there were four female chiefs and only one male chief. And the future looked even better for the next generation. Of the 1,055 students attending the schools, 533 were girls. None of this was a coincidence!

Then Steven stood before the entire community. He commands respect, and everyone listened carefully. He described how Dave, Erik, and I had come here and worked with the community to build the school. He referred to the school as the "ignition," and he thanked God because he said that I "had been the ignition."

That night Chris and I went to Steven's hut. It was pitch black, and as we walked along the dirt road, surrounded by mountains and enveloped by cornfields, I heard the eerie nighttime sounds and recalled the tales of haunted hills. I couldn't believe I had lived there for five months, mostly by myself, with only my mountain bike and tent. I told Chris that I didn't know how I had made it.

We reached Steven's hut and took seats on logs outside. Instead of a traditional kerosene lantern, Steven had an LED lantern, powered by solar energy, which cast us in a soft light. His wife and several children sat on the ground nearby.

I wanted to find out what happened to the chief. Understanding why he died was the least I could do for him.

Speaking quietly and without emotion, Steven told me that during the construction of some buildings in the village, the chief was accused of stealing six bags of cement. The police investigated and concluded the charge was true. He was then sentenced to prison, a year and a half of hard labor. Steven said the chief didn't serve his entire sentence because he got sick. When he returned to the village, he had AIDS.

His account was almost too terrible to hear. And confusing. Who accused him of committing a crime? And why? When I was living there, Mr. McCrory had accused the chief of the same thing, and I knew that it wasn't true. Steven said he didn't know who had made the accusation.

I asked if he believed it. He said he had heard they didn't have any evidence, but this was a time of political transition, and "the government was against him." Steven said he himself was "badly hurt" when the chief was imprisoned, "because the government at that time was harsh." When the chief was released, he never spoke of his arrest. He just talked about "old village stories" and his health. "I believe he knew he was dying," Steven said, "because he had been suffering for a long time."

I kept asking for more information, for more details, as if I were trying to solve a mystery. Was the chief's brother complicit? Were the other village chiefs involved? Was McCrory? Steven simply didn't know. I couldn't unearth the secrets buried in those hills.

As the night wore on, Steven talked about the challenges we had faced in building the first school. I hadn't realized how much opposition there had been. "People were saying bad things about you," Steven said. "McCrory was a candidate for Parliament. He strongly believed that if he could convince people that you should be paying them to build that school, and that the chief was keeping their money, then he would get more votes. And that's exactly what he did. He persuaded them to believe as he believed, and that made people against you." Mr. McCrory's tactics worked: he won his election and served in the Parliament. "He used you to win," Steven explained.

"I guess we both won," I said. "He got the votes, and we got the school built. But there were a lot of losers."

I reminded Steven that Mr. McCrory's children used to follow me around, and Steven said they had attended the school, and now his grandchildren did. Mr. McCrory's political career, however, was short-lived; he lost his reelection.

I wanted to know what made Steven different. Why didn't he believe Mr. McCrory when almost everyone else did? "I knew it was about politics, and those are always changing," he said. "But the school will stand forever."

★   ★   ★

Indeed it will. That afternoon, after the ceremony, I wanted to ask Steven about his daughter, Ruthie, his first child, who was born when I lived there. I remembered how he had held her with so much pride and joy. But I was apprehensive about asking, because if she had not survived, I didn't want to bring back a painful memory. Finally I decided that I had to know.

Steven smiled. He said she lived in a nearby village, but he would send for her.

A half hour later she arrived, a beautiful young woman, bright, confident, and articulate, with braided hair and wearing a stylish African dress patterned in brown and yellow. When Steven introduced her, she beamed with pride. So did he.

Steven looked at me and said, "I'm an illiterate man. But my daughter attended all of these schools, and she is a teacher, and she will lift up our family name for generations."

Ruthie told me that as a young girl, she had attended the school in Misomali that we built. Then she had attended the four other schools, after which she went to secondary school. She now taught in a nearby village. "My father," she told me, "had a vision for a future generation. My dream is that my own children, and the children of this village, will go to school beyond what I accomplished."

My time with Ruthie and Steven saved me from my feelings of loss and betrayal. Those dark emotions were washed away by a deeper and more inspirational understanding of my return to this village. I kept thinking about the word *ignition*: the act of starting a fire so the engine can work. It was a profound metaphor. All we did those many years ago was light a fire. From the very beginning Steven had been the ignition. Now the school itself had become the ignition for all who attended.

They were lighting fires that no one can ever put out.

Epilogue

That's the power of starting this kind of a fire: it can blaze any-where, and no one can put it out. If Steven was the ignition, so too were Rayia and Johnny, Komba Dumbia and Ram Chaudhary, Father Felix and Geshe and Jim Parke and the thousands of stu-dents and adults who participate in buildOn each year in the United States and abroad. We are all capable of lighting fires, of changing the world. That doesn't mean you have to quit your job and move to Harlem or Africa, but in most cases you have to confront your fears and you have to ask yourself: What am I willing to do to make a real difference in my community, my church, my country?

I ask myself that every day: What commitments am I willing to make? How hard am I willing to work toward that end? What am I willing to sacrifice? At times I've probably gone too far. I put at risk my relationship with my brother Dave, but those wounds have healed. (Dave continues to be a successful real estate developer, including beachfront property in Costa Rica. He now lives in Boul-der, Colorado, where he loves to go camping with his son, Zachary.)

The time and effort I've invested in buildOn has paid off. Over the past twenty years, our students have contributed more than 1 million service hours, and in 2012 more than 94 percent of buildOn seniors not only graduate but go to college. (In many of their schools, the four-year high school graduation rate hovers between 50 and 60 percent.) By 2012 we were working with four thousand students in seventy-two high schools.

We've documented the strength of our programs. A study by Brandeis University's Heller School for Social Policy and Management in 2010 said our programs led to ten direct outcomes for our students, including improved academic engagement, expanded civic engagement, improved leadership and teamwork, and an expanded sense of possibility or hope. Brandeis also found a causal link between those outcomes and increased academic achievement, and concluded that our students felt an increase in "empowerment" and a renewed "belief in one's ability to determine one's own life."

We've been equally successful overseas, where we have now built 525 schools. In 2012 we broke ground on a new school every five days in Haiti, Nicaragua, Mali, Malawi, Senegal, or Nepal. Our work in Mali was noteworthy. The year 2012 saw the country convulsed by a bloody civil war, by a military coup that overthrew a democratic government, and, in the north, by an influx of Islamist rebel groups with ties to al-Qaeda—but buildOn never left.

Edward L. Glaeser, an economics professor at Harvard, says that "there are basically no countries with very low levels of education that have managed to be democratic over the long-term, and almost every country with a high level of education remained a stable democracy." We believe that, so despite the turmoil, we constructed thirteen more schools in Mali in 2012, increasing our number there to 191. The country can suppress insurgents with guns, but if it's going to have a stable future, it lies in those schools and others like it.

Just as Brandeis studied our domestic programs, the Academy of Educational Development (AED), a nonprofit development organization, evaluated our operations in Mali and Malawi in 2010 and confirmed that buildOn programs "have significantly increased access to and quality of education and have inspired communities to send their children to school. . . . Men and women now open bank accounts, participate in community associations, and [have the capacity for] income generation." The report said that girls used to be held out of school rather than have to walk long distances to other villages, but now "gender equity" in education is possible and happening.

The evaluation noted that through buildOn's methodology, *"new norms* about the potential of community-wide action can take hold and increase the collective strength of the communities. Project schedules can be met, *even in rural Africa*, given sufficient diligence and management." The italics are mine. These comments are significant because we don't see ourselves as creating "new norms." We've been doing the same thing for twenty years. The problem lies with the old norms, in which so many NGOs did not recognize what was possible, even in rural Africa.

The AED evaluator, Christine Beggs, was so impressed with our work that when she returned from Africa she intended to raise the $32,000 for buildOn to construct another school in Mali.

That's one of the things I love most about my work: people learn about us, are inspired, and then take the next step to get involved. For example, we sponsor donor programs in which individuals fund their own school and then travel to that country, live with a host family, and help construct the new building. The donors are typically middle-aged and affluent. Some bring their children, and they're willing to spend more than $30,000 for the school, plus another $4,000 to $5,000 on travel expenses. We had thirty-three separate donor trips in 2012; that's more than $1 million spent for the privilege of living in a mud hut for two weeks while working under the hot sun. They could have spent their vacation time in Vail or Bermuda, but instead they went to West Africa or Haiti. That's an amazing testament to how far people are willing to go to break the cycle of extreme poverty. It's one thing to write a check, but our goal is to form partnerships between those who have financial resources and those who need them.

In some ways, my career has come full circle. Though I quit GE long ago, the company remained a staunch ally; its executives have served on our boards, it donates office space to us, and it matches employee contributions to our organization. Several years ago, GE began to encourage employees to raise money for our schools, and the company allowed those employees to take ten days off to help build them. And who were these lucky employees? Those in the Financial Management Program, the very program I had quit to pursue our mission. We get about thirty FMPs a year, and while I'm obviously biased, I'm not surprised that young professionals would be interested in our work, or, as they might say at GE, in broadening the metrics for a meaningful life. Other companies will follow when they realize this commitment also benefits their own bottom line. Jeff Bornstein, the chief financial officer of GE Capital (and Jim Parke's successor), told me that GE gains a recruiting and retention edge through its connection with buildOn. "It lets FMPs know that GE is about much more than earnings per share," said Bornstein, who's on our national board. Jim Parke, by the way, remains on the board as well.

Volunteers from all backgrounds flourish doing our type of service. This was made clear several years ago when I received an email from a high school student named Jake Sherin. His father, Keith Sherin, is GE's chief financial officer, a major supporter of buildOn, and a close friend. Jake asked me if he could travel with one of our teams to help build a school. I said that we had a team from the South Bronx heading out to Nicaragua in two weeks and asked if he wanted to join them. It would be a tough trip on short notice, but Jake never hesitated. He joined the group and headed to Nicaragua.

His trip occurred during the rainy season, and when the bus got stuck in the deep mud down in Nicaragua en route to the village, everyone had to walk the last mile or so through the muck. The rain never stopped. The bugs were everywhere. One student had to be evacuated for a medical reason. A teacher also had to be evacuated because an old leg injury prevented her from walking safely in the mud and the mountains. While our work on the school didn't slow down, it was the kind of trip that some parents would consider a disaster—including, I feared, Keith Sherin.

Sure enough, the day after everyone returned, I received a call from Keith, and I knew the reason why.

I asked him how the trip went for Jake.

"Did you know that Jake was living in a house with chickens and pigs?" he asked.

"I did not know that," I said, "but those things can happen."

"And did you know that he had insect bites all over his body?"

"I didn't know that either, but those things can happen. Those are the places we go."

There was a long pause, and I was waiting for the hammer to fall.

"Jimmy," he finally said, "Jake loved the experience, and it is the best damn thing that ever happened to him. He can't wait to get out there and build more schools!"

In fact, Jake was the hardest worker on the site. The other students loved him, and after receiving certification as a wilderness first responder, he became an intern and helped our staff lead teams to build two more schools.

If you're trying to live a meaningful life, it helps to have a roadmap. In my case, I've received direction from the nonviolent revolutionaries whom I've long admired, from Jesus Christ to Martin Luther King, from Gandhi to Mother Teresa. So too with the Dalai Lama, whose messages about human rights, personal responsibility, and world peace dovetailed with my own beliefs on social justice. I began reading about him when I was in college; little did I know then that I would someday meet him and that that encounter would have a great influence on my life.

As the spiritual leader of exiled Tibetan Buddhists, the Dalai Lama lives in Dharamsala, in the Indian Himalayas. To his followers, he is the reincarnation of the Bodhisattva of Compassion, an enlightened being who has postponed his own nirvana and chosen rebirth to help alleviate human suffering. He is perhaps better known for leading Tibet's struggle for freedom against the Chinese, for which he won the Nobel Peace Prize in 1989.

My encounter with him was quite unexpected. In 1997 I stopped off in Kathmandu for a few days before heading out to a distant village to work on a school project. I connected with some friends who were American activists for Tibetan freedom. One, Erin Potts, had cofounded the Milarepa Fund with Adam Yauch of the Beastie Boys. Fascinated that I had interviewed Mother Teresa, they encouraged me to do the same with the Dalai Lama and gave me the fax number of someone who could arrange it. I was skeptical, but when I returned to the States I sent the fax. The following morning I received a reply fax that asked me when I could come. I couldn't believe it. I was back in Nepal six months later, took a flight to Dharamsala, and suddenly found myself in the home of the Dalai Lama.

An American friend from Kathmandu agreed to assist me with filming the interview and met me in Dharamsala. On our first day, we were invited to film and photograph His Holiness as he greeted Tibetans who had lined up, forty strong, on the steps of his house. These Tibetans are nomadic yak herders, chiseled, humble, and tough. They had been persecuted and chased from Tibet by the Chinese Army and now had made the dangerous journey on foot over the Himalayas to seek refuge here. They revere the Dalai Lama as the leader of their faith, as he holds the Tibetan people together. They bowed low when they saw him, most touching their heads to the ground at his feet. Some wept. The Dalai Lama lifted them up and placed a scarf around the neck of each, a sacred gift.

On my second day, as I waited in a greeting room inside the Dalai Lama's home, I thought about the significance of the audience I was about to have. I had read many of the Dalai Lama's books and had often visited the refugees in Kathmandu. I had walked inside the Jokhang Temple, one of the most sacred temples in Tibet. I saw the Potala Palace, where he had grown up, and then hitchhiked across part of the Tibetan Plateau to Shigatse and Old Tingri, where I then traveled on horseback with a yak herder into the mountains so I could visit the Rombuk Monastery. How bizarre, even tragic, that the Dalai Lama himself could no longer visit these places in his homeland, whereas I could come and go anytime. On these journeys, I had witnessed the devotion of all Tibetans to Buddhism and their love for the Dalai Lama.

He spoke to me for well over an hour, on film, and what came through most memorably was his intelligence, compassion, and sense of humor. He ended every answer with a kind of half-chuckle and a smile, which seemed designed to put me at ease. He discussed everything from science to politics to religion, but I was struck by his comment about who influenced him the most. He cited Ling Rinpoche, his childhood mentor and instructor; Chairman Mao, who took over his country and would certainly have influenced his life; and, of all people, Thomas Merton, whose writings had inspired both my father and me. I was astounded, as the moment brought together these different parts of my life and seemed to affirm the basic tenets of my own beliefs.

Perhaps the greatest gift from the interview occurred before it actually began. I was standing outside his greeting room, when I saw a poem he had written. It was hanging on the wall and titled "Never Give Up." A black-and-white photo of the Dalai Lama was on the sheet above the poem. I took out my notebook and wrote it down, word for word, and was still writing when I was called for the audience. It was a plea for compassion and resilience:

Never Give Up

Never give up
No matter what is going on
Never give up
Develop the heart
Too much energy in your country
Is spent developing the mind
Instead of the heart
Develop the heart
Be compassionate
Not just to your friends

But to everyone
Be compassionate
Work for peace
In your heart and in the world
Work for peace
And I say again
Never give up
No matter what is happening
No matter what is going on around you
Never give up

These ideas seemed to validate so much of my own life. "Never Give Up" perfectly captured the determination of exiled Tibetans, and that struggle is why I've always identified with them. But "never give up" had long been my own mantra, certainly since we founded buildOn, and I believe it's essential for anyone who wants to make a difference in the world. You're going to have setbacks almost every day; you're going to encounter skeptics; you will experience failure. But that's when you have to summon the courage to never give up. As Frederick Douglass said, "If there is no struggle, there is no progress."

Geshe, the Buddhist monk who lived with me briefly in Harlem, knew how important that poem was to me, and the year after I first saw it, he somehow got a replica, including the photo, from Dharamsala. I framed it, and it hung in my apartment in Harlem and then in our house in Connecticut.

Now, since Jack's medical crisis began, those words speak to me as never before. There were reasons I was in the Dalai Lama's house: to meet with the very embodiment of compassion and justice, to make the connection to Merton, but also to read that poem, to absorb it, for it would be a clarion call to our entire family and a lodestar for Jack. *Never give up.*

After Jack left the New York University Langone Medical Center in March 2011, we took him back to school at the end of the month.

That alone showed his tenacity. He would try to attend half-days until June, but he continued to experience neurological spikes and seizures. We hoped the medications would work well enough to keep him in class, but he often ended up in the nurse's office, seizing or vomiting. He missed 88 percent of first grade.

He was on at least six new medications, each one with horrifying potential side effects: organ failure, lethal rash, tremors, cognitive slowing, constipation, insomnia, nausea. One warning read, "May cause suicidal thoughts or actions in a small number of people." The potential bad stuff was too terrible to contemplate, but the alternative was to allow the seizures, which, unchecked, would cause brain damage and eventually put Jack in a coma. We had no choice.

Even without side effects, the regimen was a colossal burden. Jack was required to take pills eleven times a day, including one for his gastrointestinal system that might be impaired by his antiseizure drugs, and another to combat nausea. He has to get blood drawn once a week to monitor overall drug levels and any toxic side effects that the drugs may have on his organs. Over time, the blood draws were reduced to once every two weeks, but the scar tissue on his arms had already begun to build up. Yet here's the amazing thing: Jack never complained about them. How many kids do you know who would just sit there while a nurse jabbed a needle into their arm, searching for veins that have already been poked and punctured? That's what Jack endures, without tears or recrimination.

I am proud of him, but this isn't the pride you feel when your child gets a high mark in school, performs well on the soccer field, or does a kind deed for someone. This is pride in his courage, but it comes with heartbreak.

All of this has tested Quinn too, whose activities have often come to a halt because Jenny has had to tend to Jack. Sometimes Jack will strike Quinn due to some neurological spiking or impulse. (My friends tell me that most big brothers will hit their little brothers, regardless of medical conditions.) But Quinn has an endless supply of affection for Jack. He is typically not a hugger and hugs Jenny or me only when we initiate it, but even after Jack has done something unkind to him, Quinn will spontaneously run up to him, throw his arms around him, and yell, "Jackie! Jackie!"

We're grateful that Jack remembers those moments more vividly than his seizures, which apparently fall into some memory void. If he's drawing when he's having one, he might just keep on drawing when he comes to, unaware of what just happened. When I think he has fully emerged, I'll ask him, "Jack, can you hear me?"

Eventually he looks up and says, "Yes of course I can hear you. Why are you asking?"

But he is aware of his limits. Once, when I was walking him into school, he began tapping his head, trying to think of his teacher's name, muttering to himself, "Come on, come on, you can remember." He finally asked me, "When will I be able to remember things again?"

I told him the truth. "It will take time and patience," I said, "but we're working on it."

On another occasion, we were on the beach and Jack was trying to fly a kite, but he kept seizing. At one point, I was with Quinn in the ocean when I looked up and saw Jack fall over. Jenny held him while Quinn and I came rushing out of the water. It was his fifth seizure, and we knew what we had to do. We had to give him a heavy dose of Klonopin, which inhibits brain activity and puts him in a haze for two or three days. Giving it to him made my heart sink. We were in such a special place, and now Jack wouldn't be able to experience it. With the sun sparkling off the water and the sound of other kids playing in the ocean, he sat down on my lap. He had no idea what was about to hit him, no inkling that he was about to be put into a drug-induced fog. I put my sunglasses on because I didn't want him to see me cry, and I just tried to talk to him and enjoy him for the ten minutes or so before he slipped into the clouds. His body soon became heavy, and he couldn't stand on his own. It was time to leave the beach. I picked up my son and carried him to the car.

Jenny and I grieve over these struggles, but then we are reminded of Jack's strength. As a parent, I'm not sure that anything can prepare you for such an experience, but my work with kids in this country and abroad has given me some context. Do I get angry and frustrated over Jack's condition? Of course. But I've never asked why this has happened, in part because I've seen how much suffering there is in the world. Hardship doesn't discriminate, so I focus on the progress.

I have taken Jack and Quinn to service projects in Harlem and the South Bronx, and a strong bond has formed between Jack and our students. He looks up to them because they're teenagers who are paying him lots of attention. The students know of Jack's condition, either because they've seen a seizure or because I've told them. They see him painting a mural or digging in a community garden, and they are unfailingly kind and patient with him. They love him. I believe they are also inspired by him, and I will later remind the students, when they're feeling discouraged, "If Jack isn't giving up, you shouldn't either."

And Jack is not giving up. That first spring after his diagnosis, he wanted to play baseball in our neighborhood Little League. In the second game, we went to the field, and he was doing fine, but then, when his team was batting, he had a seizure and fell off the bench. When he regained his awareness, he wanted to go out onto the field. I explained that his team was still at bat. Next it was his turn to hit. The coaches pitch until the batter makes contact, and I envisioned Jack, dazed and barely able to walk, standing at the plate, flailing at the ball but never hitting it, getting more discouraged with every pitch. I suspect that everyone else who had just seen Jack was anticipating the same thing.

The first pitch came. Jack swung the bat—*crack!* He hit the ball solid and ran to first base with a single. All the parents cheered. I was both elated and relieved and immensely proud—not just that he hit the ball but that he didn't back away from the challenge.

Triumphs come in small packages. After our first stint at Langone Medical Center, Dr. Bluvstein made us promise that we wouldn't let Jack sleep in the top bed of his bunk bed; though it had a rail, she felt it was too dangerous, and he could fall out while seizing. We agreed and set his mattress on the floor, much to Jack's dismay. He begged us almost every night to sleep in the top bunk. Quinn, meanwhile, had his own room, but he decided he wanted to sleep next to Jack. We now had two kids on the floor, but Jack still wanted to get back up on that top bunk. Dr. Bluvstein wouldn't agree.

Then one Saturday morning Jack and I decided we'd build up the rails and make it impossible for anyone to fall out. We sketched out a plan, took measurements, wrote out a materials list, and went to the lumber yard. We picked out the wood together, had it cut to size, and bought the wood screws and glue. We went home, sanded the wood, and began to put it all together. We got out the drill (Jack's favorite part), and I let him drill the holes and drive in some of the screws. The project wasn't as big and wild as the heli-dozer, but our rail system was a work of art. Much more important, it was a great achievement for Jack, a testament to his will. He would not give up until he got back in that top bunk. He's slept there ever since, and Quinn sleeps right below him.

Jack's progress at school has been halting, but not for lack of effort. His school has been extremely supportive, giving him extra attention, but by the end of second grade he was still reading a full grade level behind. Jenny and I were conflicted about whether to hold him back from the third grade, and we researched this for weeks. Some studies showed that holding a child back provides only a temporary academic bump and can hurt self-esteem. But Jack had missed virtually the entire first grade and was still battling seizures. It is understood that kids *learn to read* up to third grade, and then they *read to learn* after that. Holding our son back a grade might affect his self-esteem, but we felt it was critical to give him a fighting chance to catch up. We made the decision for Jack to repeat second grade and were trying to figure out how to tell him, but before we could, he approached Jenny one day after school. "You know," he said, "I missed all of first grade, and I haven't been able to stay up with the kids. Do you think I could do second grade again?"

Jack went through a phase in which he asked "Why me?" or

"Why did I have to go to the hospital and not Quinn?" Those are good questions, tough to answer. We try to explain that different things happen to different people. There is really no good reason, but working together we can overcome these challenges. We have a friend whose ten-year-old son has type 1 diabetes. We were with him for a couple days, and Jack was fascinated by—and perhaps took comfort in—watching the boy test his blood sugar and change his insulin pump, and do so as part of his normal routine.

Part of me recognizes how resilient kids are, not only those like Jack who have a medical issue but the children I've met who may be orphans or homeless or hungry. Yes, they can adapt and survive, but let's not celebrate too much. I'm reminded of a comment from a Haitian woman who heard an American praising the strength of the Haitian people and their ability to "bounce back." "Yes," the woman said, "we can bounce back, but *it hurts* to bounce."

Jack keeps bouncing back, and he's already beaten the enormous odds against him.

Not long after we left the Langone Medical Center, I read one of Dr. Devinsky's books on epilepsy. It explained that the more anti-seizure medications that a patient takes without success, the odds of controlling the seizures diminish. I asked Dr. Bluvstein about this, and she confirmed that if a patient tries eight or more meds, the chances of controlling those seizures drop to below 1 percent.

I was sick. By now we had already tried nine different meds for Jack. Overcome with despair, I asked Dr. Bluvstein if these numbers held true for Jack. "Yes, they do," she said. "I know the situation seems grim, but you need to know that 99 percent of the kids who get what Jack got never walk or talk again."

"How can this be?" I asked. "Why is Jack part of the 1 percent? How has he beaten these crazy odds?"

"I don't know," she said. "I can't give you a medical or scientific reason. I believe he must be touched by an angel."

I have come to believe that as well. I also believe that this angel is the man for whom Jack was named, my father, who is surely protecting and watching over him and Quinn every day.

So we count our blessings. Jack still rides his bike, and he loves to play basketball. The faster pace makes it easier for him to stay focused than when playing a sport like baseball. He loves sailing, the faster the better; Jenny believes that slicing through the waves and the sound of the water calm the pyrotechnics in his head. He took summer classes in 2012, and it was his best educational experience yet. He would come home from school wanting to do his homework. He went to the library, joined a book club, and read three books in one day. The teacher was very good. She was also young and pretty, and Jenny suspects that Jack had a crush on her, which may have been additional motivation. That's not sustainable, but we'll take progress in any form.

We continue to adjust the medications, in search of a magic elixir, and by the early summer of 2012 Jack had gone without a seizure for twenty-five or twenty-six days in three consecutive months. Until then, he had never made it that long.

Many boys look up to their father as their hero. In our house, Jack is my hero: tough, unwavering, and courageous. He's also taught me a lot. I realized long ago that I could never truly walk in the shoes of the people I wanted to help. I tried, but it wasn't possible. Yes, I could live in their community and experience their pain as well as their joy, but I always had something they didn't have: resources. I could buy food or medicine or drive off or even fly away. I controlled my destiny. But that feeling changed when Jack was stricken. His disease mocks our brightest doctors, humbles modern medicine, and renders money useless. Those who feel they've lost control over their life, even for a moment, well, I can now walk a few steps in their shoes.

I have not given up hope, however, because I have maintained my faith. This has been the ultimate test, but so far, this faith has survived the cruelest of storms. My faith is deeply rooted in Catholicism but has grown from my experiences with people from all religions and traditions and with believers from all over the world. I hold that faith in God links us all, and I reject expressions of religious superiority. There is one summit, but many paths to get there.

Mine is not a "blind faith." As Thomas Merton wrote in *The New Seeds of Contemplation*:

> *Faith is not an emotion, not a feeling. It is not a blind subconscious urge toward something vaguely supernatural. . . . Faith is first of all an intellectual assent. It perfects the mind, it does not destroy it. It puts the intellect in possession of the Truth which reason cannot grasp by itself. It gives us certitude concerning God as He is in Himself; faith is the way to vital contact with God Who is alive.*

My faith is centered on God and God alone, and it is this faith that has given me the strength and hope during my darkest hours of defeat and despair, whether in Misomali or Harlem, in South Africa or the South Bronx, in Haiti, Detroit, or Nepal. It is this faith that comforted me during my last moments with my dad and gives me strength when Jack is seizing out of control. And it is this faith that will strengthen Jack as he continues his heroic journey toward recovery. Through this faith, God will give him the courage to never give up. It is only through this faith that Jack can be healed.

While my choices have led me on a unique path, you have your own choices to make and your own path to follow. But each of us has the power to take action, to light a fire and be the ignition for others. We can contribute and find inspiration in whatever enriches our lives. We can go forth with courage, compassion, and commitment. The scope doesn't matter. What's important is what Mother Teresa often said: "Do small things with great love."

Each night before I go to sleep, I enter Jack and Quinn's room to meditate. Then I say the Lord's Prayer, which I said with my own father hours before he died. Those were the last words he spoke, and sometimes when Jack wakes up, he says that same prayer with me. One night I entered and found him sitting up in his bed. His hands were folded and his lips were moving as he softly repeated those sacred words to himself. I closed my eyes and prayed with him silently.

Your will be done.

Acknowledgments

Can one person change the world? The best short answer I've heard comes from a buildOn student from the South Bronx. "Yes," she said, "but not by yourself."

The story in these pages is proof that we are all deeply connected to one another and can accomplish nothing by ourselves.

It is only through God's grace that any of this is possible. In moments of desperation, God picked me up, guided me along, and protected me. God spoke clearly and inspired me through meditation and the people in my life. I thank God.

I thank my wife, Jenny. That she agreed to our second date is a small miracle. That she married me, moved to Harlem, and still loves me so vastly is further proof that God exists. Her courage, serenity, and grace are a constant source of inspiration. Her intelligence and gentle touch have guided me more than anyone will ever know. She is a voracious reader and wonderful poet, so not a single word in this book was reviewed by any editor until Jenny had read it. And as a mother Jenny is a wonder to behold. She is selfless, kind, patient, firm, and loving beyond all description. She is love flowing upon love. I love you, Jenny. Thank you.

I also thank Jack and Quinn. I am inspired by your courage and resiliency. You give me purpose and joy, and every day I am delighted by your curiosity, laughter, and love.

Acknowledgments

My brother Dave is a fearless soul. Without him, buildOn would not exist and I'm pretty sure I would be dead. I love you Dave. Thank you for your courage, honesty, and love.

My mom has never missed a single buildOn gala. Not one. There is no one more proud of me. She loves me no matter what, and not a conversation goes by without her telling me so. I love you too, Mom—from the bottom of my heart. Thank you.

My dad taught me the meaning of unconditional love. He taught me how to work hard and how to play hard. He taught me about integrity and dignity. But his greatest gift was his faith. He taught me to pray and showed me where to find God. At the end of his life, he taught me how to die, and through that, how to live. I love you, Dad. I miss you every single day. Thank you.

My uncle Bob is one of the kindest, gentlest, and most spiritually connected people I've ever met. He's also hilarious! Thank you for sharing so much about your childhood and time with Dad. It has deeply enriched my life.

My siblings Mari, John, and Peter have all been supportive of buildOn from the early days. Thank you all—especially John, for inviting me to Calcutta and arranging an interview with Mother Teresa.

Marc Friedman has been part of every key decision I have made at buildOn. He has been crucial to the success and growth of our mission and instrumental to the writing of this book. Marc is my closest, most loyal friend. He is a beautiful and cherished member of our family. Thank you, Marc. I love you, brother!

When I married Jenny, I had no idea just how blessed I was to have become part of her family. I read once that crisis does not so much build character as reveal it. Our medical crisis revealed that the Freres family is selfless, loving, generous, and kind. They were with us in the emergency room on day one. As days turned into months, they remained by our side and provided a loving home for Quinn. No words can truly express my gratitude to Kris, Ron, Kelsey, Derek, and John (Rothert). Thank you, and may God bless you always!

As the CFO of GE Capital, Jim Parke had become an expert in assessing risk. The day I walked into his office, he knew that the odds were stacked against us. I was certain Jim would join the skeptics and cite the many reasons why we would fail. But he didn't. He believed in our cause, and he believed in me. His belief gave me the confidence to keep going, and it gave others the confidence to trust us. Jim Parke is more than a board member, a mentor, and my greatest advisor—he is a close and trusted friend. Thank you, Jim.

Many nonprofit organizations lose their way. That ours has flourished is a direct tribute to our extraordinary boards of directors who have shared their expertise, guidance, and encouragement.

When I met John Myers, buildOn was growing but had a limited scope and limited resources. Then John stepped up to the plate. At a single fundraising breakfast, John raised enough money to change buildOn forever. Thank you, John.

Geoffrey Norman has been a remarkable mentor and friend, and his lovely wife, Christina, and their daughters have all contributed immeasurably to buildOn. Thank you for all of this, Geoffrey, and for being there when my dad passed.

Keith Sherin is one of buildOn's most powerful advocates, and one of the most genuine and generous people I have ever met. He has befriended my family and trusted us with his. Thank you, Keith, especially for your friendship.

Jeff Bornstein is one of our most passionate and driven board members. He has aligned more resources for this cause than anyone. Because of his vision, many at GE not only volunteer with our youth locally but also build schools in developing countries. We are emulating this model in multinational corporations around the world. Thanks, Jeff.

I have always been very moved by the intelligence, drive, and humility of Kathy Cassidy. She has quietly raised transformative amounts of money for buildOn. Thank you for your example, Kathy.

Denis Nayden's leadership and immense generosity have inspired us to build more than thirty schools in Haiti since the earthquake in 2010. Randi Hedin has funded the construction of dozens of schools, has traveled to four continents to help build them, and started a buildOn chapter in Seattle. Dennis Kass has been a member of our board for more than ten years, and I am grateful for his guidance. John Raffaeli is the first person to take his entire family to West Africa (or anywhere) to help construct a buildOn school, and is also a close friend to my family. Thank you.

Missy Kiernan was a young attorney when she drew up our bylaws and helped us incorporate Building with Books. She soon joined our national board and has been an outstanding member ever since. Jane Hackney is one of the most dedicated volunteers ever to serve at buildOn—from her time as the treasurer of our fledgling organization to serving on our Global Leadership Council. Thank you.

Don Torey and Ralph Layman have been outstanding leaders for more than a decade. From strategic guidance to building schools, they have been instrumental to our ability to scale. Joe Dionne was one of the first members of our board and marshaled tremendous support for the organization. Bob Lievense, another former board member, taught me that "you cannot manage what you do not measure" and helped me draft our first Key Performance Indicators. Thank you.

More thanks to Jennifer Hill and Allan Hackney. Don Epperson was one of our first board members and along with Allan Hackney leads our chapter in Boston. Mark Webb, thank you for your work on the board and for helping our family.

Other board members who deserve special recognition include Amin Aladin, Jim Bell, Diahann Billings-Burford, Suzie Ivelich, Jim Reynolds, Karen Seitz, and Melissa Thomson. Thank you all for serving with such brilliance, passion, and dedication.

So many others associated with buildOn deserve special recognition. Abby Hurst, who was instrumental in scaling our work in urban high schools, leads by example and with grace and compassion. I am grateful for all she has contributed to buildOn and cherish her friendship.

Acknowledgments

Erik Dorf invested two years of his life as a full-time volunteer for Building with Books. He brought enthusiasm, intelligence, and a great sense of humor to the work site every single day. He put his life on the line for this cause.

BuildOn has had more stalwart volunteers than I could possibly mention, but among the most dedicated from the earliest days are Jim McKinney, Tim Owens, Jennifer Nix, Pat Wheeler, Jon Donahue, Bob Davis, Gail Sulkes, Karen Vogel, Kathy Felker, Amy Becker, Brad Tewksbury, Chris Tewksbury, and Joe Fanelli.

I have written about many heroic people, and they deserve the greatest recognition: Edna and Alfonso, Elenese and Domingo, Gordon and Teca Greathouse, and Izary Lizias; Daniel Massamola, Charles Olkers, Reggie September, and Leonard; Kurt Fenske, Andrew Gatoma, Chief Misomali, and Steven Tenthani; Father Felix and Rinpoche Lobzang Tsetan; Rayia Gaddy and her parents, Arnaz and Rachel, and Johnny. My thanks also to Mother Teresa and the Dalai Lama for their generosity and inspiration.

I thank my literary agent, Todd Shuster, for helping to get this book off the ground with enthusiasm and integrity. Todd introduced me to Jim Hirsch, and we connected immediately. I entrusted him with the story of my life, and along the way he became one of my closest friends. Jim, this book would not have happened without you. Thank you.

Many thanks to those at Simon & Schuster, especially Dominick Anfuso, Leah Miller, Alessandra Bastagli, Jonathan Karp, and Mike Szczerban, all of whom were unwavering supporters. Everyone I have met during the writing of this book—publishers, editors, publicists, and marketers, as well as my agent and cowriter—has enriched my life and made this a wonderful, enlightening, and unforgettable experience.

Many coworkers at buildOn have contributed to this book, including Rosann Jager, Missy Shields, Alhousseyni Maiga, and Maurice Muchene. Thank you.

Carrie Pena is brilliant, cheerful, and driven. I have had the privilege of working closely with her for many years at buildOn and especially on this project. I'm grateful for her insight and especially her incredible loyalty to this cause.

For two decades I have worked with some of the most compassionate and determined people on the planet. They are working every day with urban youth across America and in remote villages around the world. They ensure our fiscal excellence, spread the word about buildOn, and align the funding needed to do what we do. I am proud, humbled, and inspired by every single person who works for buildOn. Thank you!

About the Authors

After college, Jim Ziolkowski backpacked and hitchhiked around the world, seeking adventure. What he found instead was a village celebrating the opening of its first school, and it changed his life. Within two years of returning to the United States, Jim quit a fast-track career in corporate finance with GE to start a nonprofit organization, now called buildOn. Its goal is to break the cycle of poverty, illiteracy, and low expectations in America's poorest inner cities as well as in rural villages in developing countries. Under Jim's leadership, buildOn's volunteers have contributed more than 1 million hours of service to their communities, and the organization has constructed more than 525 schools worldwide. Jim lives in Stamford, Connecticut, with his wife and children.

James S. Hirsch is a bestselling author who has written broadly and insightfully on race, sports, and the human drama behind topics ranging from the military to medicine. His books include biographies of sports icons Willie Mays and Rubin "Hurricane" Carter; narratives on POWs in Vietnam and race riots in the South; an investigation into diabetes, America's most serious health epidemic; and a collaboration with Governor Deval Patrick of Massachusetts. Prior to becoming an author, Hirsch worked for twelve years as a staff writer for the *New York Times* and the *Wall Street Journal*. He lives in the Boston area with his wife, Sheryl, and their children, Amanda and Garrett.

SIMON & SCHUSTER
READING GROUP GUIDE

WALK IN
THEIR SHOES

Jim Ziolkowski left behind a lucrative career in finance to help break the cycle of poverty, illiteracy, and low expectations he saw in America's inner cities and nations abroad. His idea was not that he could change the world, but that anyone could do it.

Walk in Their Shoes is Jim's personal story and the story of thousands of young women and men who believe in the power of service to redeem and transform. From the South Bronx to Detroit and from Haiti to Nepal, they are changing the world one community at a time.

Discussion Questions

1. Can one person change the world? Is it a ridiculous or naïve quest, or can an individual really make an impact?

2. The theme of "ignition" runs throughout the book, as people spark change in their own lives and communities. Can you think of a time when someone close to you has made one small action that ignited a larger change?

3. Who has changed your world? Jim identifies the Dalai Lama, Mother Teresa, and his dad as inspirations. Who are the individuals who have inspired you to exceed your own expectations?

4. Have you ever been motivated by the strength of others as they face their fears? When in your own life have you confronted fear? Did you overcome it?

5. Has there ever been something you wanted to do, a leap you wanted to take, but didn't?

6. Jim quit his job, turned his life upside down, and moved to Africa in order to start buildOn. Are there ways to change the world that involve less drastic change?

7. For many buildOn students the experience of building a school in the developing world has its most profound impact when they return home and see their own community through new eyes. How has travel impacted your own life and your perception of the world? Did it make you more present and grateful in your own community when you returned home?

8. Jim tries to "walk in their shoes" by living and working along-side the people of Malawi and Harlem. Is it ever possible to really experience how someone else lives? Is it important to try?

9. On a trip to build a school in Nicaragua Johnny writes his poem "Two Worlds" (page 182), which contrasts life in Nicaragua with his life back home in the United States. What does that poem tell you about what we need versus what we want?

10. Rayia's experience serving veterans changed her perception of what service means. Have you ever had an experience that challenged your preconceptions about a group of people?

11. Jim writes on page xi, "Was our dream a long shot? Of course. But I believed in the cause, in the power of service to redeem and transform, and that was all I needed. That's all anyone needs." Have you seen the power of service to others in your own life?

12. Why do you think the passage about the "sleeping sickness of the soul" from Albert Schweitzer's *Reverence for Life* moved Jim so deeply (page 17)? What words have you relied on at crucial moments in your life? Is there still time to "wake up your soul?"

Enhance Your Discussion

- **Include an educator!** If you are discussing this book in a group setting, invite a teacher or other educator to join the discussion.

- **Include a student!** We were all students once, but some of us may have forgotten what it was like! Include a high school student in your discussion group.

- **Get out there and serve!** Talking about changing the world is a good thing, but acting on that impulse is even better. Put the book down and find a place where you can give back to your community!

Author Q&A

Do you ever wonder what your life would have been like if you'd stayed at GE Capital?

I was lucky to have found out early what I was supposed to do with my life, so I don't look back. I have been deeply influenced by people like Rayia and Steven. Their strength and courage fuels my passion for our work. There is nothing I would rather be doing. I know this is a gift and I'm deeply grateful.

I now realize that 90 percent of success is grit, the refusal to give up. And grit is clearly fueled by passion and belief in what you do. I don't know if I would have had enough passion to succeed at GE, but I have tremendous admiration for our friends at GE that do. They succeed at the very highest level and have found a way to give back and to maintain a strong sense of purpose in their life.

Are there choices you wish you could make over?

I really don't have any major regrets, and I realize I'm lucky in this regard also. Buddhists believe that if you live each day as if it is your last and truly live in the moment, then you will never have any regrets. Though I am very far from achieving this, I strive for it every day. It's helpful.

Looking back, would forty-seven-year old Jim have any advice for twenty-four-year old Jim?

If I were talking to the twenty-four-year old version of myself, I would simply say, "hang in there." The heaviest burdens and the greatest fears that I've faced arose from not knowing what the future would hold. We can never know what is around the next corner. This can be exciting and sometimes terrifying. If, when I was twenty-four, I would have known how hard it was going to be get buildOn off the ground and what was going to happen in Malawi, I probably would have chickened out. But if I could have seen just a little further down the road, my fears and anxiety would have disappeared. Hang in there!

If a reader is feeling a "sleeping sickness of the soul," what would you recommend he or she do?

If you're young and you have a dream of doing something bigger with your life, take that first step. Confront the challenges in front of you one at a time and don't let yourself be intimidated. Responsibilities mount as time passes, so you may never again be in a position to take a chance and pursue your dream. Take that first step now. Then take the next step and keep walking!

Even if you are not young and the responsibilities are already piled high, it is not too late. It's never too late to open your eyes! Opportunities will arise to serve others and find greater purpose in your life without neglecting your responsibilities. There is no need to take a giant leap. Just take the first small step and keep walking.

You are inspired by your faith. What advice do you have for those who are disillusioned by religion or trying to find their faith?

Some of the best advice on faith came from Gandhi. At the height of the nonviolent struggle for the liberation of India Gandhi was leading millions of people. And they were converting to Hinduism because of him. When Gandhi realized what was going on, he firmly protested by saying, "our innermost prayer should be that a Hindu should be a better Hindu, a Muslim a better Muslim, a Christian a better Christian."* He urged us to dig deeply into our own faith and discover the beauty and value within it.

You may not agree with everything that your church preaches or teaches, and that's healthy. I certainly don't agree with everything that the Catholic Church teaches, but I am strongly aligned with the principles of social justice and liberation theology. We must not only serve the poor but also be in solidarity with them. I know that if I were to switch to another religion I would find flaws in it. And, of course they would find many flaws in me! We are human and so are the institutions and churches we belong to. There are few instances when a church has become better because we left it. Hang in there and work for change!

Will buildOn ever work in my city?

Establishing a buildOn afterschool program requires a serious investment of resources, financial and otherwise. As an organization we have made the decision to deepen our programs in some of the most challenged communities and high schools in the United States. Over the next three years, our plan is to reach more students in the cities where we already have a presence, rather than bring our after-school programs to new cities. Once service becomes a bigger part of the culture and fabric of these communities, we will expand to new places.

Because we have a proven methodology that is replicable almost anywhere, our growth is only limited by the amount of financial resources we have to invest.

Having said all that about our afterschool programs, any person in any city or community anywhere can set up a buildOn chapter and help build schools in developing countries. Literally. You can orga-

---

* *Young India*, January 19, 1928.

nize your family, friends, and/or community and raise the funds to construct a school (about $30,000) and then travel to the village where the school is being built, live with a host family, and actually help build the school.* There are no boundaries!

buildOn works to address gender balance issues in the countries where it builds schools. Does its programming in the United States also address this issue?

The cornerstone of our methodology in developing countries is gender balance. Through a holistic approach beginning with the covenant and including our local leadership model, all members of the community have a stake in gender balance. As a result, 50 percent of the students in buildOn schools are girls. We strongly believe that equal access to education is the foundation for real change.

In the United States the challenge is reversed. It is more difficult to engage young men in our programs and their communities than it is to mobilize young women. But succeeding at gender balance in our afterschool programs is critical. In general, boys who are not involved in afterschool programs are up to six times more likely to be convicted of a crime than those who are involved. We work very hard to engage boys at the same level that we do girls.

How does buildOn decide which countries to build schools in?

There is a direct correlation between illiteracy and extreme poverty, so we go to countries that are among the highest on the human poverty index.† Because long-term program sustainability is essential, we also look for a reasonably stable government and ministry of education that can provide teachers for the schools that we build. We assess

* buildon.org/chapters.
† http://hdr.undp.org/en/statistics/indices/hpi/.

the need for schools on the ground level, surveying communities to ensure the need for schools and the desire to help build the schools. Our selection process is comprehensive, but it is the most important part of our methodology. If it is not done correctly, we will fail to engage the communities and cannot build the school.

Given your travel schedule, how do you balance work and family?

I'm not sure I have a good answer to this question. I spend a lot of time thinking about balance and I always try to prioritize my family, but sometimes I fail.

What books have most influenced you?

I have quoted many of my favorite books, and they include *War and Peace* by Leo Tolstoy, *New Seeds of Contemplation* by Thomas Merton, *Why We Can't Wait* by Reverend Martin Luther King Jr., and *Autobiography: The Story of My Experiments with Truth* by Mohandas Gandhi. Not long after Jack became ill I picked up *Man's Search for Meaning* by Viktor Frankl and found meaning in what we were going through. There are many other books that have had tremendous influence on me, such as *The Long Loneliness* by Dorothy Day, *Long Walk to Freedom* by Nelson Mandela, *Les Misérables* by Victor Hugo. The list goes on!

I recently read *For the Benefit of All Beings* by His Holiness the Dalai Lama. This is a wonderful book. As I was writing this book I read *Tattoos on the Heart* by Gregory Boyle. I loved it! It is heartbreaking, hilarious, and inspiring all at once.

Can One Person Change the World?

I hope that this book will be the beginning of a larger conversation as we each seek the answer to this question for ourselves.

I invite you to join this conversation online at facebook.com /buildOn or to reach out to me on Twitter @JimZbuildOn.

Of course, I'd love for you to join the buildOn movement in its work to empower people around the world through service and education. Visit buildOn.org/getinvolved to

- Launch your own campaign to build a school

- Join or start a buildOn chapter

- Empower a buildOn student right here in the United States

The only way to change the world is to confront your fears, to take that first step. You can be the ignition that sparks a fire that changes the world!